Technology-Enhanced Language Teaching and Learning

Advances in Digital Language Learning and Teaching

Series Editors: Michael Thomas, Liverpool John Moores University, UK; Mark Peterson, Kyoto University, Japan; Mark Warschauer, University of California – Irvine, USA

Today's language educators need support to understand how their learners are changing and the ways technology can be used to aid their teaching and learning strategies. The movement toward different modes of language learning – from presence-based to autonomous as well as blended and fully online modes – requires different skill sets such as e-moderation and new ways of designing and developing language learning tasks in the digital age. Theoretical studies that include practical case studies and high quality empirical studies incorporating critical perspectives are necessary to move the field further. This series is committed to providing such an outlet for high quality work on digital language learning and teaching. Volumes in the series focus on a number of areas including but not limited to:

- task-based learning and teaching approaches utilizing technology
- language-learner creativity
- e-moderation and teaching languages online
- blended language learning
- designing courses for online and distance language learning
- mobile-assisted language learning
- autonomous language learning, both in and outside of formal educational contexts
- the use of web 2.0/social media technologies
- immersive and virtual language-learning environments
- digital game-based language learning
- language educator professional development with digital technologies
- teaching language skills with technologies

Enquiries about the series can be made by contacting the series editors: Michael Thomas (m.thomas@ljmu.ac.uk), Mark Peterson (tufsmp@yahoo.com) and Mark Warschauer (markw@uci.edu).

Also available in the series

Autonomous Language Learning with Technology: Beyond the Classroom, Chun Lai
Autonomy and Foreign Language Learning in a Virtual Learning Environment, Miranda Hamilton
Digital Games and Language Learning: Theory, Development and Implementation, edited by Mark Peterson, Kasumi Yamazaki and Michael Thomas
Language Teacher Education and Technology: Approaches and Practices, edited by Jeong-Bae Son and Scott Windeatt
Online Teaching and Learning: Sociocultural Perspectives, edited by Carla Meskill
Task-Based Language Learning in a Real-World Digital Environment: The European Digital Kitchen, edited by Paul Seedhouse
Teacher Education in Computer-Assisted Language Learning: A Sociocultural and Linguistic Perspective, Euline Cutrim Schmid
Teaching Languages with Technology: Communicative Approaches to Interactive Whiteboard Use, edited by Euline Cutrim Schmid and Shona Whyte
Video Enhanced Observation for Language Teaching: Reflection and Professional Development, edited by Paul Seedhouse
WorldCALL: Sustainability and Computer-Assisted Language Learning, edited by Ana María Gimeno Sanz, Mike Levy, Françoise Blin and David Barr

Forthcoming in the series
Teaching Languages with Screen Media: Pedagogical Reflections, edited by Carmen Herrero and Marta F. Suarez

Technology-Enhanced Language Teaching and Learning

Lessons from the Covid-19 Pandemic

Edited by
Karim Sadeghi, Michael Thomas and Farah Ghaderi

BLOOMSBURY ACADEMIC
LONDON • NEW YORK • OXFORD • NEW DELHI • SYDNEY

BLOOMSBURY ACADEMIC
Bloomsbury Publishing Plc
50 Bedford Square, London, WC1B 3DP, UK
1385 Broadway, New York, NY 10018, USA
29 Earlsfort Terrace, Dublin 2, Ireland

BLOOMSBURY, BLOOMSBURY ACADEMIC and the Diana logo are trademarks of
Bloomsbury Publishing Plc

First published in Great Britain 2023
Paperback edition published 2024

Copyright © Karim Sadeghi, Michael Thomas, Farah Ghaderi and Contributors, 2023

Karim Sadeghi, Michael Thomas, Farah Ghaderi and Contributors have asserted their right
under the Copyright, Designs and Patents Act, 1988, to be identified as
Authors of this work.

For legal purposes the Acknowledgements on p. xxiii constitute an
extension of this copyright page.

Cover design by James Watson
Cover image © shutterstock.com

All rights reserved. No part of this publication may be reproduced or transmitted
in any form or by any means, electronic or mechanical, including photocopying,
recording, or any information storage or retrieval system, without prior
permission in writing from the publishers.

Bloomsbury Publishing Plc does not have any control over, or responsibility for, any
third-party websites referred to or in this book. All internet addresses given in this
book were correct at the time of going to press. The author and publisher regret any
inconvenience caused if addresses have changed or sites have ceased to exist, but can
accept no responsibility for any such changes.

A catalogue record for this book is available from the British Library.

A catalog record for this book is available from the Library of Congress.

ISBN: HB: 978-1-3502-7101-2
PB: 978-1-3502-7105-0
ePDF: 978-1-3502-7102-9
eBook: 978-1-3502-7103-6

Series: Advances in Digital Language Learning and Teaching

Typeset by Newgen KnowledgeWorks Pvt. Ltd., Chennai, India

To find out more about our authors and books visit www.bloomsbury.com
and sign up for our newsletters.

We would like to dedicate this work to teachers and learners across the globe, and in particular language teachers and learners, who lost their lives or a family member during the global Covid-19 pandemic, hoping that we have all learnt the lessons, health-wise, technology-wise and human-wise.

Contents

List of Figures	xii
List of Tables	xiii
List of Contributors	xiv
Foreword: Don't Mention the Pandemic *Jozef Colpaert*	xix
Acknowledgements	xxiii

1 Introduction: Options and Issues in CALL   1
  Karim Sadeghi, Michael Thomas and Farah Ghaderi

Part 1 Emergency CALL at the Time of a Pandemic

2 A Distracted Learning Pandemic: The Aftermath of Synchronous
  Online Courses   13
  Larry L. LaFond

3 Italian as a Second Language in Schools during the Covid-19
  Pandemic: Exploring Teachers' Perspectives   29
  Stefania Ferrari

4 From Emergency Transitions to Teaching English Online: Three Cases   43
  Carla Meskill, Wuri Kusumastuti and Dongni Guo

Part 2 Responses to CALL during the Emergency

5 Anger, Excitement, Shame and Pride: Adult English Learners' Attitudes,
  Perceptions and Emotional Experiences towards Online Learning   59
  Lisa Cox and Juyoung Song

6 Study Abroad from Home: Development of L2 Learner Autonomy in an
  Unprecedented Online Programme during the Covid-19 Pandemic   75
  Akihiko Sasaki and Osamu Takeuchi

7 Technology-Enhanced Out-of-Class Autonomous Language Learning in Times of the Covid-19 Pandemic: A Shifting Perspective for Advanced Learners   89
Simone Torsani

8 Invisibly Vulnerable: A Corpus-Based Investigation of Media Representations of Australian EAL/D Students in Covid-19 Lockdown   103
Jessica Morcom and Jianxin Liu

Part 3 Technology Integration into Teaching at the Time of the Pandemic

9 Lockdown with *La Casa de Papel*: From Social Isolation to Social Engagement with Language   121
Antonie Alm

10 Online Learning in the Time of Coronavirus: Paradigmatic Lessons Learnt through Critical Participatory Action Research   135
John I. Liontas

11 Technology-Mediated Writing Tasks in the Online English Classroom: Focus on Form via Synchronous Videoconferencing   151
Valentina Morgana and Michael Thomas

Part 4 E-Assessment during the Covid-19 Pandemic

12 Formative Assessment in Synchronous Language Teaching in Higher Education during the Covid-19 Pandemic   167
María Luisa Carrió-Pastor

13 E-Portfolios as a Technology-Enabled Assessment: Surviving or Accommodating Covid-19   183
Ricky Lam, Marcus Lau and Joanna Wong

14 Keeping Them Honest: Assessing Learning in Online and Digital Contexts   197
Peter Davidson and Christine Coombe

Part 5 Beyond Emergency CALL, Post–Covid-19 Lessons

15 Moving Back into the Classroom while Moving beyond Current Paradigms: Lessons for Post-Covid Language Education 213
Melinda Dooly

16 Deconstructing the 'Normalization' of CALL: Digital Inequalities, Decolonization and Post-Pandemic Futures 227
Michael Thomas

17 Conclusion: Learning the Lessons from the Pandemic? 241
Michael Thomas, Karim Sadeghi and Farah Ghaderi

Index 249

Figures

2.1	A student's home arrangement of technology during class meetings	20
4.1	English language teaching online: A generative framework	46
7.1	The recourse to autonomy before the Covid-19 pandemic and its increase during the pandemic	95
8.1	Customization of online search settings	107
8.2	Cluster analysis – word frequency query top 50	110
8.3	The 'students' node word cloud	112
9.1	Study conditions under lockdown	125
9.2	L2 Netflix viewing during lockdown	127
9.3	Blogging and commenting	129
12.1	Collaborative chat for formative assessment	177
12.2	Teacher–student communication in the class forum during the Covid-19 pandemic	178

Tables

2.1	Undergraduate and Graduate Survey Responses: Sources of Distraction	19
5.A1	Participants' Countries of Origin	72
5.A2	Participants' Educational Backgrounds	72
5.A3	Participants' US Residency	72
6.1	Timetable and Class Format	79
7.1	Autonomy before and during the Pandemic	94
8.1	Key Search Terms	108
8.2	Sample News Sources	109
8.3	Summary of 'Students' in the Corpus Sample	111
8.4	'Students' Themes – International Students	113
8.5	'Students' Themes – School Students	113
9.1	Correlations between Commenting and Social Engagement	129
10.1	Digital Platforms and Their Features	143
11.1	Research Design	156
11.2	Intergroup Analysis – t test	159
11.3	Intragroup Analysis – t test	160
11.4	Results and Descriptive Statistics of the Grammar Pre- and Post-test	160
11.5	Results for the Students' Perception Questionnaire	161
12.1	Assessment Grid Used to Indicate the Results of the Assessed Activities for Each Student	174

Contributors

Antonie Alm has a PhD from UCLA and is Associate Professor at the University of Otago, New Zealand. Her research interests lie in L2 motivation and engagement, learner autonomy, and informal language learning. Antonie is on several editorial review committees and works as an associate editor for the *CALL Journal* and the *JALT CALL Journal*.

María Luisa Carrió-Pastor is Professor of English Language at Universitat Politècnica de València, Spain. Currently, she is the Head of the Department of Applied Linguistics, the coordinator of the doctorate degree 'Languages, Literature, Culture and, Their Applications' and a member-at-large of AILA Executive Board. Her research areas are contrastive linguistics, pragmatics and the study of academic and professional discourse, both for second-language acquisition and discourse analysis. Some of her publications are available at https://www.researchgate.net/profile/Maria_Carrio-Pastor; https://orcid.org/0000-0002-3040-5362.

Christine Coombe has a PhD in foreign/second-language education from the Ohio State University, USA. She is currently Associate Professor at Dubai Men's College, Higher Colleges of Technology, UAE. From 2011 to 2012, she served as president of the TESOL International Association. Christine has authored/edited fifty-seven books.

Lisa Cox is an ESL instructor at Jefferson Community and Technical College, Louisville, Kentucky, USA. Her research interests include students with limited or interrupted formal education, students with refugee backgrounds, adult literacy, multimodal composition and online teaching and learning.

Peter Davidson teaches business communication and technical writing at Zayed University in Dubai, UAE, having previously taught in New Zealand, Japan, the UK and Turkey. He has co-edited a number of books, mainly on assessment and technology. He has 120+ publications and has delivered 140+ conference papers and 85 workshops in 16 different countries.

Melinda Dooly holds a Serra Húnter fellowship as Researcher and Senior Lecturer in the Department of Language and Literature Education and Social Science Education at the Universitat Autònoma de Barcelona, Spain. Her principal research addresses technology-enhanced project-based language learning, intercultural communication and twenty-first-century competences in teacher education. She is lead researcher of GREIP: Research Centre for Teaching and Plurilingual Interaction.

Stefania Ferrari is currently Associate Professor in Second-Language Teaching Methodology at Eastern Piedmont University in Italy. Her main research interests are second-language acquisition, second-language pragmatics and task-based language teaching. She collaborates with local authorities and schools in Northern Italy for the implementation of projects dedicated to the inclusion of migrant students.

Farah Ghaderi holds a PhD from University Putra Malaysia and is Associate Professor of English Literature at Urmia University, Iran. She acts as executive manager of *Iranian Journal of Language Teaching Research*. Her main research areas include travel and gender studies, otherness, education and postcolonial studies. Her recent research has focused on gender and intercultural encounters and education and has appeared in *RELC Journal*; *Interventions*; *Journal of Multicultural Discourses*; *Gender, Place and Culture*; *Victorian Literature and Culture*; *Iranian Studies*; and *Angelaki*. Her co-translated work (Robert J. C. Young's *Postcolonialism: A Very Short Introduction*) was published in Iran in 2012. Her most recent publication is the co-edited volume, *Theory and Practice in Second Language Teacher Identity* (2022).

Dongni Guo is a doctoral student and graduate assistant in the Department of Educational Theory and Practice, State University of New York, Albany, USA. Her research focuses on online language instruction, specifically how virtual visuals and interaction with digital screen promote language comprehension. She explores teaching strategies through embodied and situated learning frameworks.

Wuri Kusumastuti is a doctoral student and research and teaching assistant in Language and Technology of Educational Theory and Practice, State University of New York, Albany, USA. She researches second-language learning, autonomous language learning online, online language teaching, blended learning, adult education, authentic materials, teacher education, culturally based pedagogy and languages for specific purposes. She is a trained Oral Proficiency Interview (OPI) Proctor for the Indonesian Language Test, American Council on the Teaching of Foreign Languages (ACTFL).

Larry L. LaFond is Professor of English at Southern Illinois University Edwardsville, USA, where he has taught online and hybrid courses in TESOL and linguistic theory for over twenty years. He has previously published on issues of access, the ethics of assessing online learning and strategies for engaging students in online environments.

Ricky Lam is Associate Head and Programme Director of the Master of Education in the Department of Education Studies at Hong Kong Baptist University. His research interests include L2 writing assessment, digital portfolios and language assessment literacy. His publications have appeared in numerous top-tier journals. Ricky is the author of *Portfolio Assessment for the Teaching and Learning of Writing* (2018, Springer) and *Using Portfolios in Language Teaching* (2019, New Portfolio Series 4).

Marcus Lau double majored in English Language & Literature and Language Education at Hong Kong Baptist University. Since 2017, Marcus has dedicated himself to supporting learners with special educational needs as well as exploring some significant topics in L2 writing classrooms. Prior to his graduation, he took part in the Student-Tutor Writing Consultation Programme (SWCP), volunteered to organize an English project in Budapest, Hungary, and participated in an overseas immersion programme at the University of Queensland, Australia.

Jianxin Liu lectures in ESL and literacy education at Charles Sturt University, Australia. He is interested in applied linguistics, additional language education, digital literacies and multimodal academic communication. He has produced sizeable publications in these areas.

John I. Liontas is Associate Professor of ESOL/FL Education at the University of Florida, USA, editor-in-chief of the award-winning encyclopaedia, *The TESOL Encyclopedia of English Language Teaching* (2018), active member in (inter)national learned societies, distinguished thought leader, and multiple award-winning author, researcher and practitioner in SLA, idiomatics and emerging digital technologies.

Carla Meskill is Professor of Educational Theory and Practice, State University of New York, Albany, USA. She researches best uses of media and technologies in classrooms, online instruction and educator professional development. Research on these and related topics is widely published.

Jessica Morcom teaches at a primary school in New South Wales, Australia. Her research centres on school EAL/D curriculum, pedagogy and technology integration. She is also interested in the intersection between language education and well-being.

Valentina Morgana is Adjunct Professor of English Linguistics at the Università Cattolica del Sacro Cuore in Milan, Italy. She holds a doctorate in education from the Department of Languages of the Open University, UK. Her research interests include Applied Linguistics (MALL and TBLT) and Corpus Linguistics. Her recent publications focus on mobile English language learning and technology-mediated task-based language teaching.

Karim Sadeghi has a PhD from the University of East Anglia, UK, and is Professor of TESOL at Urmia University, Iran. He is the founding editor-in-chief of *Iranian Journal of Language Teaching Research* (the only Iranian journal in the humanities with a Scopus-SJR-Q1 top 15% ranking) and serves on the editorial board of several national and international journals, including *RELC Journal, Research in Post Compulsory Education, TESOL Journal, Language Testing in Asia* and *Heliyon Education* (as associate editor). He was selected as Iran's top researcher in the humanities and social sciences in 2013 and in English language/applied linguistics in 2018. His recent publications have appeared in *RELC Journal; System; Assessing Writing; Journal of Multilingual* and *Multicultural Development* and *English for Specific Purposes Journal*. His recent publications include *Assessing Second Language Reading* (2021), *Theory and Practice in Second Language Teacher Identity* (2022) and *Talking about Second Language Acquisition* (2022).

Akihiko Sasaki, PhD, is Professor of EFL and Applied Linguistics at Mukogawa Women's University, Hyogo, Japan. His research interests include L2 teaching and learning, self-regulation and learning strategy use in technology-enhanced L2 learning, and teacher education. His academic work has appeared in international and domestic journals.

Juyoung Song is Professor in English and TESOL at Murray State University, USA. Her research interests include second-language education, multilingualism and language teacher education, particularly issues regarding language ideology, identity, and emotion. She has published articles in such journals as *TESOL Quarterly*, *The Modern Language Journal* and *Journal of Sociolinguistics*.

Osamu Takeuchi, PhD is Professor of Applied Linguistics at Kansai University, Osaka, Japan. His research interests are L2 self-regulation, L2 learning motivation and technology-enhanced learning. His recent publications include 'Language Learning Strategies: Insights from the Past and Directions for the Future' in *Second Handbook of English Language Teaching*.

Michael Thomas is Professor of Education and Social Justice and Chair of the Centre for Educational Research (CERES) at Liverpool John Moores University, UK, and Principal Fellow of the Higher Education Academy. He holds PhDs from Newcastle University and Lancaster University, respectively, and has taught and conducted research at universities in Germany, Japan, England and Wales over a twenty-five-year period. He is author or editor of over thirty books and peer-reviewed special editions on computer-assisted language learning, digital natives, project-based pedagogy, online education and pedagogical theory. He is founding editor of four book series, including *Digital Education and Learning*, *Advances in Digital Language Learning and Teaching* and *Global Policy and Critical Futures in Education*.

Simone Torsani is Lecturer in Second Language Acquisition and Foreign Language Teaching at the University of Genoa, Italy, where he is member of the scientific board of the PhD course in Digital Humanities. His research in technology-enhanced language learning mainly focuses on distance language teaching, especially writing, assessment and autonomous learning in non-institutional contexts.

Joanna Wong is a graduate of the BA in English Language & Literature and BEd in English Language Teaching programme at Hong Kong Baptist University. During her undergraduate career, she keenly participated in various public speaking contests, conferences and poetry writing activities both locally and internationally. Before embarking on her journey of teaching, she had also gained invaluable experience as a part-time instructor for English enhancement and DSE speaking courses.

Foreword: Don't Mention the Pandemic

Jozef Colpaert

During the two years of the pandemic, as editor of *Computer Assisted Language Learning*, I have been rather reluctant to accept articles with the words 'pandemic', 'Covid' or 'Corona' in the title or abstract. So why have I written this foreword in a book that is about 'lessons to be learnt from the pandemic'? Well, simply, because the focus is not on the pandemic itself, but on what we have learnt. It is not about the pandemic, it is about the New Normal.

My biggest fear was that things would return to the 'Old Normal' once the pandemic subsided. At the time of writing this foreword, at the very top of the fifth wave, principals start informing their teachers that 'all lectures and tutorials will again take place face-to-face. Some classes might use an online format for specific pedagogical reasons'. Apparently, we have learnt very little. Let's try an auto-ethnographic approach that might shed a different light on the problem.

My personal view on things is based on what I have read, seen, experienced, and analysed as citizen, educator, researcher, designer, editor, reviewer, conference organizer and father. It is just a humble opinion statement, but I think it may help frame the chapters in this book in the right way. The problem is so multifaceted that it is difficult to find the right angle of attack. We no longer see the forest for the trees. So what are the aspects that we can discuss?

Let's start with two positive elements: teacher resilience and technological affordances.

What surprised me most was the reaction of teachers worldwide. Their resilience, their initiatives and their sudden shift to 'Emergency Remote Teaching'. There was not enough time for organizing a specialized course or even for providing them with basic information: they just did what they thought they had to do. And we witnessed more change than in the past forty years. This entails serious consequences for teacher education and training. We should stop considering teachers as ignorant and resistant beings who need to be trained. We should empower, enable and equip them to explore and experiment on their own. To learn, to share and to apply what they have learnt. And the academic world should listen. Models such as the Technological Pedagogical Content Knowledge Model (TPACK) are based on a rather derogatory view of teachers in this respect. A technology that requires knowledge and training is not a well-designed technology. Teachers' digital literacy is not the ability to cope with ill-designed system features. It is the ability to design, to formulate expected affordances based on a motivational conceptualization and an educational specification and to select technologies accordingly. Is this just a *boutade*? Let's see …

Fortunately for education, there was technology to make this 'Emergency Remote Teaching' possible. A wide variety of meeting tools, increased network capacity, learning management systems, Massive Online Open Courses (MOOCs) interactive apps, student response systems, games and virtual spaces enabled activities that were simply unimaginable four years ago. And we all, as students or teachers, discovered new affordances such as discussions in break-out rooms, co-construction in shared documents, telecollaboration, autonomous learning, peer evaluation and asynchronous coaching.

On the other hand, we also had to deal with some less-positive elements about our education system, about educational technology, about developing regions and about our minds.

In many countries where both parents work full-time, we soon discovered that our entire education system serves primarily as a giant childcare facility. Closing schools poses a huge problem for the economy. Parents have to look for alternative childcare, stay at home or try to combine babysitting with their own telework. Hence the pressure to keep schools open at all costs. The primary concern of politicians (as well as public opinion) is to keep schools open for the sake of the economy, rather than out of concern for the student's mental health and learning progress.

Second, despite the strong qualities of available technology, educational technology still has serious shortcomings. First of all, there is a serious lack of dedicated functionalities developed by design for learning, teaching and evaluation. The main focus is on the use of generic meeting, communication and construction tools. In the case of CALL, more advanced linguistic–didactic functionalities such as answer evaluation, feedback and remediation have been researched and developed since the 1980s, but they have not yet been implemented in a significant number of applications.

Perhaps this is a luxury problem. In developing regions, there simply was not enough technology, if at all, so students and educators there were hit hardest by this crisis. These regions urgently need not only vaccines, but also technology in order to provide alternative forms of education, especially in rural areas.

Last but not least, our minds. The psychological aspect. Surprisingly, many people enjoyed the peace and quiet, and the absence of perfunctory obligations. Many students achieved better results because there were less distractions. Other students were confronted with the emptiness of their existence and learnt that life is about more than drinking buddies, social media and festivals. Both teachers and students complained about the lack of connection. Relatedness is an important universal innate psychological need. The reason why MOOCs perform poorly and why they show huge drop-out rates is that they do not provide enough functionalities to increase the sense of belonging in the system. Even more surprisingly, and this is confirmed by motivation specialists, the need for autonomy turned out to be even stronger than the need for relatedness.

So we have identified two opportunities and four challenges that most people were able to witness. But, digging a little deeper, I am convinced that our main concern should be design.

What we have also learnt from this pandemic is that our education is still too much instruction based, despite all our efforts to introduce activating teaching strategies, autonomous learning, coaching and collaboration. Teachers should be trained more in design than in educational technology. They should be able to design their own pedagogical approach taking into account their specific context, circumstances, learning objectives, learners and infrastructure, as well as their own needs, goals and preferences.

Teachers should become designers. But what does design mean? It has become a fashionable term. We are all into design thinking, design-based research or instructional design, design as a product quality, design as a creative process. Personally, I tell my students that design is about opening fans (ranges of possibilities) and about making informed choices in a substantiated way. Design is about the three As: Application, Adaptation and Approximation. Application of theory and accepted findings in the fields of pedagogy, linguistics and psychology. But this application is not enough: we also need to adapt to specific learners, goals, circumstances and contexts. But even adaptation is not enough: we should realize that the learning environments we design will always be a hypothetical solution on the pathway of our cyclic-iterative endeavour. I call this process 'educational engineering', based on the definition of engineering as 'the strategy to apply when not enough knowledge is available'. And this lack of knowledge has become apparent during these two years.

The focus should not be on the learning environment as a product, but on design as a process. It is not about emergency remote teaching procedures, but about the strategy, rationale and principles we can formulate for designing the best possible multimodal learning environment. A flexible environment where by adjusting the parameters of instruction, individual learning, coaching and collaborative learning, we can choose other face-to-face or remote, synchronous or asynchronous, individual or collaborative activities.

Design is important for education, but also for the future of CALL. Technology in itself does not carry an inherent, measurable and generalizable effect on learning. Only a holistic learning environment can have this effect, to the extent that it has been designed in a justifiable and methodological way. And this brings me to the three Ts: terminology, transdisciplinarity and technology.

Every self-respecting discipline needs a clear, well-defined and accurate terminology. Unfortunately, in the CALL world, the real pandemic may be the use of pervasive and persuasive terms such as virtual exchanges, blended learning, flipped classrooms or digital pedagogy. These terms have probably been coined to name new and largely unknown phenomena, but very few remember their originally intended meanings, and many use these terms with different connotations in mind.

The second challenge for CALL is its multi-disciplinarity. There are so many disciplines involved (linguistics, pedagogy, psychology, technology, design) that it has become very difficult, if not impossible, to work with multidisciplinary teams in an interdisciplinary way. It has taken me years to understand that CALL is not just another discipline among others, but that it is a boundary-transcending discipline. CALL connects disciplines on a higher level of abstraction. CALL is transdisciplinarity.

Finally, I started my career with interactive language courseware and will probably end my career with it. The future of CALL depends on dedicated technologies with linguistic–didactic functionalities developed by design for language learning, teaching and testing. The principle is simple: the added value of a technology is the extent to which the affordances of that technology match the requirements of the designed learning environment. And this is where it all comes together.

This book presents itself perfectly in line with this approach. It offers a kaleidoscopic view on the post-pandemic evolution of language teaching and learning. Its chapters mention a wide variety of aspects such as challenges and affordances, attitudes and perceptions, autonomy and socialization, assessment and evaluation, e-portfolios and meeting tools, paradigms and research methods, and critical pedagogy.

The contributing authors do not use persuasive terminology, nor do they rely on hype-related arguments. This book will hopefully lay the foundation for a new era in which we will design motivational multimodal learning environments where psychology comes first, where pedagogy is paramount, where technology is the logical conclusion of this design exercise and where we will have forgotten all about the pandemic. Let's focus on flexible, adaptive and smart learning environments for diversity and inclusion, fairness and equity, learning disabilities and poverty, well-being and global citizenship.

Acknowledgements

The completion of this project has been a team undertaking. We are first of all indebted to the authors and contributors who kindly accepted our invitation to join us in this venture and collaborated fully until the very final stage of the production; without their contributions we wouldn't have been able to start this work. The professionalism of the work owes itself to a wonderful team at Bloomsbury who made sure that our initial proposal was warmly received, smoothly evaluated and skilfully developed into this final shape. We are in particular indebted to Maria Giovanna Brauzzi, the commissioning editor and our main contact person at Bloomsbury Academic, as well as her assistants and production team, including Laura Gallon, Anna Elliss, Evangeline Stanford, Peter Warren and the rest of the team, for so effectively working us through all stages of submission, review, editing and production. We are also very obliged to proposal and manuscript reviewers whose generous and constructive feedback allowed us to fine-tune the volume.

1

Introduction: Options and Issues in CALL

Karim Sadeghi, Michael Thomas and Farah Ghaderi

Background

Among others, Liontas (2002) rightly predicted that the 'e-volution of computer and video medium' in the form of 'technological advances made in the field of hypertext, hypermedia, artificial intelligence, machine translation, software engineering, and wireless communication networking' (p. 316) will drive the future of education. CALL (computer-assisted language learning) has now extended to include digital options such as blogs, wikis, social networking, podcasting, Web 2.0 applications, language learning in virtual worlds and interactive whiteboards (Davies et al., 2011). Considered a luxury at the time of Liontas's prediction over two decades ago and intended primarily to offer remedial support and reinforcement of learning, digital technology (as the aftermath of the Covid-19 pandemic which has affected more than 385 million people and claimed nearly 5.7 million lives worldwide at the time of writing this chapter in February 2022) is now seen as a necessity of human life in general and language education in particular. CALL has now by necessity surpassed its initial applications for traditional drilling and practising using a computer and includes all forms of digital technology as well as online (such as virtual learning environments (VLEs)) versus offline and remote (or web-based distance learning) as opposed to in-classroom learning contexts. In line with the major theme of this volume (technology-enhanced language learning and teaching or TELLT), this chapter aims to introduce TELLT, briefly reviewing its historical background and considering the options in delivering such language instruction as well as issues and challenges in integrating digital technology to second-/foreign-language education in technologically deprived contexts. This book is not about emerging CALL technologies during the Covid-19 pandemic, but rather, it focuses primarily on how language teachers and learners, who were earlier less familiar or unfamiliar with general CALL technologies, had to adopt them on an emergency basis.

CALL: Terminological Diversity and a Brief History

CALL, also invariably known as computer-aided instruction (CAI) and computer-aided language instruction (CALI), can be traced back to the first mainframe computers following the PLATO (Programmed Logic for Automated Teaching Operations) project at the University of Illinois (Marty, 1981), which was used for teaching Russian reading; similar programmes were developed by 1980 for teaching English as a Second Language (ESL), French, German, Spanish and Italian (Chapelle, 2001). With the arrival of mini or personal computers towards the end of the 1970s, however, CAI and CALL became buzzwords in instructional settings. According to Davies and Higgins (1982), since CALI focused primarily on teaching (instruction) rather than on learning, and given the emphasis on student-centred approaches to instruction, CALI gave way to CALL in the 1980s. CALL is now an umbrella term referring to all its variants such as mobile-assisted language learning (MALL), technology-assisted language learning (TALL), technology-enhanced language learning (which emerged around the early 1990s, at the University of Hull) and the like. There is no shortage of terminologies related to CALL, and various other terminologies may be coined in the future with different combinations of its core concepts: technology/computer, language and learning. Whatever the terminology, all such acronyms refer, in one way or another, to the application of digital technology (those with which we are familiar and unknown ones that may appear in the future) for facilitating language education. Despite variations in terminology, CALL is now a well-established and reputed field and includes several professional associations in different parts of the world (such as EUROCALL, CALICO, IALLT, AisaCALL, JALTCALL and PasCALL, to name the most prominent examples), some publishing their own journals like *ReCALL* and the *CALICO Journal*, as well as a flagship journal with the same title as the field itself, published by Taylor and Francis: *Computer Assisted Language Learning*.

The term CALL has accordingly been developed to primarily cater for 'learning' rather than 'teaching', which is increasingly being assigned a secondary role in language education circles; we believe, however, that without appropriate teaching which aims to facilitate the learning process, optimal learning may not be easily achievable; hence the focus of this book on using technology for learning *and teaching* languages, with the latter referring to CALL use for language assessment as well as for initial (pre-service) language teacher education purposes. The term 'technology-enhanced language learning and teaching' that we have coined for this volume subsequently implies the use of other forms of digital technology (as well as computers) and their application to teaching a language (in addition to learning it). This is in line with Levy's (1997, p. 1) definition of CALL as 'the search for and study of applications of the computer in language teaching and learning', rendering CALL as an approach to language instruction where digital technologies are used to aid presentation (teaching), and reinforcement and assessment of learning. Had it not been due to its heavy reliance on teachers and teaching, TALL could have moved forward effortlessly during and after the Covid-19 pandemic; however, the recent global experience once more highlighted the key role teachers and teaching play in the success of language learning.

In term of historical stages, Warschauer and Healey (1998) divided CALL into three phases: Structural/Behaviorist CALL (developed in the 1950s and implemented in the 1960s to 1970s), Communicative CALL (1970s to 1980s) and Integrative CALL, integrating multimedia and the Internet (1990s onwards). The post–Covid-19 CALL is certainly a distinct stage, and we can add a new phase to the above phases: Forced CALL (2020 onwards) which subsumes the earlier period (Integrative) and is expected to include new emerging technologies that will appear in the future to account for emerging and unplanned CALL needs of language teachers and learners. Although this volume is not specifically on emerging CALL technologies during the Covid-19 period (since it takes time for such technologies to emerge), it does document some early experimentations with already existing CALL technologies used innovatively in contexts for which they had not been meant – that is, their use for unplanned, emergency contexts. Next, we briefly review the affordances computer technology has offered language learning and teaching.

CALL Affordances

We use the term 'affordances' here to refer to the opportunities offered by using computer technology (including personal computers, laptops, smartphones etc., and relevant programmes like multimedia, games, virtual reality (VR) and so on) for language learning and teaching. Since the 1970s, when personal computers found their way into the lives of learners who could afford them, a revolution was expected to occur in language education since language instruction was made more individualistic. From the very start, computers could be trained to offer personalized instruction at the level appropriate to learners' language competence and learning rate. The role of the computer became that of a personal tutor that was able to interact with individual learners and offer instruction, practice and feedback on various language skills and sub-skills. The invention of the internet and the World Wide Web towards the late 1980s and early 1990s brought more affordances to the application of computers for language education. In addition to interaction that could happen with the computer, human beings could facilitate the learning process either online or offline in the form of asynchronous or synchronous computer-mediated communication (SCMC) and collaborative learning among learners, and communication between learners and teachers was made possible from a distance.

With the current giant advances in computing and digital technologies, a new landscape has been created for more authentic, real-time, visual communicaions such that even before the pandemic, numerous language schools across the world (and particularly in tech-savvy contexts) would offer at least a part of their education online or in a blended format. While the experience of fully fledged CALL was not new to students and teachers living in such contexts, there were millions of learners and teachers in technologically poor parts of the world who did not have access to any such affordances until the pandemic hit. The planned version of CALL had then to be modified and deployed in contexts not ready for such an intervention due to lack of infrastructure, the needed software and hardware, internet access, digital literacy of students, teachers and parents, economic conditions and the like. As such, despite its numerous potential uses, students and teachers in these contexts were not able to take full advantage of CALL's benefits. Even today when most learners and teachers across the globe have now had a sense of CALL in one way or another, not all its affordances are accessible in all contexts, for one or more of the reasons mentioned above. CALL's major affordances have been related to using computer technology for teaching and learning almost all language skills and sub-skills and primarily pronunciation, vocabulary, grammar, reading, listening and offering feedback on writing and speaking, in both individual and collaborative settings as well as in synchronous and asynchronous modes. Studies have also highlighted the effect of CALL on learners' motivation, autonomy, positive attitude and emotional gains. To better grasp the full range of the affordances offered by CALL, we next review some of the recent studies documenting the benefits of using computers and other digital technology for language learning and teaching, hoping that more students and teachers in technologically under-resourced contexts will one day have access to similar advantages.

There are numerous studies supporting the effectiveness (as well as challenges) of using digital technologies for teaching and learning (especially within the context of second-language education) and the number is surging after 2020 with a focus on emergency TELLT (e.g. Krajka, 2021; Tao & Gao, 2022; Willermark & Islind, 2022; Wong & Moorhouse, 2021; also *System* has published a Special Issue (2021–2) with twenty-six articles devoted to online language learning during the Covid-19 pandemic). Experimenting with Italian students and using VLE-enhanced language learning programmes based on the *WebCT* platform, Polisca (2006), for example, found that the online programme fostered students' motivation and improved the quality of independent learning and concluded that 'VLE-supported group work produces better results than individual, non-VLE-enhanced work' (p. 499). In a recent meta-analysis of the effects of 3D virtual worlds (3DVWs) in language learning, Wang et al. (2020) analysed thirteen primary studies (with fifty variables) conducted between 2008 and 2019 and found that the use of 3DVWs in language education led to significant overall linguistic gains and affective gains. Similarly, Peng et al.'s (2021) meta-analysis of seventeen MALL studies (2008–17) revealed a significant effect of mobile technologies in language learning.

The affordances of smartphones and multimedia messaging systems in developing informal language learning outside the classroom have been documented by Wigglesworth (2020). Formal learning using mobile phones has also been found to be effective in learning vocabulary in Spanish as a second language (Hanson & Brown, 2020): while students reported low enjoyment using a spaced repetition flashcard application called Anki and were reluctant to use it, those who used it more performed better at the end of the semester.

Studying serious digital games (as opposed to commercial off-the-shelf games which are produced for entertainment) with sixty-six English as a foreign language (EFL) students, Chen and Hsu (2020) found that these games significantly improved vocabulary learning as well as content knowledge (history) and that the students reported enjoying the learning experience. Video captioning as another technological tool has also been reported to improve low–intermediate Chinese EFL learners' vocabulary learning in a multimodal listening activity (Hsieh, 2020). Similarly, in the context of Iran, Hassanzadeh et al. (2021) found that computer-aided concept mapping (compared to a traditional outlining technique) boosted university EFL students' lexical diversity in a process-based writing course. Likewise, mobile-supported task-based language teaching (TBLT) has been found to lead to improved performance in vocabulary and conversation comprehension as well as increasing awareness of fluency- and accuracy-based speaking strategies compared to traditional paper-based TBLT; however, no gains were reported for grammar (Fang et al., 2021).

As far as the skill of reading is concerned, Yang and Qian (2020) experimented with computerized dynamic assessment (CDA), comparing the results with traditional teaching and assessing of reading, and found that the CDA group significantly outperformed the control group after four weeks of learning. Studying the effects of VR tools like Google Cardboard and Expeditions on Chinese as a Foreign Language learners' speaking proficiency development, Xie et al. (2021) found that the content and vocabulary of the VR group improved significantly compared to that of the non-VR group; the qualitative data also lent support for VR's role in facilitating preparation and encouraging active learning. In the context of writing, Chang et al.'s (2021) experiment with 113 third-grade Taiwanese children indicated that a game-based writing environment led to improvements in textual cohesion as well as improving their attitude to writing. Experimenting with forty-eight Taiwanese EFL learners paired with American college peers, Wu et al. (2020) found that online flipped writing instruction not only enhanced foreign language students' writing proficiency, but also prevented students from demotivation (as a result of positive learning experiences and developing cross-cultural awareness). In the process of a five-year study (2014–19) with STEM students, Brudermann et al. (2021) also found that online, unfocused indirect corrective feedback greatly contributed to accuracy in writing development.

Working with twenty-five L2 Spanish learners, Lenkaitis (2020) investigated the potential of videoconferencing on learner autonomy and found that SCMC via Zoom fostered learner autonomy and created an authentic language learning experience. Technology in the form of voice telecollaboration has also been found to boost pre-service language teachers' intercultural learning (Sardegna & Dugartsyrenova, 2021), and a similar finding has been reported with study abroad students with regard to the effect of Padlet (a social media tool) on promoting intercultural awareness (Lomicka & Ducate, 2021). Telecollaboration as a technological tool has also been documented to build more favourable views of Colombian pre-service English teachers towards themselves as well as leading to positive attitudes to confront detrimental effects of native-speakerism ideologies (Gonzalez, 2020).

On the emotional side, examining online peer feedback in wiki environments in the context of a university English for Specific Purposes (EAP) course, Ma (2020) found that online peer feedback promotes a friendly, supportive and non-threatening environment and contributes to EAP writing both affectively and tangibly. SCMC has also been reported to mitigate foreign language anxiety, with VR-based interaction being the most fun and the most effective learning environment, compared to audio and video-based SCMC (York et al., 2021). Mobile technology assisted learning has also been found to promote the use of certain strategies by Chinese learners not normally employed in teacher-fronted classrooms, such as satiation and emotion control strategies, as well as increasing the number of metacognitive and commitment control strategies (Gao & Shen, 2021).

CALL Challenges

Apart from issues to do with access to technological hardware and software, there are few disadvantages reported for the applications of digital technology in planned language education compared to their numerous benefits in facilitating the learning process. The age of Covid-19 has, however, revealed more challenges with respect to the emergency use technology, especially in the context of economically deprived countries and less affluent areas within developed countries. Most such challenges are due to the fact that, as Moser et al. (2021) recognize, CALL was meant for *planned* teaching and learning, the nature of which is fundamentally different from 'the abrupt shift from face-to-face contexts to *remote learning*' (emphasis in original; p. 1). Studying Polish schools' transition to emergency language educating during the Covid-19 pandemic, Krajka (2021), for instance, identifies some challenges with forced online teaching as being students' lack of concentration and demotivation, behavioural issues such as using insulting comments, technical issues like old operating systems and weak connection, classroom management problems in delivering feedback, assessment, monitoring work, organizing pair/group work, time management and fatigue for students, and work overload for teachers and the like.

In a systematic review of fifty-five published studies about the global English language teaching community's responses to the Covid-19 pandemic, Moorhouse and Kohnke (2021) discover the main challenge as being instructors' lack of competence in online teaching and consequently their struggle in adapting their pedagogy to teaching online. Another key observation of their review is the existence of a digital divide between teachers working in different geographical contexts or those with different financial conditions, leading to challenges such as lack of suitable devices and internet connection issues. In a Turkish university context, with most students coming from economically less-stable countries, Sadeghi (in press), for example, identifies the main challenges of using digital technologies at the time of the Covid-19 outbreak, when classes were delivered from a distance, as being technological, economic, social, familial and emotional – challenges similar to those reported by others implementing CALL in contexts with limited technological resources. In a guest-edited volume in *System*, Tao and Gao (2022) review the twenty-six articles comprising the special issue, some of which reported challenges of CALL during the Covid-19 transition period, and conclude that in addition to technical issues common to all studies, there was a wide range of challenges associated with educational, socioeconomic and digital settings of the contexts involved.

Not all challenges associated with CALL appeared at the time of the Covid-19 outbreak; some of the reported challenges were already there, especially in technologically deprived contexts, even before the pandemic. For instance, in a survey of ninety-five Iranian teachers of young learners, Taghizadeh and Hasani Yourdshahi

(2020) reported that although teachers in general had a positive attitude towards the integration of technology in their teaching, most did not have the required technical knowledge and skills, and they did not receive any training to prepare them for such teaching; other major challenges that they faced were limited computing facilities and lack of support from schools and institutes. While concluding that new technologies, including MALL, can greatly contribute to learning language skills, Peng et al. (2021) warn that 'new technologies might also expose learners to incomprehensible input and inaccurate feedback, or distract them with innovative software or hardware, leading to an emphasis on technological means over pedagogical goals' (p. 278). Indeed, we acknowledge that digital technology affords significant potential for language learning and teaching but also underline the challenges faced by learners, teachers, parents, educational authorities and governments in transferring to a remote and an online education system during the Covid-19 pandemic. It was with a view to learn from such challenges for the post-Covid period that this volume was brought together.

The Structure of This Book

In addition to this introductory chapter and a Foreword by Jozef Colpaert, with its sixteen other chapters, this book is organized around five parts: In Part 1, 'Emergency CALL at the Time of a Pandemic', Larry L. LaFond reports a distracted learning pandemic in synchronous online teaching, and then in Chapter 3, Stefania Ferrari reflects on the challenges to the teaching of Italian as a second language in schools during the Covid-19 pandemic. This is followed by Carla Meskill, Wuri Kusumastuti and Dongni Guo's report about three cases of moving to online teaching in three different countries in Chapter 4. In Part 2, 'Responses to CALL during the Emergency', Lisa Cox and Juyoung Song offer an account of the emotional experiences of adult immigrant and refugee students in online English (ESL) classes in Chapter 5. Then in Chapter 6, Akihiko Sasaki and Osamu Takeuchi report the development of L2 learner autonomy in unprecedented online classes in a Japanese study abroad programme from home, and Simone Torsani in Chapter 7 investigates the role of technology in learner autonomy at the time of the Covid-19 emergency. This is followed by Jessica Morcom and Jianxin Liu's corpus-based investigation of media representations of Australian EAL/D students in Covid-19 lockdown in Chapter 8.

In Part 3, 'Technology Integration into Teaching at the Time of the Pandemic', Antonie Alm reviews Netflix for language learning in Chapter 9, and John I. Liontas offers the way forward for second-language teaching and learning through critical participatory action research in Chapter 10. Valentina Morgana and Michael Thomas's account of focus-on-form English writing tasks in synchronous online learning in Chapter 11 closes this part. In Part 4, 'E-Assessment during the Covid-19 Pandemic', María Luisa Carrió-Pastor looks at the integration of data-driven learning instruction through a multimodal corpus of language objects at the time of the pandemic in Chapter 12. Ricky Lam, Marcus Lau and Joanna Wong then introduce e-portfolios as a technology-enabled assessment in Chapter 13, and Peter Davidson and Christine

Coombe consider opportunities and challenges in assessing learning in online and digital contexts in the Chapter 14. In Part 5, 'Beyond Emergency CALL: Post-Covid-19 Lessons', Melinda Dooly, in Chapter 15, proposes lessons for post-Covid language education, and in Chapter 16, Michael Thomas writes about the future of post-pandemic CALL and examines the link between normalization, decolonization, social justice and technology-enhanced language teaching. The volume ends with the editors' concluding chapter, which reflects on the volume as a whole and identifies a research agenda for future research in CALL in the post-pandemic language classroom.

References

Brudermann, C., Grosbois, M., & Sarre, C. (2021). Accuracy development in L2 writing: Exploring the potential of computer-assisted unfocused in an indirect corrective feedback in an online EFL course. *ReCALL, 33*(3), 248–64.

Chang, W.-C., Liao, C.-Y., & Chan, T.-W. (2021). Improving children's textual cohesion and writing attitude in a game based writing environment. *CALL, 34*(1–2), 133–58.

Chapelle, C. (2001). *Computer applications in second language acquisition: Foundations for teaching, testing and research*. Cambridge University Press.

Chen, H.-J., & Hsu, H.-L. (2020). The impact of a serious game on vocabulary and content learning. *CALL, 33*(7), 811–32.

Davies, G., & Higgins, J. (1982). *Computers, language and language learning*. CILT.

Davies, G., Walker, R., Rendall, H., & Hewer, S. (2011). Introduction to computer assisted language learning (CALL). Module 1.4. In G. Davies (Ed.), *Information and communications technology for language teachers (ICT4LT)*. Thames Valley University. Retrieved 5 January 2022, from http://www.ict4lt.org/en/en_mod1-4.htm.

Fang, W.-C., Yeh, H.-C., Luo, B.-R., & Chen, N.-S. (2021). Effects of mobile supported task-based language teaching on EFL student's linguistics achievement and conversational interaction. *ReCALL, 33*(1), 71–87.

Gao, C., & Shen, H.-Z. (2021). Mobile-technology-induced learning strategies: Chinese EFL university students learning English in an emergency context. *ReCALL, 33*(1), 88–105.

Gonzalez, J. J. V. (2020). Prospective English teachers re-examining ideologies in telecollaboration. *CALL, 23*(7), 732–54.

Hanson, A. E. S., & Brown, C. M. (2020). Enhancing L2 learning thorough a mobile assisted spaced-repetition tool: An effective but better pill? *CALL, 33*(1–2), 133–55.

Hassanzadeh, M., Saffari, E., & Rezaei, S. (2021). The impact of computer-aided concept-mapping on EFL learners' lexical diversity: A process writing experiment. *ReCALL, 33*(3), 214–28.

Hsieh, Y. (2020). Effects of video captioning on EFL vocabulary learning and listening comprehension. *CALL, 33*(5–6), 567–89.

Krajka, J. (2021). Teaching grammar and vocabulary in COVID-19 times: Approaches used in online teaching in Polish schools during pandemic. *The JALT CALL Journal, 17*(2), 112–34.

Lenkaitis, C. A. (2020). Technology as a mediating tool: Videoconferencing, L2 learning and learner autonomy. *CALL, 33*(5–6), 483–509.

Levy, M. (1997). *CALL: Context and conceptualisation*. Oxford University Press.

Liontas, J. I. (2002). CALLMedia digital technology: Whither in the new millennium? *CALICO Journal, 19*(2), 315–30.

Lomicka, L., & Ducate, L. (2021). Using technology, reflection, and noticing to promote intercultural learning during short-term study abroad. *CALL, 34*(1–2), 35–65.

Ma, Q. (2020). Examining the role of inter-group peer online feedback on wiki writing in an EAP context. *CALL, 33*(3), 197–216.

Marty, F. (1981). Reflections on the use of computers in second language acquisition. *System. 9*(2), 85–98. doi:10.1016/0346-251x(81)90023-3

Moorhouse, B. L., & Kohnke, L. (2021). Responses of the English language teaching community to the COVID-19 pandemic. *RELC Journal, 52*(3), 359–78. Retrieved 5 January 2022, from https://doi.org/10.1177/00336882211053052.

Moser, K. M., Wie, T., & Brenner, D. (2021). Remote teaching during COVID-19: Implications from a national survey of language educators. *System, 97*, 1–15. Retrieved 5 January 2022, from https://doi.org/10.1016/j.system.2020.102431.

Peng, H., Jager, S., & Lowie, W. (2021). Narrative review and meta-analysis of MALL research on L2 skills. *ReCALL, 33*(3), 278–95.

Polisca, E. (2006). Facilitating the learning process: An evaluation of the use and benefits of a Virtual Learning Environment (VLE)-enhanced independent language-learning program (ILLP). *CALICO Journal, 23*(3), 399–515.

Sadeghi, K. (in press). (Un)Learning English 'offline' at the time of COVID-19 pandemic: The story of language education at a technologically deprived context. *Language Teaching Research*.

Sardegna, V. G., & Dugartsyrenova, V. A. (2021). Facilitating pre-service language teachers' intercultural learning via voice-based telecollaboration: The role of discussion questions. *CALL, 34*(3), 379–407.

Taghizadeh, M., & Hasani Yourdshahi, Z. (2020). Integrating technology into young learners' classes: Language teachers' perception. *CALL, 33*(8), 982–1006.

Tao, J., & Gao, X. (2022). Teaching and learning languages online: Challenges and responses. *System, 107*, 1–9. Retrieved 5 January 2022, from https://doi.org/10.1016/j.system.2022.102819.

Wang, C.-P., Lan, Y.-J., Tseng, W.-T., Lin, Y.-T. R., & Gupta, K. C.-L. (2020). On the effect of 3D virtual worlds in language learning – a meta-analysis. *CALL, 33*(8), 891–915.

Warschauer, M., & Healey, D. (1998). Computers and language learning: An overview. *Language Teaching, 31*(2), 57–71.

Wigglesworth, J. (2020). Using smartphones to extend interaction beyond the EFL classroom. *CALL, 33*(4), 413–34.

Willermark, S., & Islind, A. S. (2022). Several educational affordances of virtual classrooms. *Computers and Education Open, 3*, 1–9. Retrieved 5 January 2022, from https://doi.org/10.1016/j.caeo.2022.100078.

Wong, K. M., & Moorhouse, B. L. (2021). Digital competence and online language teaching: Hong Kong language teacher practices in primary and secondary classrooms. *System, 103*. Retrieved 5 January 2022, from https://doi.org/10.1016/j.system.2021.102653.

Wu, W.-C. W., Yang, J. C., Hsieh, J. S. C., & Yamammoto, T. (2020). Free from demotivation in EFL writing: The use of online flipped writing instruction. *CALL, 33*(4), 353–87.

Xie, Y., Chen, Y., & Ruder, L. H. (2021). Effects of mobile assisted virtual reality on Chinese L2 students' oral proficiency. *CALL, 34*(3), 225–45.

Yang, Y., & Qian, D. D. (2020). Promoting L2 English learners' reading proficiency through computerized dynamic assessment. *CALL*, *33*(5–6), 628–52.

York, J, Shibata, K., Tokutake, H., & Nakyama, H. (2021). Effect of SCMC on foreign language anxiety and learning experience: A comparison of voice, video and VR-based oral interaction. *ReCALL*, *33*(1), 49–70.

Part 1

Emergency CALL at the Time of a Pandemic

2

A Distracted Learning Pandemic: The Aftermath of Synchronous Online Courses

Larry L. LaFond

Background

In the mid-spring of 2020, university teaching and learning around the world underwent a sudden and necessary pivot from face-to-face (f2f) to online teaching due to the global Covid-19 pandemic. The degree to which any individual university was affected depended on a variety of interacting factors, for example, how much of that university's curriculum was already taught online, how many faculty had experience in online teaching or how well local infrastructure could support a full online curriculum. Some institutions initially thought that the pandemic would be brief, but as the virus spread and death tolls rose, most universities decided that safety concerns compelled them to continue fully online during the 2020–1 school year. By fall of 2021, with greater experience with masking, social distancing, testing and vaccination, some f2f classes gradually re-emerged.

Lessons have been learnt about how to remain physically safe during a pandemic, but what has been learnt about the dynamics of teaching and learning in this context? Distance learning and asynchronous online classes are not new, but the sudden shift to 100% online meant that many instructors had a steep learning curve to move their classes rapidly to the synchronous online modality. One widespread strategy, made feasible and economical through refinements in technology over the past decade, involved shifting teaching from f2f to synchronous videoconferencing platforms such as Skype, Zoom, Microsoft Teams or Google Meet.

The availability of *synchronous* environments mistakenly led some to assume classroom pedagogies would easily transfer online, a notion quickly dispelled when faculty attempted to teach classes using similar methods as their f2f classes. After just a few weeks, students who endured long online lectures began to learn and retain less and began experiencing physical, emotional and psychological ailments.

This chapter explores some of those cognitive challenges that students experienced, using the reported experiences of students who had not regularly taken synchronous online courses before the pandemic. Following a literature review of some key issues affecting synchronous online learning, the research questions, design of the study and data collection are presented. The chapter concludes with discussion of the data and reflection on lessons learnt about online education during the pandemic.

Literature Review

That emerging technologies may distract students is not a new phenomenon. Early discussions of these distractions focused on the f2f classroom and, later, distance education (initially, *correspondence studies*). The launch of televised university classes in the 1950s brought new hope that technology would transform distance learning. A few decades later, institutions like the University of Phoenix were ready to take advantage of revolutions in distance education and began offering fully online degrees in 1989. Many students in the early 1990s were just experiencing their first use of email and the internet, but these new tools were not typically inside university classrooms. By 2000, course management systems (Blackboard, WebCT, etc.) had become more commonplace and internet usage more widespread. The development of cell phones that could link with the internet in 2001 created a new set of distractions in the classroom.

During the past two decades, many studies have discussed detrimental effects technology may pose in both the classroom and online learning (Burak, 2012; Foerde et al., 2006; Grewal & Harris, 2009; Sana et al., 2013). Research on these emerging technologies also considered how these technologies may be used in (asynchronous) teaching, what best practices might be developed and how readiness deficits may be addressed (Hung et al., 2010; Kebritchi et al., 2017; LaFond, 2002). Online education was also examined through the lens of different learner variables such as age, motivation, time management and attention. For example, Cercone (2008) proposed online learning designs tailored to adult learners, recognizing that older adult learners often have special obstacles related to work and family pressures, age-related insecurities and unfamiliar technologies.

Although research on online teaching and learning has continued for many years, there is little doubt that a new context arose in March 2020, when the World Health Organization declared the outbreak of Covid-19 as a pandemic. The announcement prompted universities to rapidly seek convenient, cost-effective solutions to continue their course offerings remotely. Since some pedagogical and course management functions were already being conducted online by many instructors (grade books, readings, assignments, discussion boards, videos), the idea of shifting fully online seemed a prudent solution. This decision was further buttressed by the studies in the previous decade that showed that online technologies could be a credible platform for student learning and provide positive learning outcomes (Chen et al., 2010; Kauffman, 2015; Yukselturk & Bulut, 2007). At the time, a majority of university courses were f2f with designated meeting times, and since many instructors were unprepared to instantly deliver pedagogically sound asynchronous classes, the promise of newly developed synchronous conferencing tools were thought to be an answer; consequently, the f2f course schedule was moved to synchronous online.

Optimism about synchronous online learning was soon tempered by the reality of what happened when students' *full* academic schedules became online synchronous. It took only a few weeks before students and faculty alike experienced levels of distraction unlike any they had seen before. Most could not resist the temptation to open new tabs on their computer screens or multitask in other ways during meetings or class sessions. Environmental disruptions added to the distraction. Less was being learnt.

It had taken only a few years for Zoom to move from being a new upstart company in 2011, to domination of the web-conferencing world (Aboulezz, 2021). Within the new context of the pandemic, Zoom achieved the status of a household name. Consequently, when a newly observed malady appeared, it was given the name, 'Zoom fatigue', regardless of the synchronous platform being used. A number of studies have considered how student behaviours changed, how students developed physical and psychological ailments and how they became less productive in the wake of the pandemic (Fauville et al., 2021; Nadler, 2020; Peper et al., 2021; Vaskivska et al., 2021).

Distracted learning is the primary symptom of the shift to synchronous online learning this chapter explores. Students sometimes think that opening a new tab on their computer screen during an online course is harmless and efficient. Some argue that this digital doodling enhances their concentration, especially during long meetings. Some embrace multitasking, despite the broad evidence that the term 'multitasking' is misleading, since what brains are really doing is rapidly shifting between tasks, something that Ophir et al. (2009) showed actually consumes more time to perform a task and leads to poorer performance.

Burak's (2012) study of 774 students revealed great disparities between online and f2f multitasking behaviour, with the online environment manifesting high prevalence of multitasking, together with negative outcomes, including poorer learning outcomes and reduced GPAs. The impact of the *synchronous* courses on student learning has now become a burning question as we begin to process the impact of the pandemic, and studies are appearing that consider numerous questions (Daniel, 2020; Fisher et al., 2021; Murphy, 2020; Tsang et al., 2021). Some researchers have highlighted the difference between emergency remote teaching and well-planned online courses (Hodges et al., 2020; Iglesias-Pradas et al., 2021), with cautions against confusing one with the other or normalizing emergency measures.

Online and distance education have undergone a great deal of scrutiny for many years; however, the unique circumstances of the latest global pandemic require further thought. For one, many of the previous investigations were focused on particular learner variables that distinguished learners of differing ages, technical expertise, attentional focus, and online access. These concerns have not disappeared, but the context has changed and now prompts us to consider what factors the new situation poses. Much of the literature proceeds from an instructional design perspective, while fewer studies supply a qualitative analysis of the voices of learners who have endured new challenging conditions. It is precisely this gap that the current study addresses by focusing on the perspectives of learners.

Finally, it may be important to note the place of this chapter within this larger volume related to technologically enhanced language teaching and learning. After all, the early sections of this book are focused on issues related to CALL (Levy, 1997), particularly as used in direct language instruction. However, the varying technological enhancements associated with CALL are deployed within a teaching context; hence, their usefulness is highly dependent upon the quality of the content training that pre-service language teachers have received and the models that have informed their development. For this reason, the proficiency pre-service teachers develop in the use of CALL technologies is often dependent upon more general proficiencies they have developed in their teacher preparation programs. The quality of their own educational experiences, as will be shown, were significantly affected by the pandemic context.

Research Questions

Four questions that surface from the literature review relate to how we might better understand the experience of teaching and learning in the pandemic context, and what guidance we might take from that understanding. Specifically,

1. How does synchronous online learning in a pandemic context differ from earlier types of f2f or online learning?
2. Do findings regarding variables previously studied (e.g. age, level of study, attentional focus) need to be revisited in light of the pandemic context?
3. Did teaching modality during this pandemic impact levels of distraction and, ultimately, degree of learning success?
4. How might synchronous online courses be taught more effectively in the present context?

Methodology

Participants

Participants were students taking either undergraduate linguistics courses as part of their major or minor, or graduate students pursuing advanced degrees in either linguistics or Teaching English to Speakers of Other Languages. All students ($n = 288$) were at one of three universities in the North Central region of the United States. The average age of the undergraduate students ($n = 247$) was approximately twenty-one years, and approximately thirty-four years for graduate students ($n = 41$). Undergraduate students were taking courses in the principles of linguistics, syntactic analysis, history of the English language, American dialects, psycholinguistics and phonology. Graduate students were taking courses in grammar pedagogy, world languages and cultures, second-language acquisition and advanced linguistic theory. All of these students' courses were being taught in an online synchronous environment, using Zoom.

Instrument

There were two separate data collection instruments used. During the regular 2020–1 academic year, a survey using three open-ended questions was administered:

1. What challenges did you face related to understanding the content of our course in the online environment?
2. How has level of distractedness during these Zoom meetings compared to courses you have taken f2f?
3. What are some actions that either you or your instructor could take to reduce distractions or the temptation to multitask?

Surveys administered during Fall 2021 used those three open-ended questions, but were also followed by two closed-ended questions:

1. In which learning environment do you experience the greatest number of distractions or do the most multitasking?
2. Which of the following items has been a distraction to you during one of our classes this semester? (Select all that apply.)

The choices given for the first closed-ended question were these: (a) f2f classes, (b) asynchronous classes (no scheduled online meeting times), (c) synchronous classes (scheduled online meeting times) or (d) I have not experienced distraction or multitasked in any of these environments.

For the second closed-ended question, the choices were these: (a) other people around me who are not taking the class, (b) pets, (c) environmental noise, (d) other screens open on my computer or other media near me, (e) dropped internet connection or computer problems, (f) other and (g) does not apply – I have not been distracted at any time.

Data Collection

In the Spring 2020, Summer 2020, Spring 2021 and Summer 2021 semesters, data was collected from students at the end of their courses. During the Fall 2021 semester, data was collected during the third week of class. Participation in the survey was voluntary. The survey was placed on online course management pages and collected over a one-week window. Written responses to open-ended questions by graduate students fell within a range of 96–270 words, overall averaging 152 words. Responses to the open-ended questions by undergraduates fell within a range of seven to eighty-five words, overall averaging twenty-two words. The close-ended survey response rate was 72%, and the open-ended response rate was 68%. These were considered very good response rates, given the voluntary nature of the respondent pool.

Data Analysis

The high response rate to the closed-ended survey permitted the use of raw percentages as part of an analysis of the two questions. A qualitative analysis of responses to the open-ended question was conducted by establishing content categories relevant to the research questions. This task involved coding pattern content, but since the analysis was inductive, coding categories were derived directly from the text data. Once repeated themes were identified, those themes were given codes that were then used to mark each instantiation of that theme in the data. This iterative process led to the identification of three major categories derived from the data: distraction (D), fatigue (F) and reduced social interaction (RI).

Results

Most students who participated in the survey stated that their online learning experience during the pandemic involved high levels of distraction, although undergraduates and graduates reported somewhat different evaluations of the sources of the distractions and whether these distractions were worse than their normal experience with f2f or online courses. There were slight variations in how instructors used specific tools in Zoom (e.g. whiteboard, lecture, screen sharing, breakout groups, polling and chat) in these classes, but questions asked in the surveys were looking at the overall experience of students in their courses.

Responses from undergraduate students on the closed-end survey indicated that they experienced the greatest amount of distraction or did the most multitasking in synchronous online courses: 100% more than in asynchronous online courses and 600% more than in f2f courses. Responses from graduate students painted a different picture, with the majority of them (53%) indicating that they experienced the greatest amount of distraction, or did more multitasking, in asynchronous courses, while 47% of them found the synchronous environment more distracting. None of the graduate students found f2f classes the most distracting.

Differences in response patterns also appeared for the closed-ended question regarding the sources of the distractions. Text messages or messages on social media were the most common source given, although this source was selected by 100% of the undergraduates and only 70% of the graduates. Other differences included 80% of the undergraduates reporting dropped internet connections or computer problems, while graduates selected this choice 53% of the time. Also, undergraduates reported more distractions stemming from other people around them not taking the class (60%), while graduates reported this 47% of the time. Both graduates and undergraduates reported significant distractions with other screens open on their computers or other media near them (60%, undergraduate, and 53%, graduate). A full listing of their survey responses regarding sources of distraction may be seen in Table 2.1.

There were three open-ended questions posed to both graduates and undergraduates related to their experiences with the online synchronous course they were currently taking. These questions invited them to discuss the challenges the synchronous environment posed for understanding course content and the level of distractedness they faced during Zoom meetings and offer any suggestions they had about actions that could be taken, either by the instructor, or themselves, to reduce distractions.

An analysis of the content of these open-ended responses yielded three very frequent themes: distraction (arising from a variety of sources including the mode of learning, external environmental issues and 'multitasking' – i.e. engaging in multiple activities, seemingly at once, but actually in rapid succession), fatigue (displayed with an array

Table 2.1 Undergraduate and Graduate Survey Responses: Sources of Distraction

Undergraduate Students	(%)
Other people around me not taking the class	60.00
Pets	30.00
Other environmental noise	30.00
Other screens open on my computer or other media near me	60.00
Text messages or messages on social media	100.00
Dropped internet connection or other computer problems	80.00
Other	0.00
Does not apply – I have not been distracted at any time	0.00
Graduate students	**(%)**
Other people around me not taking the class	47.058
Pets	35.294
Other environmental noise	41.176
Other screens open on my computer or other media near me	52.941
Text messages or messages on social media	70.588
Dropped internet connection or other computer problems	52.941
Other	11.764
Does not apply – I have not been distracted at any time	5.882

of physical and psychological symptoms) and reduced interactions (mostly related to impoverished interactions between students and between student and professor).

Distraction

Nearly all students reported significantly increased levels of distraction, much of it due to the synchronous learning mode, multitasking or other environmental factors. Some students made explicit comparisons between online and f2f learning:

> The level of distractedness during these zoom meetings has increased drastically compared to in-person instruction. I am guilty of checking my phone/replying to emails during zoom class rather than giving my undivided attention to the course material. (Graduate A)

The lure of multitasking was also explicitly mentioned in many comments; however, as we see in these two undergraduate comments, multitasking, learning mode and environmental factors interact with one another:

> I think it's just so easy to pull up another tab and multitask on my personal computer when having a Zoom class. It's easy to get bored quickly and begin multitasking. I prefer in person classes because I am surrounded by a learning environment. At home I do not feel I am at school, therefore not taking it as seriously. (Undergraduate A)

Figure 2.1 A student's home arrangement of technology during class meetings.

> I think the level of distractedness rose during Zoom. You are not in a classroom setting where not only are you forced to pay attention to a certain extent, you are removed of all other distractions created near you because you are in learning environment. In a classroom, you do not have to worry about people coming to talk to you or thinking that you can multitask. (Undergraduate B)

One student, a computer science major and linguistics minor, provided a photograph of his assortment of screens and electronic devices he had open before him during class meetings.

Being at home was frequently mentioned as a source of distraction for both undergraduates and graduates. The presence of pets added to this concern.

> Honestly, being at home makes me far more distracted than I would be in a classroom setting. My dog pestering me, my phone right next to me, my screen in front of me, and my endless supply of snacks definitely makes it easier for my mind to wonder [*sic*]. (Undergraduate C)

> I have three cats and a dog and I often was distracted by them jumping on my desk, barking, or needing let in/out of my room and I felt like I was always debating turning my camera on and off if there was a pet onscreen, because I didn't want to distract my classmates as well … Zoom classes require much more self-discipline, which, over a long semester, can be hard to muster. (Graduate B)

Graduate B raises an issue also mentioned by others, how the onscreen movements or behaviour of one student potentially distracts another, as with this undergraduate:

> I am personally not too distracted during class. I try to stay focused and not do other things. I am more distracted by others doing things unrelated to class. It annoys me when people are obviously doing something else and not participating

in class … there are students who do not turn on their cameras even in breakout rooms, nor say anything. I find that disrespectful and I have to wonder why they are taking the course in the first place. (Undergraduate D)

A few students expressed that they were not concerned about the distractions they experienced, including one who felt that there were also positive aspects to the videoconferencing environment.

I would have just as easily been distracted in real life. There was no difference in how quickly my mind would wander, but it is more acceptable to be distracted in a zoom class, and not only that, but you can also use your computer to just pull up games or other websites while still remaining in the zoom call. (Undergraduate E)

Distractedness is sort of a mixed bag. There are the minuses you're expecting, like other applications pulling my attention away. But there are also some plusses. For one, I always used noise-cancelling headphones, and those combined with your microphone and connection's good quality meant I could hear you more clearly with less auditory distraction than I might have in a real classroom. (Undergraduate F)

Fatigue

It is hard to separate the fatigue experienced as a result of online coursework from the general malaise felt by many people, students or not, during the pandemic. Disrupted lives, lost jobs, displacement from student housing and loss of social connectedness were experienced by a number of these students. Fatigue attributed to the learning modality appeared prominent in student responses. Some reported increased anxiety, low motivation or minor physical irritations related to the online platform:

I prefer watching the zoom meeting which the background of it is black than going to other website's [sic] with multicolor and bright white backgrounds because I don't want my eyes to feel like burning. (Undergraduate G)

I will have to admit that at the very end of the class meetings my mind kind of drifts away and I can't process what is going on sometimes. (Undergraduate H)

All my roommates are on different schedules and this further complicated me finding a quiet space for the class period. My roommates would take calls and typically did not wear headphones for school meetings. These things wore on my patience and my ability to focus on class. (Undergraduate I)

On Zoom, it is hard not to look down at your phone during class due to burnout. Every week, we are meeting on Zoom numerous times with many different professors and it gets old quick, especially since we have been doing this for over a year now. Things were just easier face-to-face; it was easier to pay attention. (Undergraduate J)

These complaints were even more pronounced among graduate students, who at two of the three universities in this study had lengthy night courses.

> I feel as though distractions and multitasking are inevitable in an online, synchronous class that is 3 hours long at night. By this point, people are tired and ready to be done for the day so focusing for the entirety of a class at this time and in this manner is hard to do. (Graduate C)

> I was completely mentally drained from zoom by the time online evening classes came around … and the combination of it being 2 hr 45 min and online just did not work well for how I learn. (Graduate D)

Along with fatigue, some made reference to loss of attention and motivation:

> I feel as though online synchronized meetings are never ideal … This semester I have 3 classes that are all online 6–9 pm. This semester is also when I am experiencing the most trouble paying attention during the synchronized meetings. I usually tend to lose motivation and energy by the end of class. (Graduate E)

Reduced Interaction

Loss of social connectedness has been a prominent characteristic of the pandemic. Based on student responses, online courses both exacerbated the problem and displayed signs of it. Students found reduced interactions a noticeable feature of synchronous learning.

> In a physical classroom, there was always moments before class or opportunities to ask peers questions relating to the class. This could be over anything like homework, concepts, what pages are assigned, or to reconfirm due dates … The few minutes before class to ask casual questions among peers while the professor isn't specifically involved is something I severely missed. It is hard to do college alone from your bedroom. (Undergraduate K)

> I definitely think being there in person to be able to answer questions more freely and being around classmates in person, bounce ideas off each other and such, would have helped with understanding the content of the course. (Undergraduate L)

Some of the loss of interaction was attributed to the specific features of online videoconferencing, particularly muting.

> It definitely feels harder to participate and ask questions when you have to mute and unmute constantly as not to interrupt others. (Undergraduate M)

It's intimidating just to hit the unmute button. So, when you are going to hit the unmute button, it feels more like a performance. To illustrate this, it would be like having an in-person classroom where each time someone wants to speak, ask a question, or contribute they have to stand up and go to the front of the room. (Graduate F)

Suggestions

Students offered a wide variety of suggestions about how synchronous environments could be improved, many of which were pithy and direct. One said that if she had to take another synchronous online course, she would be sure to 'take her dogs on a longer walk before class', presumably so that she would not need to potty the dog during class (Graduate G). Another suggested, 'Try as best as possible to go back to face-to-face' (Undergraduate N). There were conflicting recommendations based on individual preference. One student stated,

> Breakout rooms tend to keep my focus better than lecture-style zoom meetings. I could definitely eliminate distractions on my end as well, but sometimes it is very difficult when my attention is not fully on a subject. (Graduate H)

Another remarked,

> I think it would help if we went into breakout rooms less. Once we are broken into small groups, not only does it give me anxiety, which makes learning a lot harder, but once we come back to the main session, it is extremely hard to refocus. (Graduate I)

There were suggestions that synchronous online courses should have 'less lecture and more discussion' (Undergraduate O) or, somewhat less terse,

> I think for online synchronous classes to work they need to be discussion based and involve a lot of participation. Otherwise, they should just be pre-recorded so that students can watch in their own time and even speed up the recording so they can focus more. (Undergraduate P)

In one instance, a student suggested that the university should be doing more to assist,

> I think the school could advertise more places on campus we could take these classes or have these meetings that are a bit more secluded, as this would at least help to get students away from distractions such as roommates or pets. (Undergraduate Q)

Quite often students remarked that they needed to take responsibility themselves to improve their class experience:

> I should have my phone away from me or on do not disturb so that I am not receiving notifications. I definitely prefer the asynchronous style, as it allows

me to work at my own pace when I am certain I am free of distractions. (Undergraduate R)

To prevent any possibility of unnecessary distractions or temptations to multitask, I plan to begin implementing note-taking during class sessions. This might help me control my focus and perhaps ask questions I didn't realize I had. (Graduate J)

Discussion

This study posited four research questions which can now receive at least provisional answers. Student responses to the closed-ended and open-ended questions suggest that synchronous online learning in a pandemic context does differ from earlier types of f2f or online learning. Much of the research on online teaching in the past was conducted in a context quite unlike that experienced during the pandemic. For example, the experience of students who previously took a mixture of classes, f2f and online, was quite different from that of students who had never previously taken an online course and now had full course loads of entirely synchronous courses.

Even for those who had previously taken many online courses, the situation had dramatically changed when all meetings, and many social interactions, in their life were moved to videoconferencing. Previous research largely explored how an online course might be taught in a pedagogical sound way. What that research did not envision was a context where students sat online from morning to night to conduct their jobs, to interact with family and to take their courses. Data from the survey reveals that whatever online learning had been in the past, it became a different beast when all of life moved online. Students experienced more distractions, less social connectedness and more physical and psychological challenges.

Data from the study also gives us reason to suspect that previously studied variables operated differently during the pandemic. For example, while older students were considered to have unique challenges pre-pandemic, they reported fewer distractors during synchronous courses in these areas. Compared to undergraduates, fewer reported distractions from text messages, dropped internet connections or other people around them. In fact, 5.88% of the older adults reported that they experienced none of the potential distractors listed. Other research examined the detrimental effects of self-focusing leading to poorer performance on cognitive tests, but Bailenson (2021) argues that studies of this type are based on tests taking less than an hour, providing 'no data on the effects of viewing oneself for many hours per day (p. 4).

Many students reported fewer distractions in f2f courses compared with online courses. Graduate and undergraduate students differed somewhat in their judgements over which involved more distractions, synchronous or asynchronous, but open-ended comments showed that some undergraduates conflated distraction and procrastination. It would not be surprising to find that procrastination occurs more frequently in asynchronous courses.

Lessons Learnt

This study asked how synchronous online courses might be taught more effectively in the present context; in short, what has been learnt? Student responses to a similar question made references to structuring classes in a more interactional way, 'more discussion, less lecture'. That recommendation is probably sound for many synchronous classes, pandemic or not, and it could address some of the interactional deficit experienced in synchronous classes. There were also various suggestions regarding breakout rooms (pros and cons), greater campus availability of distraction-free spaces and a reassessment of course scheduling, particularly whether synchronous online is appropriate for a once-a-week class meeting for several hours. Again, these suggestions appear reasonable.

Students admitted there was more they could do themselves to enhance their focus. Some suggested that taking written notes, as in an f2f course, might help attention and lessen distractions. Some spoke of getting away from their house, where it was tempting to treat the course too casually. Others said they needed to do a better job of getting prepared for class, turning off notifications and reviewing content. All of this revealed a belief that preparation for the class meeting would help with engagement and focus.

Beyond modifying class procedures and scheduling, there are also a variety of practical technical options that can be taken to address the fatigue that has been associated with synchronous online learning. The literature is growing related to these modifications (Bailenson, 2021; Flanigan & Titsworth, 2020; Peper et al., 2021). For example, one issue students face is, ironically, their face. Gazing at ourselves while we attempt to learn is distracting and tiring. Bailenson (2021) illustrates this with the following analogy: 'Imagine in the physical workplace, for the entirety of an 8-hr workday, an assistant followed you around with a handheld mirror, and for every single task you did and every conversation you had, they made sure you could see your own face in that mirror' (p. 4). Unfortunately, our students have found themselves in an analogous circumstance during the pandemic. While it may be difficult to convince them to hide the self-view, those who do so may experience positive effects.

One student considered taking her dog on longer walks before class. Videoconferencing does create a situation where one sits in the same spot for extended periods, and this reduction in mobility is also associated with greater lethargy and less focus. Students can become frozen in place, which leads to excessive close-up eye contact with a screen full of faces. Besides hiding the self-view, reducing the size of the videoconferencing window can reduce the cognitive load and intensity of the course session (Bailenson, 2021).

These solutions, however, sidestep one obvious question: should synchronous courses be the mode of choice at all in a context such as the one from which we are emerging? In similar circumstances, perhaps not. Considering our students' experiences with synchronous online courses during the pandemic, we must view emergency remote learning as something quite different from carefully planned online courses. At least in terms of distractions, purely synchronous teaching may be the least favourable option for many learners. If we once again find ourselves in a position of a complete, rapid movement to online teaching, it may be better to consider asynchronous or hybrid options, or any other solution that avoids subjecting our students to negative effects of relentless videoconferencing.

References

Aboulezz, O. (2021). How Zoom won the pandemic. *Digital Innovation and Transformation*. Retrieved 8 March 2021, from https://digital.hbs.edu/platform-digit/submission/how-zoom-won-the-pandemic/.

Bailenson, J. (2021). Nonverbal overload: A theoretical argument for the causes of Zoom fatigue. *Technology, Mind, and Behavior, 2*(1). Retrieved 6 April 2021, from https://doi.org/10.1037/tmb0000030.

Burak, L. (2012). Multitasking in the university classroom. *International Journal for the Scholarship of Teaching and Learning, 6*(2). Retrieved 12 June 2021, from https://doi.org/10.20429/ijsotl.2012.060208.

Cercone, K. (2008). Characteristics of adult learners with implications for online learning design. *AACE Review, 16*(2), 137–59.

Chen, P., Lambert, A., & Guidry, K. (2010). Engaging online learners: The impact of Web-based learning technology on college student engagement. *Computers & Education, 54*(4), 1222–32. Retrieved 20 February 2021, from https://doi.org/10.1016/j.compedu.2009.11.008.

Daniel, S. (2020). Education and the Covid-19 pandemic. *Prospects, 49*(1), 91–6. Retrieved 9 December 2021, from https://doi.org/10.1007/s11125-020-09464-3.

Fauville, G., Luo, M., Muller Queiroz, A., Bailenson, J., & Hancock, J. (2021). Zoom exhaustion & fatigue scale. *Social Science Research Network, 4*(August–December), Retrieved 27 July 2021, from https://doi.org/10.1016/j.chbr.2021.100119.

Fisher, M., Dorner, M., Maghzi, K., Achieng-Evensen, C., Whitaker, L., Hansell, F., St. Amant, J., & Gapinski, S. M. (2021). Liminality, disruption, and change: A prismatic look at pandemic education. *Prospects, 51*, 523–40. Retrieved 9 July 2021, from https://doi.org/10.1007/s11125-021-09563-9

Flanigan, A., & Titsworth, S. (2020). The impact of digital distraction on lecture note taking and student learning. *Instructional Science, 48*(5), 495–524. Retrieved 25 September 2021, from https://doi.org/10.1007/s11251-020-09517-2.

Foerde, K., Knowlton, B., & Poldrack, R. (2006). Modulation of competing memory systems by distraction. *Proceedings of the National Academy of Sciences, 103*(31), 11778–83. Retrieved 9 July 2021, from https://doi.org/10.1073/pnas.0602659103.

Grewal, S., & Harris, L. (2009). Learning virtually or virtually distracted? The impact of emerging internet technologies on pedagogical practice. In N. Panteli (Ed.), *Virtual Social Networks: Mediated, Massive and Multiplayer Sites* (pp. 18–35). Palgrave Macmillan UK. Retrieved 8 June 2020, from https://doi.org/10.1057/9780230250888_2.

Hodges, C., Moore, S., Lockee, B., Trust, T., & Bond, M. (2020). *The difference between emergency remote teaching and online learning.* Retrieved 15 September 2022, from https://er.educause.edu/articles/2020/3/the-difference-between-emergency-remote-teaching-and-online-learning.

Hung, M., Chou, C., Chen, C., & Own, Z. (2010). Learner readiness for online learning: Scale development and student perceptions. *Computers & Education*, *55*(3), 1080–90. Retrieved 16 January 2020, from https://doi.org/10.1016/j.compedu.2010.05.004.

Iglesias-Pradas, S., Hernández-García, Á., Chaparro-Peláez, J., & Prieto, J. (2021). Emergency remote teaching and students' academic performance in higher education during the Covid-19 pandemic: A case study. *Computers in Human Behavior*, *119*, 106713. Retrieved 29 December 2021, from https://doi.org/10.1016/j.chb.2021.106713.

Kauffman, H. (2015). A review of predictive factors of student success in and satisfaction with online learning. *Research in Learning Technology*, *23*. Retrieved 29 December 2021, from https://doi.org/10.3402/rlt.v23.26507.

Kebritchi, M., Lipschuetz, A., & Santiague, L. (2017). Issues and challenges for teaching successful online courses in higher education: A literature review. *Journal of Educational Technology Systems*, *46*(1), 4–29. Retrieved 8 December 2021, from https://doi.org/10.1177/0047239516661713.

LaFond, L. (2002). Learner access in the virtual classroom: The ethics of assessing online learning. *Kairos*, *7*(3). Retrieved 8 December 2021, from https://kairos.technorhetoric.net/7.3/coverweb.html.

Levy, M. (1997). *Computer-assisted language learning: Context and conceptualization*. Oxford University Press.

Murphy, M. (2020). Covid-19 and emergency eLearning: Consequences of the securitization of higher education for post-pandemic pedagogy. *Contemporary Security Policy*, *41*(3), 492–505. Retrieved 8 December 2021, from https://doi.org/10.1080/13523260.2020.1761749.

Nadler, R. (2020). Understanding 'Zoom fatigue': Theorizing spatial dynamics as third skins in computer-mediated communication. *Computers and Composition*, *58*, 102613. Retrieved 2 December 2021, from https://doi.org/10.1016/j.compcom.2020.102613.

Ophir, E., Nass, C., & Wagner, A. (2009). Cognitive control in media multitaskers. *Proceedings of the National Academy of Sciences*, *106*(37), 15583–7. Retrieved 8 January 2022, from https://doi.org/10.1073/pnas.0903620106.

Peper, E., Wilson, V., Martin, M., Rosegard, E., & Harvey, R. (2021). Avoid Zoom fatigue, be present and learn. *NeuroRegulation*, *8*(1), 47. Retrieved 4 March 2022, from https://doi.org/10.15540/nr.8.1.47.

Sana, F., Weston, T., & Cepeda, N. (2013). Laptop multitasking hinders classroom learning for both users and nearby peers. *Computers & Education*, *62*, 24–31. Retrieved 9 June 2022, from https://doi.org/10.1016/j.compedu.2012.10.003.

Tsang, J., So, M., Chong, A., Lam, B., & Chu, A. (2021). Higher education during the pandemic: The predictive factors of learning effectiveness in Covid-19 online learning. *Education Sciences*, *11*(8), 446. Retrieved 2 March 2022, from https://doi.org/10.3390/educsci11080446.

Vaskivska, H., Palamar, S., Kravtsova, N., & Khodakivska, O. (2021). Transformation of the learning process in higher education institutions under the influence of the of pandemic Covid-19. *Wiadomosci Lekarskie (Warsaw, Poland: 1960)*, *74*(6), 1505–9. Retrieved 13 October 2021, from https://doi.org/10.36740/WLek202106140.

Yukselturk, E., & Bulut, S. (2007). Predictors for student success in an online course. *Journal of Educational Technology & Society*, *10*(2), 71–83.

//3

Italian as a Second Language in Schools during the Covid-19 Pandemic: Exploring Teachers' Perspectives

Stefania Ferrari

Introduction

In Italy in February 2020, school buildings were gradually closed, forcing teachers to work for the remaining part of the school year with the mediation of technology. Such a sudden technological shift was not the result of a planned innovation, but a forced choice: the only alternative available to continue to do what used to take place in the classroom. In other words, the health emergency resulting from the Covid-19 pandemic and the consequent migration of teaching activities to the web led teachers to seek new solutions for a number of aspects: from lesson planning to material development, including changes in methodological choices. Everything happened on the field, day by day, without the time to plan and experiment in advance.

The exceptional nature of the situation, together with the new challenges posed by the actual pandemic phase, calls for urgent research on the distance learning/teaching process. With the aim of contributing something new to the current debate, this work explores the online teaching experience in the field of Italian as an additional language in mainstream education. Through a series of extensive semi-structured interviews, distance teaching from the teacher's perspective has been investigated focusing on a number of issues: not only lesson planning, material and activity choices, teaching strategies and techniques employed, but also teachers and students' familiarity with technologies before the pandemic, teacher training during the pandemic, organizational aspects and collaboration with families and among colleagues.

In the following pages, after presenting the Italian context in terms of inclusion projects and briefly discussing the first surveys on distance teaching in Italy during 2020, the methodology employed for the present research is described, and the main results are discussed. Finally some concluding reflections and post-Covid lessons are presented.

The Teaching of Italian as an Additional Language in Italy

In the European context, educational support policies for newly arrived migrant children and more generally students with migrant background are organized following two main models: a *separated* one, which includes preparatory classes before accessing mainstream education, and an *integrated* one, where newly arrived students are welcomed in mainstream classes. The Italian model is generally defined as *integrated*, as students enter school attending classes with corresponding age and level of instruction, while they can access special courses dedicated to the teaching of Italian as a second language, if made available by their institution. Comparing different European support policies, a recent report (European Union, 2013) defines the Italian model as a *non-systematic* support model:

> The model is characterized by randomness of the support provided. Countries that are attributed to this group have no clearly articulated policy on the national level to support the integration of newly arrived migrant children or such policy exists, but is not effectively resourced and implemented. The support provided at regional, local and/or school level is highly fragmented as teachers, parents and local communities are largely left to their own devices. (p. 8)

The document describes the diverse approaches of the Italian school system, where institutions, associations or educational agencies variously support schools in inclusion projects, promoting Italian L2 teaching activities. At the national level, the role of external institutions in the implementation of such projects leads to strong local disparities: there are areas where projects have a certain solidity and others where supports are occasional. This element is certainly a peculiarity of the Italian situation: on the one hand, schools are stimulated in the creation of networks at the local level and encouraged to promote an integration between the various bodies dealing with minors and immigration; on the other hand, the success of such projects is determined by the ability of individual schools to create an active dialogue with local institutions. This is an additional challenge to effective inclusion, since it requires collaboration among different actors: schools, on the one hand, and local authorities, on the other.

In such a context, the pandemic and the consequent distance teaching generated different responses, with significant variations between institutions, even in the same local area. In many cases, the quality of inclusion projects was seriously at risk. The present work aims at investigating how schools and institutions dealt with the teaching of Italian as a second language during the period of school closure in 2020.

The First Surveys

Distance teaching during the health emergency rapidly brought about the publication of different studies, especially at the international level. At the time when the present research was carried out, most of these works were devoted to foreign-language learning, mainly in university contexts (e.g. Atmojo et al., 2020; Fansury et al., 2020; Febriani et al., 2020; Ferdig et al., 2020; Gao & Zhang, 2020; Hartshorne et al., 2020; Hodges et al., 2020; Lo Presti, 2020; MacIntyre et al., 2020).

Concerning the Italian school context, the first data came from four researches undertaken through spring and early summer 2020 and conducted, respectively, by the Ministry of Education,[1] CENSIS,[2] INDIRE[3] and SIRD.[4] The survey, 'A Comparative Study on Online Teaching Methods Adopted in Italian Schools in the Emergency Period COVID-19', carried out by SIRD (Girelli, 2020; Lucisano, 2020) is of particular interest for the present work since it shares with this study not only the main themes under investigation, but also their observation from the teacher's perspective. Moreover, as this is a wide-ranging study representative of the teaching population, it is a useful touchstone in identifying similarities and differences between mainstream teaching and Italian L2 teaching.

The SIRD survey showed that the critical issue in distance learning was students' participation: a quarter of the school population was unable to take part in distance class activities. Online schooling was therefore characterized by being first of all less accessible and inclusive, despite the effort teachers demonstrated by contacting students even personally through phone calls, messages and social media. The lack of internet connections or technological devices in families and an insufficient digital culture among both students and teachers, associated with the need to abruptly adapt teaching methodologies to the new context, were some of the possible reasons for such a limited participation. As the SIRD survey reported, teachers claimed that they had to face distance teaching without any specific preparation: despite the fact that over half of the respondents were trained in the use of multimedia and technologies in the classroom, most of them had not been able to actively adapt teaching technologies to online teaching. Data showed how teachers mainly preferred to adopt more traditional strategies, rather than shifting towards innovative solutions, with synchronous or asynchronous frontal lessons as the most common choice reported. Furthermore, as online activities required a remodelling of teaching programmes, teachers testified to a significant additional workload. Even with increased efforts, difficulties in managing online learning environments and involving students strongly reduced the effectiveness of learning and inclusion.

The Study

The present research focuses on the teaching of Italian as an additional language during the period of closure of school buildings in Italy between the end of February and the beginning of June 2020. As the Italian educational support policies for newly arrived migrant children are unsystematic, the present research refers to a limited geographical area – three provinces of Emilia Romagna region in Northern Italy – where the teaching of Italian as L2 is managed according to two models: on the one hand, projects carried out in collaboration with local authorities involving external experts with specific qualifications for teaching Italian as L2; on the other hand, activities promoted by entrusting additional assignments to in-service teachers, even in the absence of a specific qualification. Besides the level of specific training, external experts and in-service teachers differed with regard to the number of schools and students with which they usually work. External experts collaborated with five to ten different schools, carrying out various teaching modules of twenty-five to thirty hours and working generally with seventy to a hundred-and-twenty students each. Their activities were organized in group levels, which included both absolute beginner classes as well as more advanced groups. In-service teachers worked with smaller groups of two to ten students belonging to their own institution, teaching mainly beginners, with modules lasting ten to thirty hours.

Participation in the survey was on a voluntary basis, and teachers were contacted through their schools or training institutions. Data was collected in July 2020, thus encouraging a retrospective reflection on the experience of distance learning/teaching. In more detail, fourteen teachers participated in the survey, all women, aged between thirty and sixty-five, engaged in the teaching of Italian as L2 for a period ranging from ten to fifteen years. Seven of them worked as external experts on projects financed by local authorities, both in primary and secondary schools, while the remaining seven were in-service teachers with additional assignments for the teaching of Italian as L2. Of these, three worked in primary schools and four worked in secondary schools.

For data collection, in order to observe the perspective of teachers, extensive oral interviews were preferred to an online questionnaire. Oral interviews gave space to active listening, promoting a more intimate sharing of the experience. The interviews lasted from forty-five minutes to two hours. To ensure a certain degree of comparability among data, the interviewer had a list of questions to refer to, grouped into the following macro-areas:

- teaching context description;
- teachers and students' mastery of language teaching technologies;
- teachers and students' access to digital devices;
- start-up and organization of distance learning/teaching;
- distance learning/teaching tools and platforms;
- teaching strategies;
- institutions and colleagues' support;
- relationship with families;
- students' response to distance teaching.

All participants were surprisingly willing to share their experience; they all expressed interest in the investigation, which was considered mainly as an opportunity to evaluate the thoughts, emotions and choices of the past months of schooling, as it appeared in many of the emails received after the interview:

> It was very useful for me to participate in this research, it has helped me to sort out my ideas. These have been months of intense work and considerable emotional overload. I feel we have a lot to share amongst colleagues, if we really want to bring home something new from this experience. Despite years of teaching behind me, never before I found myself wondering so much about what I was doing. Unlike

what usually happens, we were not experimenting with a predefined goal or a structured training project, for many days the focus was simply on not getting lost.

Since the participation in the survey was on a voluntary basis, it should be noted that informants can be considered as particularly 'active' teachers involved in projects that in some way represent good practices in the field of Italian L2 teaching. The answers therefore indicate the perception of professionals who only partially represent the diversified world of Italian L2 teaching. In this sense, the study certainly does not have the ambition to be exhaustive, but rather aims at highlighting processes that may have been activated also in other contexts.

Once interviews were collected and transcribed, a content analysis was conducted, firstly marking distinct content elements and key points in each interview and secondly forming broader categories to describe the content of the informants' responses. The process involved two coders who analysed the corpus cooperatively.

Results

Results of the qualitative analysis conducted on the interviews are presented by grouping data around a series of themes. In this section, firstly, we discuss teachers and students' familiarity with technologies before the pandemic; secondly, we address aspects related to the organization of teaching activities: this includes both the possibility to access devices and the actions undertaken to contact students in order to start teaching lessons online. Thirdly, we focus on teaching programmes, activity and material selection, and subsequently, we describe the main teaching strategies adopted. Finally, we present reflections on the relationship with colleagues and families, concluding with post-Covid lessons.

Teachers' Familiarity with Language Teaching Technologies

The first issue addressed in the interviews was the familiarity with language teaching technologies. Of fourteen teachers interviewed, nine reported they had attended at least one training course on new technologies and language or curricular teaching. In particular, the external experts testified to a systematic use in class of multimedia materials, such as courses on CD-ROMs or educational websites, both in their classes or as recommended additional resources for students' autonomous work. All teachers regularly used interactive whiteboards, computers and audio–video materials in their lessons in the classroom. Several schools they worked with already systematically used platforms for sharing materials and homework in mainstream classes, although informants underlined that such teaching supports were not always easy to access for newly immigrated students. At any rate, no teacher had previous experience in the management of Italian L2 courses partially or entirely online.

As for the participation in training courses on language teaching technologies during the health emergency, ten teachers stated they took part in dedicated seminars, while four declared they considered the use of the platforms rather intuitive. In addition, three of the external experts opted for the organization of self-training and resource sharing groups, even with colleagues working in other projects. Referring to the quality of the training courses available at that time, teachers suggested a certain degree of dissatisfaction, as most of these initiatives were dedicated to the technical aspect of teaching platforms, rather than targeting their use for language teaching, in particular for Italian L2.

What emerged from all the interviews, regardless of the quality or quantity of previous training experiences, was a sense of unpreparedness. Despite the significant previous experience of the participants in the field of Italian L2 teaching, moving classes on the web required a complete review of their teaching strategies: teachers felt that they were starting off unprepared, without specific reference points, but they were determined to face the emergency and work at their best.

Students' Familiarity with Language Teaching Technologies

As for the students' familiarity with digital devices, a rather varied panorama emerged. Overall, teachers underlined how children were less autonomous than teenagers, even in schools where digital platforms were regularly used for resource sharing. Despite the spread of smartphones and tablets among students, especially at secondary levels, teachers highlighted how the autonomous use of technologies mainly concerned games and the social dimension, but not their educational application.

As we will see in more detail in the section dedicated to educational choices, students' limited autonomy with teaching technologies significantly influenced the work of Italian L2 teachers. Furthermore, interviews showed that newly arrived students attended Italian L2 online activities regularly, while in many cases they did not participate in distance mainstream classroom lessons. The presence of specific projects dedicated to the teaching of Italian L2 reduced the number of cases of dropout, ensuring at least a minimum level of lesson attendance during the period of school closure.

Access to Digital Devices

Closely connected to the topic of familiarity with language learning technologies is that of access to digital devices. For teachers, no difficulties emerged, while for students, the situation was more problematic. As teachers reported, smartphones were in many cases the only tool available, especially in the initial phase of distance teaching. Despite the fact that individual institutions slowly provided students with computers, tablets or access cards where necessary, the lack of computer skills and the presence of more than one child of school age in the household often limited the effectiveness of the interventions implemented. Smartphones therefore continued to be, for many, the only device for accessing online lessons.

This situation led L2 teachers to plan tailor-made courses, organizing lessons considering mainly the sort of device students could access, rather than the actual range of features offered by available platforms. In the same course, lessons could take place in different digital spaces: at the initial stage, trying not to exclude anyone, more informal applications such as Skype and WhatsApp were used. When possible, platforms like Zoom or Google Meet were introduced later on. In order to promote inclusion, a part of Italian L2 online classes were dedicated to IT literacy or specific training sessions for using teaching platforms employed in mainstream classrooms.

Where available, the cultural–linguistic mediators also played an important role in promoting access to mainstream online lessons:

> Many schools made tutorials for the use of platforms, but they turned out too complex for migrant families. We simplified and translated such access guides and we used them as a basis for individual mentoring or peer-to-peer support.

Briefly, interviews suggested how the presence of an Italian L2 teacher in the school, together with the possibility of drawing on mediation services, made it possible to reach, inform and include students who otherwise would not have been able to access online lessons independently.

Starting Online Activities

The organization and start-up of online activities were acknowledged by all the informants as the most complex phase. School closures caught everyone unprepared. Only five out of fourteen teachers started distance teaching in February, while the majority did it two to three weeks after school closure (more precisely, eight in March and one in April). The difference in time frames was closely linked to the quality of each inclusion project. Institutes with stable projects were able to start Italian L2 classes quickly; in other contexts, especially where it was difficult for the school itself to activate online teaching, the personal commitment of the single Italian L2 teacher played a significant role.

In particular, the initial phase was described as extremely expensive in terms of resources. It required careful monitoring, and students and family were often contacted one by one. Where L2 Italian teachers and mediation services had the opportunity to work together, online activities were activated more rapidly and successfully:

> At the beginning an enormous effort has been necessary. With the help of the mediation service, we called one by one all the migrant students and their families. The school started the official contact, and I participated with the help of interpreter as a bridge not only to get in touch with every single family but also to be sure they did understand what would have happened.

Informants also reported cases where Italian L2 online lessons were not made available, as some schools, even with a relevant number of migrant students, had major difficulties in activating online lessons for mainstream classes and therefore did not consider the teaching of Italian L2 as a priority at that time.

Data again confirmed how the presence of projects with a certain stability and dedicated resources was essential to make available and accessible not only Italian L2 classes, but also curricular lessons.

Teaching Strategies

The most extensive part of each interview concerned the description of choices in terms of syllabus design and teaching strategies. From a purely organizational point of view, the first aspect to draw teachers' attention was the need to create a balance between the organization of each Italian L2 project and the new context of distance teaching. More specifically, as Italian L2 is not a curricular subject but is organized as a project with a limited number of teaching hours, it rarely covers the entire school period. Particularly for external experts, in some cases, it was no longer possible to provide in every school Italian L2 support during the period of school building closure, as resources allocated to this activity had already been depleted, while in others, teachers had to start their online activities with a group of students they had not met before. At the time of school closure, only a part of Italian L2 classes had already started. In these cases, course planning and development was more complex as teachers had to carry out needs analysis and formative assessment online.

Besides, as external experts worked in different schools, they had to coordinate their weekly commitments. As a result, during distance teaching, the time schedule had to be adapted to students and schools' needs, thus resulting in a higher number of lessons to teach with different groups and levels. In addition, there was a need to balance Italian L2 lessons with mainstream activities, in terms of both timetable and curriculum design. Furthermore, mainstream teachers often required additional support to Italian L2 teachers in order to develop materials for bilingual students. In other words, online teaching led to an overload of commitments for many interviewed teachers, especially for external experts:

> My overall weekly working hours have doubled, compared to pretty much halved class time. I worked many hours unpaid, but it was the only way not to leave students alone.

If it was easier for curricular teachers to organize their work commitment by adapting it to the demands of distance teaching, this flexibility was not always feasible for external experts. All L2 teachers acknowledged the importance of reviewing the duration of their synchronous activities: if lessons generally lasted two hours once a week, online it was more effective to organize shorter and more frequent meetings, mainly because students' online attention span was reduced when compared to classroom presence:

> If in classroom we meet for a two hour slot once or twice a week, online you need to meet students more often preferably on a daily basis. It's a question of feasibility. At the beginning we tried to keep the classroom attendance timetable, so they were a bit uncomfortable in the sense that we immediately realised that it was impossible to do a two-hour lesson online with fifteen-year-old students. Then at that point ... I decided to teach classes one hour a day.

To summarize, in contexts where teachers have been able to work flexibly, adapting their lesson timetable to the needs of students and online learning, classes worked better, while where this was not done, lessons were less effective. Data suggested an intrinsic weakness of projects dedicated to Italian L2: as they were mainly based on external funding, unlike in the case of curricular teaching, it was not always possible to adapt their organization to distance teaching demands.

Concerning teaching choices, interviews showed a constant attempt to seek solutions appropriated to the various contexts. Altogether, distance classes were provided in four ways: (a) organizing online synchronous lessons dedicated specifically to Italian L2 learners; (b) offering individual online tutoring to support class activities; (c) regularly providing simplified materials to curricular teachers; and (d) teaching together with the curricular teacher, thus involving all students in the class where the bilingual learner was enrolled. More in detail, the first solution was generally adopted with absolute beginners: when the online curricular activities were not accessible to L2 learners, the class council preferred to encourage exclusive participation in Italian L2 activities. There were also cases, particularly in secondary school, where this choice was made by the individual student, who assiduously attended L2 activities, but was absent during many class proposals. The second solution was preferred for intermediate and advanced students, particularly in secondary schools. Italian L2 teachers prepared texts or simple video lessons to be used for self-study, eventually integrating them with brief tutoring sessions. The third solution was adopted in two types of situations: on the one hand, in schools where even in mainstream classes synchronous lessons were not implemented and, on the other hand, in schools where class teachers asked for explicit support from Italian L2 teachers. The fourth solution, less frequent and reported only by three out of fourteen teachers, was an example of good teaching practice stimulated by the emergency. In schools where a previous collaboration between class teachers and Italian L2 teachers already existed, a slot was created to experiment using inclusive teaching activities with the whole curricular class, favouring a merged endeavour between the class teacher and Italian L2 teacher.

Describing examples of individual lessons, however, a substantial difference emerged between in-service teachers and external experts' choices: for the former, online teaching triggered mainly transmittal modes, while for the latter, more interactive modes were adopted. The first comment below represents the approach of an in-service teacher, while the second that of an expert one:

> Unfortunately, the lesson became almost frontal. Google Meet, unfortunately, forced frontal lessons and I cannot hide it, the centrality of students was completely lost. We worked so many years for inclusion, students should be at the centre of the lesson and then with online teaching we inevitably found ourselves teaching from the pedestal. In my opinion there was a step backward.

> Compared to how lessons have changed, I'd say they changed for the better. I had the opportunity to give more space to each student and his/her needs, to go straight to what is necessary, to focus more our attention on language.

In-service teachers reported lessons organized mainly as follows: a video or a page from a textbook, usually shared synchronously as opening stimulus, followed by structured comprehension activities and grammar focus. In many cases, teaching materials were based on simplified rewriting of study materials assigned by mainstream class teachers. Despite the fact that in-service teachers acknowledge at least theoretically the importance of training students to use language in interaction, they were not able to give space to such kind of work during online lessons. In contrast, external experts described the distance experience as a chance to give an even more specific attention to spoken interaction. Among the most frequently used activities reported by external experts were the use of games, silent books, communicative tasks or problem-solving activities. Lessons were mainly dedicated to the interaction between students in pairs or in small groups, with feedback tailored to students' spoken or written production:

> We played a lot as it was useful to make lessons more stimulating and interactive, I was seeking students' active participation.
> We generally started each lesson with a problem to solve, and we worked on it interactively. For example, in order to develop writing skills, we wrote a formal email to the town mayor to find out when the gyms were meant to reopen.

Relating to the most practised skills, all external experts stated to focus mainly on the oral dimension of language and group work:

> Online lessons gave me the opportunity to work much more on oral production and interaction rather than written production. I think this was a positive result.

In other words, distance teaching, at least for external experts, stimulated a greater focus on oral communication and interaction, also offering a chance to enrich the variety of linguistic inputs to which students were exposed:

> Online teaching forced me to experiment on the use of many educational resources, as well as multimedia content of various types, authentic materials, and even the feedback was more rigorous and targeted.

In any case, interviews showed how online teaching did not lead to a real increase in the use of technologies for teaching; on the contrary, it forced teachers to reduce it in order to focus on language learning:

> Online teaching/learning has forced me to eliminate many things in order to get to the essentials, because I did strip away tools we generally use like books, computer, miming, in order to penetrate language. To discover language and its use. While maybe in classroom you present a Power Point, a video or an audio recording, to me, personally, distance has brought me back to spontaneity, to simple one to one or group interactions. In classroom I used to use the computer a lot, I used to work on individual written production, here I have gone back to the spoken words.

Despite the various examples of teaching strategies documented by the interviewees, many teachers highlighted a sense of general disappointment regarding the final results, especially where the evaluation of the effects of their educational choices were concerned.

The experience of distance teaching was inevitably an opportunity to actively reflect on teaching, on materials and activities that were more functional in this context, as well as appreciating the overall needs of students, which not only included language learning, but also the emotional and social dimensions:

> It has been an opportunity for an extraordinary professional growth. I have developed a certain mental and organisational flexibility and I have given even more importance to the continuous diversification of input and activities, so as to keep students' motivation at its highest. I constantly looked back at my teaching habits and more than anything I realised in class sometimes we do not listen to students, while online we were forced to.

In summary, beyond individual experiences, online teaching was acknowledged as a moment of professional growth, a space that has reopened questioning on how and what to teach, and even more significantly for teachers with lengthy professional experience.

The Relationship with Colleagues

The emergency situation and the consequent organizational and teaching challenges certainly favoured a stronger relationship among colleagues, although with some differences between external experts and in-service teachers. External experts stressed the importance of collaboration with other L2 colleagues. Online teaching led to an intensification of both coordination meetings and informal exchanges. In contrast, for in-service teachers, there were no opportunities to work with other L2 professionals. However, for both groups, a strengthening of relations with curricular teachers and mediation services emerged.

In summary, the online experience resulted in closer cooperation between colleagues, not so much through institutional moments, but rather through informal contacts. During distance teaching, the dialogue between colleagues moved from traditional exchanges to work out bureaucratic or organizational issues, to moments mainly dedicated to teaching and educational choices. Faced with the complexity of the situation, teachers felt the urgency of sharing teaching strategies and solutions adopted with colleagues.

Relationship with Families

In general, Italian L2 teachers have no direct contact with students' families, as curricular teachers deal with such relationships. With online teaching, in contrast, this professional figure also comes into contact with families, particularly during the start-up phase:

> We used the mediators and WhatsApp to get in touch with families. Usually, parents do not get in touch with the Italian L2 teacher, we had the opportunity to start a direct contact, at least with children in primary and middle schools.

Interviews highlighted how online teaching allowed an access to private family spaces, and teachers had the opportunity to learn more about the family context of each student. Indeed, in discussing the relationship with families, a word that resonates in all the interviews is actually 'intimacy'. All interviewed teachers recognized the key role of families during distance teaching. The experience undoubtedly opened for parents a 'window' into their children's school; for many, it was an opportunity to observe and witness first-hand school activities, to get to know teachers and to monitor attentively the ways in which their children took part in lessons. Many teachers, in fact, emphasized the presence of a family member during lessons:

> Mothers got more interested, more engaged in school life. Truly, next year, we should create a stronger alliance in this direction.

In summary, online learning highlighted the importance of positive and active relationships with families. In the case of migrant families, teachers usually lamented an absence from school institutional meetings. As the emergency prompted the school to find new channels and to increasingly expand one-to-one less formal communication with families, it was possible to focus on new communicative strategies. The 'intimate' relationship produced by online teaching strengthened in many cases the educational alliance between home and school, or at least, it paved the way towards a stronger connection.

Post–Covid-19 Lessons

Undoubtedly, the Covid-19 emergency exposed a series of limits of the Italian school system and its policy for inclusion: first of all, the asystematicity of dedicated projects – when present, they are usually delegated to external financing and they are limited in time and amount of resources allocated. The data discussed here show how the quality of L2 online teaching was directly proportional to the actual availability of resources devoted to trained professionals, such as mediators and expert Italian L2 teachers. However, the organization of inclusion projects in 'hourly packages' did not allow – even in more solid contexts – instructional continuity, so essential at such a delicate moment. Secondly, online teaching inevitably underlined the importance of establishing an active relationship with students' families, as their involvement in school life is a key element for successful interventions. Finally, the sudden shift of lessons to the web forced teachers, including experienced ones, to reflect and actively discuss their teaching approaches. The emergency accelerated knowledge acquisition in the use of technologies, both for students and teachers, but from the data discussed here, none recognized it as a major outcome. To the contrary, their enforced experimentation actually led, on the one hand, to analyse what is essential for teaching, and on the other, to carefully heed learners' needs. 'Attention to the relationship', 'interaction', 'variety of linguistic input', and 'active participation' were among the words and phrases most frequently used by interviewed teachers in describing the online experience. In some cases, these expressions were used to indicate what was missing and in others, to describe the path taken. Undoubtedly, what emerged from the survey was the opportunity generated by distance teaching towards a deeper reflection on personal teaching practices, rather than a greater integration of technological tools in teaching.

The months of online schooling have left professionals with a series of open questions, along with the feeling that they only partially succeeded in achieving their educational role. In other words, the emergency, with its challenges, stressed the urgent need for the development of structural and quality interventions for the linguistic support of bilingual students and for promoting inclusion and positive school achievement.

Notes

1. https://istruzioneveneto.gov.it/wp-content/uploads/2020/03/m_pi.AOODPPR.REGISTRO-UFFICIALEU.0000318.11-03-2020.pdf (last accessed 5 September 2021).
2. https://www.censis.it/sites/default/files/downloads/Diario%20della%20Transizione.pdf (last accessed 5 September 2021).
3. http://www.indire.it/2020/07/29/indagine-indire-sulle-pratiche-didattiche-durante-il-lockdown-uscito-il-report-preliminare/ (last accessed 10 September 2021).
4. http://www.sird.it/ (last accessed 12 January 2022).

References

Atmojo, A. E., & Nugroho, A. (2020). EFL classes must go online! Teaching activities and challenges during COVID-19 pandemic in Indonesia. *Register Journal, 13*(1), 49–76. https://doi.org/10.18326/rgt.v13i1.49-76.

European Union. (2013). *Study on educational support for newly arrived migrant children*. Publications Office of the European Union. Retrieved 15 September 2022, from https://op.europa.eu/en/publication-detail/-/publication/96c97b6b-a31b-4d94-a22a-14c0859a8bea.

Fansury, A. H., Januarty, R., & Syawal, A. W. R. (2020). Digital content for millennial generations: Teaching the English foreign language learner on COVID-19 pandemic. *Journal of Southwest Jiaotong University, 55*(3). https://doi.org/10.35741/issn.0258-2724.55.3.40.

Febriani, S. R., Widayanti, R., Amrulloh, M. A., & Mufidah, N. (2020). Arabic learning for elementary school during Covid-19 emergency in Indonesia. *Okara Journal, 14*(1), 67–80. https://10.19105/ojbs.v14il.3194.

Ferdig, R. E., Baumgartner, E., Hartshorne, R., Kaplan-Rakowski, R., & Mouza, C. (2020). *Teaching, technology, and teacher education during the COVID-19 pandemic: Stories from the field*. Association for the Advancement of Computing in Education (AACE). Retrieved 15 September 2022, from https://www.learntechlib.org/p/216903/.

Gao, L. X., & Zhang, L. J. (2020). Teacher learning in difficult times: Examining foreign language teachers' cognitions about online teaching to tide over COVID-19. *Frontiers in Psychology, 11*. https://doi.org/10.3389/fpsyg.2020.549653.

Girelli, C. (2020). La scuola e la didattica a distanza nell'emergenza Covid-19. *RicercaAzione, 12*(1), 203–20.

Hartshorne, R., Baumgartner, E., Kaplan-Rakowski, R., Mouza, C., & Ferdig, R. E. (2020). Special issue editorial: Preservice and inservice professional development during the COVID-19 pandemic. *Journal of Technology and Teacher Education*, *28*(2), 137–47. Retrieved 15 September 2022, from https://www.learntechlib.org/primary/p/216910/.

Hodges, C., Moore, S., Lockee, B., Trust, T., & Bond, A. (2020). The difference between emergency remote teaching and online learning. *Educause Review*. Retrieved 15 September 2022, from https://er.educause.edu/articles/2020/3/the-difference-between-emergency-remote-teaching-and-online-learning.

Lo Presti, M. V. (2020). Second language distance learning: The issue of language certification in the time of COVID-19, *European Journal of Education*, *3*(2), 89–102.

Lucisano, P. (2020). Fare ricerca con gli insegnanti. I primi risultati dell'indagine nazionale SIRD 'Per un confronto sulle modalità di didattica a distanza adottate nelle scuole italiane nel periodo di emergenza COVID-19'. *Lifelong, Lifewise Learning*, *17*(36), 3–25. https://doi.org/10.19241/lll.v16i36.551.

MacIntyre, P., Gregersen, T., & Mercer, S. (2020). Language teachers' coping strategies during the Covid-19 conversion to online teaching: Correlations with stress, wellbeing and negative emotions, *System*, *94*. https://10.1016/j.system.2020.102352.

4

From Emergency Transitions to Teaching English Online: Three Cases

Carla Meskill, Wuri Kusumastuti and Dongni Guo

Introduction

Moving to online teaching is not a simple step. Yet such a step had to be taken under emergency conditions in 2020 when schools around the globe were closed. What came to be known as *emergency remote learning* became the imperative. This emergency response differs significantly from the highly informed and intentionally designed *online instruction* that had been a success story for nearly three decades prior to the international pandemic. Under non-emergency conditions, the move to online instruction requires complex conceptual shifts and concomitant actions to ensure that the medium is used in pedagogically positive ways. Indeed, Yen et al. (2018) rightly contend that teaching digitally is neither immediate nor instinctive for many educators. In the best of times there are major conceptual challenges that need to be thoroughly deconstructed and well understood as part of becoming a skilled online educator (Gacs et al., 2020; Meskill et al., 2020). These become even more challenging under emergency circumstances (Hodges et al., 2020).

This study examined three English language teaching (ELT) educators' knowledge, perceptions of online teaching, and how these, along with local supports and constraints, shaped praxis; and how, in turn, praxis reshaped the knowledge base. We queried teachers of English as a second or foreign language from three diverse cultures and contexts: a suburban US high school, a Chinese elementary school, and an Indonesian middle school. Each shared how s/he undertook the move to online instruction, specifically the roles of their prior knowledge, the sociocultural context, and how they conceptualized the online medium. From their accounts, we learn not only about similarities and differences between knowledge, perceptions and practices, but also about sociocultural milieus and how these contributed to shaping their online instructional practices.

Online Language Education

Online language education has been a mainstay for over twenty-five years. Students at all levels from around the world have successfully studied additional languages through the careful design of online instructional experiences by their teachers. Digital resources to support this instruction abound and include social media-like platforms to practice authentic language use, authentic target language digital content, and integrated automated learning activities. In spite of this wealth of digital affordances, prior to the emergency transition to online teaching, opportunities to develop the knowledge and skills needed to teach K-12 online were widely advocated but spottily supported. This was in large part due to the absence of clear goals and aims for such opportunities (Moore-Adams, et al., 2016) especially for language education (Meskill et al., 2020).

Nation (2007) describes an ideal language course as consisting of four equally balanced strands: (1) meaning-focused listening and reading; (2) language-focused instruction; (3) meaning-focused speaking and writing; and (4) fluency development activities. What is common to these four elements is the goal for students to fully master the target language for authentic, active use. They therefore need intensive practice in authentic comprehension and production of the language (Savignon, 2018; Swain, 2000). Thus, teachers of English moving their practices online must master strategies to involve active student engagement in communicative activity in new online spaces. In addition to understanding the affordances of those spaces, this involves knowing students well and tailoring accordingly (Beasley & Beck, 2017; Meskill et al., 2002; Meskill et al., 2020). Further, online contexts of language teaching require reconceptualizing instruction in lieu of duplicating face-to-face language classrooms (Compton, 2009; Hampel & Stickler, 2005; Meskill & Anthony, 2015). Because language learning puts greater demands on interactivity and communication between and among teachers and students, it requires instructional and communicative skills that are different from teaching other subjects online (Compton, 2009). In large part, online language education depends on 'carefully designed CMC tasks in conjunction with effective strategies, such as teacher modeling and scaffolding for fully online instruction are essential to boost learner autonomy in a meaningful and productive way' (Lee, 2016, p. 94).

Bennett and Marsh (2002) suggest that teachers should develop the competence to identify differences and similarities between face-to-face and online teaching and address the strategies and techniques afforded by online teaching. In addition, based partly on Hampel and Stickler's (2005) pyramid of online language teaching skills, Compton proposes a new framework comprising three categories: technology, pedagogy and evaluation. The pedagogy category consists of five types of knowledge that novice online teachers should have: (a) knowledge of strategies for online community building and socialization; (b) knowledge of strategies to facilitate communicative competence and online interaction; (c) knowledge of language learning theories for online language learning; (d) knowledge of curriculum design frameworks for online language learning; and (e) knowledge of strategies for online language assessment

(Compton, 2009). According to this framework, proficient language teachers should be able to ground their practices in appropriate learning theories and course design frameworks for online environments and implement materials and tasks accordingly. Pedagogical knowledge guides teachers in identifying students' needs, designing successful online language courses and implementing their course designs with practice feeding back and informing ongoing development of pedagogical knowledge. This cyclical process, based on Shulman's model of pedagogical reasoning and actions, represents how teacher knowledge continually grows and changes (Freeman, 2002; Schachter & Freeman, 2020; Shulman, 1987). The elements of a tripartite knowledge base for online language teaching are discussed more fully in the following sections.

Teacher Knowledge Online

Theory and research on teacher knowledge – the knowledge teachers generate and implement in their professional work – have developed a great deal in the past decades. This knowledge has variously been viewed as interpretive frameworks (Cochran-Smith & Lytle, 2015), beliefs and orientations (Schoenfeld, 2019) and professional vision (Sturmer et al., 2013). Once conceptualized as a predetermined body of knowledge that teachers were required to master prior to teaching, teacher knowledge is now considered a complex, multifaceted genre of knowledge that is continually shaped and reshaped by any number of influences. It is the knowledge that continually develops as part of being a teacher (Hargreaves, 2001). In contrast, lay perceptions of education often view the process of becoming a teacher as learning *about* teaching – that there is some body of information one assimilated prior to venturing into the field. It is generally accepted, however, that there is no single body of knowledge (Freeman, 2002). Developing into a professional educator, rather, means the development of knowledge and views of oneself as an educator in tandem with content, students and classroom dynamics (Freeman, 2002). In a similar spirit, Shulman (1987) offers a seminal model of pedagogical reasoning and action that is a cyclical process moving from comprehension to transformation to instruction to evaluation to reflection, then generating new comprehension of purpose, subject matter, students and self, as a new cycle (Shulman, 1987). New comprehension builds on the new pedagogical knowledge developed from previous pedagogical actions.

Based on this dynamic, a cyclical profile of teacher processes, the theoretical framework we employed for this study, comprises informed teacher knowledge/perceptions, the social context and the pedagogical process as interlocking, inter-informing aspects of the profession (see Figure 4.1). This tripartite framework accounts for teacher knowledge, sociocultural contexts of practice and pedagogical processes. The cyclical design reifies knowledge shaping practice and practice shaping knowledge.

We utilize this framework to probe the emergency remote learning responses of three ELT professionals from distinct geographic and sociocultural contexts. Teachers' backgrounds and contexts of situation naturally differ from continent to continent and from demographic to demographic, especially when it comes to emergency responses to

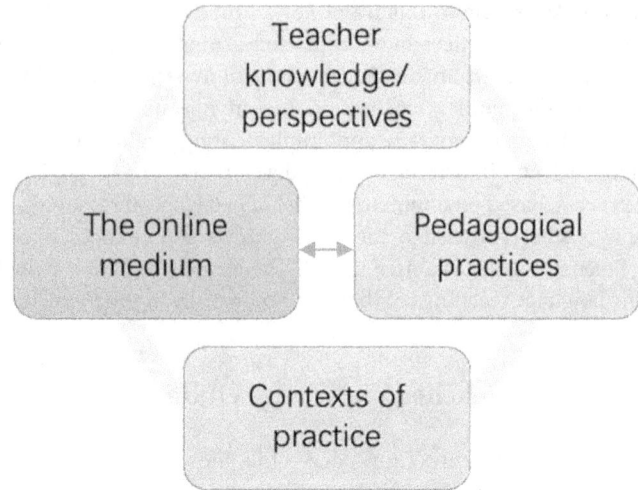

Figure 4.1 English language teaching online: a generative framework.

school closures. Such differences are reflected in teacher knowledge, their perceptions of online education and how these influence their practices teaching English online. We examine how these influenced teachers' online instructional practices along with sociocultural elements that contributed to pedagogical action.

Methodology

In order to compare and contrast the perceptions and practices of ELTs from different parts of the globe, we queried teachers from China, Indonesia and the United States about their forced transition to online instruction. By probing contextually distinct phenomena, our goal was to gain a deep sense of what was important to each teacher in each circumstance as well as what might be common among these vastly differing instructional settings. The overarching research questions that guided the inquiry were the following:

> Under emergency conditions, how do teacher knowledges and perceptions of language education and online instruction translate into online teaching practices?
> How do specific contextual factors influence these practices?

The three participants were identified via the authors' professional networks and invited to first complete a written questionnaire (Appendix). Follow-on interview questions were subsequently developed based on individual teacher responses, and forty-minute to one-hour interviews were conducted via Zoom. Our cyclical view of teacher learning was shaped by the study design, research questions and subsequent data analyses and interpretations. In the following sections, we report on each of the three participants' experiences.

US Suburban High School: Tom

Tom had been teaching English as a second language at a suburban, west coast US high school for two years. Prior to this, he taught English language arts and drama. He self-taught for the state ESOL teacher exam and passed successfully. He reported thriving with this content and 'can't get enough' of theory and practice in the field. Tom was native Australian and had lived and studied German in Germany. He was a highly motivated and animated teacher who loved his work. 'I love teaching in-person, and I also love technology that automates tasks, tracks progress and adapts to the student to give them immediate feedback'. Prior to the pandemic, he reported using tracking apps to keep tabs on individual student progress. This afforded opportunities to tailor instruction moment by moment and thus push students' learning along. 'I enjoy using tech because it gives me a greater insight into student achievement and allows me to create targeted instruction and build closer relationships with students.' Like most young people, leading up to the shift to online teaching, he had had ample time honing his social media skills. Further, he had skyped for years prior to Covid-19 'so I could easily wrap my mind around live videoconferencing'.

Tom was particularly excited about theories of language acquisition and had strong intuitions based on his own language immersion experience in this regard. He was excited about the socio-cognitive dimensions of language acquisition and his students' interests and enthusiasms fired him up; he was truly interested in and learning from what his students had to say. His online teaching practices were shaped by this stance: his online practices were wholly student centred, and he hoped to make ever more use of social media tools to promote community and instructional interaction. By using tracking apps, he spent more time working with students, individually and in small groups, and planned to use Zoom break-out rooms extensively. His overall teaching approach was to assign individual and small groups of students to work on screen-based tracked assignments while he modelled, corrected, engaged and expanded the learning; this approach translated directly into the fully online version of his teaching. Tom incorporated students' interests and experiences (students' voices) in all activities as a means for them to develop the target language – for example, each student developing a presentation of their story using Google Tour.

He preferred to encourage his students and not correct too much in favour of a focus on meaning. Regarding instructional activities to promote metalinguistic awareness, he gave the example of playing around with different accents. He believed strongly in the importance of positive role models for young people, and he reported his teaching as lively and animated as a consequence.

> Pictures, words, movements, acting out, comparing to something else, conceptually, give examples, drawing attention to patterns – a range of ways of explaining – metaphors, explain one idea in many different ways – imagine you're a painter with 3 primary colors – from that one idea you can express it many different ways – I do all of these things while looking for when the student GETS IT.

Urban Chinese Elementary: Ping

Since earning her bachelor's degree in English education, Ping first taught English online on a one-on-one basis for four years. At the time of the Covid-19 pandemic, Ping was teaching at an urban public elementary school, where she taught beginning-level English to grade three students in the regular live classroom. Her preferred practices were to make and share videos, then tutor her students individually.

Ping loved teaching English and considered herself an online language education explorer. Her four years of experience as an online English tutor for a private school provided a tremendous leg-up when it came time to transition her live teaching under emergency circumstances. No matter the format, her practices were based on students' developmental stages and her knowledge of second-language acquisition and early literacy learning. Her instruction emphasizes speaking, listening and communication skills for which she made extensive use of manipulatives and multimodal digital media. She was also especially confident about her instructional strategies, her English pronunciation and her patience working with children. Teaching several children at once online, however, differed a great deal both from the live classroom she had become accustomed to and from the one-on-one tutoring she had done previously. She found this challenging but continued to develop materials and methods to meet children's needs. Ping rewarded and motivated her students' good work with virtual and actual physical presents that she mailed to children's homes.

> Can you imagine how happy and encouraged they are when they receive gifts!

She found that these acts of recognition and connection mattered a great deal during emergency remote learning.

Rural Indonesian Middle School: John

John was a self-taught polyglot and had been an ELT instructor at the same middle school in a small village in Central Java for seventeen years. Prior to the epidemic, he had experience neither taking nor teaching courses online. He did not see himself as proficient in online socialization other than in WhatsApp groups. Where he reported knowing five languages, his proficiency was limited to reading and writing, which was what he emphasized in his language instruction.

John was representative of many ELT educators in remote areas with limited connectivity and devices (Meskill et al., 2023). Due to these constraints, he found it difficult, if not impossible, to use English when instructing his students. He argued that it is more important that students understand his instructions clearly in order to be able to do their assignments. This trend was reflected in his online teaching where most of the written instruction is in Indonesian.

> It is difficult to teach English online because students need more explanation in Indonesian Language. Prior to covid, my students had many challenges to understand the materials from English subject. They also have low motivation to

learn. The main problem that my students face is the limited inventory of English vocabulary.

John defined himself as both a passive language learner and a passive language teacher. He attended four years of college where he majored in English education. He enjoyed learning new languages by memorizing, reading and writing short texts in the target language. In his teaching, he also focused more on grammar than speaking and listening.

I usually teach my students by imitating me. Because the focus of my subject is only grammar learning. I did not give a detail explanation or activity for speaking, listening, or reading.

Because he was neither actively engaged in online communication/community prior to the Covid-19 lockdown, nor had any experience teaching or learning online, John did not feel comfortable teaching online. Even though he was provided with professional development on how to develop online material such as video sequences or online assignments, this was not sufficient for him to understand how to teach online.

I was so CONFUSED, personally I never have any experience teaching online. My ability to use online apps also limited, I have limited infrastructure, limited internet access.

The pandemic motivated him to explore online resources, but he was constrained by his students' socioeconomic conditions. He attempted hybrid teaching with his low-income students by doing home visits to check on their progress. He also called on the phone when students were missing from his online classes.

Based on my very limited experience, I was trying to implement semi-online teaching where teacher and students only have one-way communication through WhatsApp. Along the way, I am learning other apps such as google classroom, schoology, kaizala, and Microsoft 365 as my effort to find an affordable and a low bandwidth online learning platform other than WhatsApp for my students.

John used the national Indonesian language to make sure that his students were not overwhelmed. He blended his instruction by regularly calling his students' parents or doing home visits to ensure students' well-being and that they understood the subject that week. His major instructional strategies consisted of checking daily whether students had read the instructions in the WhatsApp group and had completed the assigned task. Based on this, he provided one-on-one feedback and remediation.

Teacher Knowledge, Contexts of Practice and the Online Medium

Like most young people his age in the United States, Tom reported that he had had extensive prior experience with social media and/or online teaching. He had Skyped for years prior to Covid-19 so 'knew the ropes' of video teleconferencing. Tom also considered himself a fast learner, someone who loved learning, and picked things up, including technical things, quickly and easily; he was consistently confident about accomplishing his pedagogical vision online. In China, prior to teaching her in-school third-grade class, Ping had tutored individual students online for four years. She thus had developed a solid foundation in synchronous and asynchronous communicative skill building in her online English tutoring. She reported confidence in designing and implementing her online instruction. By contrast, coming from a rural area with low connectivity, John had had little such online experience with the social and digital literacies that informed the other two teachers' transition to online English teaching.

All three teachers reported some form of support from their schools as part of the emergency transition to online instruction. While having in common the same overall purpose – to help teachers rethink their practices in light of digital affordances – the type of support varied greatly. Tom reported that 'people have been very helpful' along with a number of opportunities to grow collaboratively with his fellow teachers. There were 'staff meetings, teacher meetings, teachers share with one another.' He also managed to work independently toward online instructional fluency:

> I work things out for myself and like suggestions from others, others are challenged as they have never done this before.

Ping's transition benefitted from a number of government-supplied materials and workshops on online teaching. She was also supplied with state-of-the-art video production and post-production support when making video segments for her students. Further, like Tom, Ping consulted with other teachers. Unlike regular colleagues, however, these teachers, whom she characterized as 'expert', appeared in government-generated video recordings where they modelled best online practices. From these, Ping selected what she saw as potentially valuable strategies and integrated these into her own online class. In contrast, while John's school provided him with internet access (an expensive commodity in Indonesia), he reported that there was no professional development; nor was there a clear protocol from the school or district. He and his fellow teachers did, however, informally share strategies for dealing with a difficult situation. Also, by contrast, whereas Tom and Ping reported making extensive use of online resources, many of which were supplied through their schools, John was again limited by lack of connectivity, though he reports having made some strides researching learning platforms on his own, especially those that would work for his low-connectivity rural students.

One contextual challenge Tom cites was with the technology itself. Like many teachers during this period, he puzzled over the affordances and constraints of live video teleconferencing.

> How to humanize zoom sessions? Make it as varied as possible; times where I'm talking, encouraging them to talk back, talk to each other, show videos, slides, show screen and showing them how to do things, do a little bit then check in, that's the pattern, slowly and steadily and always checking in.

He tried to recognize whether students were engaged or not 'by laughing, talking; check in via chatbox, ask a question', and he gave students the space and time to contribute, to join in. His synchronous sessions were 'low pressure; if they're not engaging – if they are looking away, eyes glazing over – let them drift off a bit, wait then grab them back in. I think sometimes they need that down time'. And where Ping's four years as an online English tutor contributed to her overall confidence as an online educator, this experience only partially prepared her for the emergency transition. Working one-on-one is radically different from teaching a whole class via video live-streaming as her school required. In order to compensate for the communication shortcomings of the medium, she explored as many potential sources of motivation for her students as possible and experimented with a number of strategies to sustain her students' interest and attention. She found conferring with her colleagues, involving her students' parents, along with the model lessons provided by the government, helpful in this regard. In the Indonesian context, John reported that he craved models of how to teach English online that realistically reflected the connectivity and bandwidth constraints he and his students faced. Besides connectivity issues, the greatest impediments he reported were little support from parents in the home and the lack of professional development and guidance from the school and district.

All three educators reported that the most positive feature of online language instruction were opportunities to individualize instruction, a particularly important aspect of language education as students' backgrounds and developmental trajectories can vary widely. There were, however, downsides. For Tom, 'online is slower; writing on a whiteboard is quicker to get what you need; slower to locate and put the right thing up at the right time without "losing them". You also need eye contact to see "are they with me"? Online you need to take more time and have more trust that they are doing what they should.' He goes on to lament,

> Coming from a drama teacher background, online learning is nowhere near as much fun as in-person learning. Students need to move to learn.

Ping's four years' experience with online teaching gave her confidence in making this transition. She knew how to support students' active engagement and how to teach in engaging ways online. Nonetheless, she felt pressure because the content and the number of students were different from her prior online teaching circumstances. To meet these new challenges, she consulted expert teachers, watched model recordings on the internet, picked things up that she saw as valuable and then integrated these into her own online class. There were drawbacks, however. Like Tom, Ping thought online environments constrained communication and rapport among teacher and students. On the other hand, it also represented opportunity for individualization and to support students' speaking competency. Ping indicated that video recording apps made speaking practice archivable, manipulable and easily modifiable. Her instructional design reflected this perception. To take advantage of the lack of limitations imposed by time and space, she conducted and assigned many oral/communication activities for her students. In rural Indonesia, John's major reported constraint was internet speed and the availability of devices. Even though his school supplied a connection, it was limited and this limited John's ability to plan and implement high-bandwidth lessons. Even more challenging in the rural Indonesian context was the fact that students very often lack connectivity.

> Most of students do not have cell phones for online class. Even if they have, they have to take turns with their siblings or parents. In addition, many of them could not afford internet data since most of students from … come from low income families.

The result was that John could not engage his students in synchronous learning. He relied solely on WhatsApp and phone calls to communicate with students. This also impacted students' participation and their awareness of whether class was in session or not. In addition, most parents did not require their children to attend or pay attention when they did. They did not see online classes in WhatsApp as serious teaching, so they let their children wake up late and/or ignore their teachers.

In spite of very different sociocultural contexts, these three ELT professionals made the transition to online instruction. In the US context, Tom was able to make use of his native social media skills to enact tailored, authentic interaction with his students. He developed his understanding of the medium and its instructional possibilities with his teaching colleagues in formal workshops and on his own. Though he preferred the interpersonal dynamism of live teaching, he saw online affordances complementing language acquisition. In China, Ping, whose transition was supported by prior online teaching experience and government support in many forms, would rather be with her third-grade students, but also saw some inherent advantages to the online medium even though it required extra work to motivate and engage young learners. Finally, in poor, rural Indonesia, John struggled to find ways to engage his students in language activity beyond assigning and correcting exercises in their textbook.

All three teachers consistently expressed their commitment and dedication to teaching their students English. This commitment was clearly evidenced through the extraordinary efforts they expended to make this emergency transition work. Where professional support was particularly strong in Ping's situation, she nonetheless found that she needed to exercise extra effort and ingenuity to make the medium work for her. This was also true for John, who likewise took extraordinary measures to ensure his students continued to learn English regardless of the challenging infrastructure characteristic of rural areas of Indonesia.

Discussion

The design of this study was predicated on the understanding that instructional practices are shaped by teacher knowledge, understanding of online education and the contexts of instruction, with knowledge and praxis informing and shaping one another in cyclical fashion. It is clear from these three teachers' experiences that a significant portion of what goes into generative teacher knowledge involves conceptualizing the nature and affordances of the online environment and the tools at hand. This ever-developing knowledge in turn becomes situated pedagogical action. Further, teachers' knowledges differ from culture to culture and demographic to demographic. We inquired about these knowledges in three distinct parts of the world: the United States, China and Indonesia. Under emergency conditions, these knowledges were forced to give way and be applied to remote students who had otherwise experienced formal learning in live classrooms prior to the pandemic. It is instructive to note that for these three teachers, online venues offered greater opportunities for individualized instruction and authentic communication. Each teacher worked with, not against, constraining aspects of the medium to meet the specific needs of their students. The same was echoed in a recent international survey of language teachers worldwide who cited digital affordances that supported student-centredness as primary (Meskill et al., 2020).

Disruption forces new ways of conceptualizing and implementing knowledge. Novel situational structures can guide, constrain and liberate practice. These three language educators rose to the school shutdown challenge in ways both markedly similar and different depending on the contexts of their work. What is clearly uniform across the three cases is the enormous dedication to students and to the field that was reflected in their efforts to make the medium work. Providing language educators with the opportunities and the support they need to continually grow and experiment to meet such new challenges is essential. We consequently advocate for more research that conceptualizes digital technologies as social tools that can complement specific uses and contexts of use. The generative framework for undertaking such inquiry suggested here represents a step in this direction. Such a framework can support how researchers and teacher educators understand the interrelationships between pedagogical knowledge, technological affordances, contexts of teaching and learning and effective practices in online language education.

Lessons Learnt

There is much to be learnt from teachers and teaching under extraordinary circumstances. Such insights into precisely what constitutes a radical shift in thinking about and practising the craft of teaching can contribute greatly to how we shape professional development and on-demand supports for practising and future educators. Here we use the voices of three contextually diverse teachers of the English language to illuminate the interplay between individual professional knowledge and contexts and how these came to shape their forced move to online instruction. For these ELT professionals, the move to online instruction affords thoughtful observations and responses to students' learning that complement their individual trajectories and also affords more focus on productive engagement in the target language, both critical aspects of language learning not always as easily accomplished in live classrooms. Data also highlights the centrality of language-teacher knowledges in making successful transitions. To be useful, then, language educator development and support should accommodate dynamic teacher knowledges and supply tailored, on-demand supports rather than a one-size-fits-all training. These are the lessons learnt from these three teachers' experiences under extraordinary circumstances that squarely inform teacher development in teaching languages online.

References

Beasley, J. G., & Beck, D. E. (2017). Defining differentiation in cyber schools: What online teachers say. *TechTrends, 61*(6), 550–9. https://doi.org/10.1007/s11528-017-0189-x.

Bennett, S., & Marsh, D. (2002). Are we expecting online tutors to run before they can walk? *Innovation in Education and Teaching International, 39*(1), 14–20. https://doi.org/10.1080/13558000110097055.

Cochran-Smith, M., & Lytle, S. L. (2015). *Inquiry as stance: Practitioner research for the next generation*. Teachers College Press.

Compton, L. (2009). Preparing language teachers to teach language online: a look at skills, roles, and responsibilities. *Computer Assisted Language Learning, 22*(1), 73–99. https://doi.org/10.1080/09588220802613831.

Freeman, D. (2002). The hidden side of the work: Teacher knowledge and learning to teach. A perspective from North American educational research on teacher education in English language teaching. *Language Teaching, 35*(1), 1–13. http://doi:10.1017/S0261444801001720.

Gacs, A., Goertler, S., & Spasova, S. (2020). Planned online language education versus crisis prompted online language teaching: Lessons for the future. *Foreign Language Annals.* https://doi.org/10.1111/flan.12460.

Hampel, R., & Stickler, U. (2005). New skills for new classrooms: Training tutors to teach languages online. *Computer assisted language learning, 18*(4), 311–26. https://doi.org/10.1080/09588220500335455.

Hargreaves, A. (2001). *Changing teachers, changing times: Teachers' work and culture in the postmodern age*. A&C Black.

Hodges, C., Moore, S., Lockee, B., Trust, T., & Bond, A. (2020). The difference between emergency remote teaching and online teaching. *Educause Review*. Retrieved 15 September 2022, from https://er.educause.edu/articles/2020/3/the-difference-between-emergency-remote-teaching-and-online-learning.

Lee, L. (2016). Autonomous learning through task-based instruction in fully online language courses. *Language Learning & Technology, 20*(2), 81–97. Retrieved 15 September 2022, from https://scholarspace.manoa.hawaii.edu/bitstream/10125/44462/20_02_lee.pdf.

Meskill, C., & Anthony, N. (2015). *Teaching languages online*. Multilingual Matters.

Meskill, C., Anthony, N., & Sadykova, G. (2020). Teaching languages online: Professional vision in the making. *Language Learning & Technology, 24*(3), 160–75. Retrieved 15 September 2022, from http://hdl.handle.net/10125/44745.

Meskill, C., Kusumastuti, W., Guo, D., & Wang, F. (2023). Preparing English language teachers for rural education: Creative responses to online language teaching in China and Indonesia. In E. Mikulec (Ed.), *English language education in rural contexts: Theory, research, and practices*. Brill Sense.

Meskill, C., Mossop, J., DiAngelo, S., & Pasquale, R. (2002). Expert and novice teachers talking technology: Precepts, concepts, and misconcepts. *Language Learning Technology, 6*(3), 46–57.

Moore-Adams, B., Jones, W., & Cohen, J. (2016). Learning to teach online: A systematic review of the literature on K-12 teacher preparation for teaching online. *Distance Education, 37*(3), 333–48. https://doi.org/10.1080/01587919.2016.1232158.

Nation, P. (2007). The four strands. *International Journal of Innovation in Language Learning and Teaching, 1*(1), 2–13. https://doi.org/10.2167/illt039.0.

Savignon, S. (2018). Communicative competence. *The TESOL encyclopedia of English language teaching*, 1–7. https://doi.org/10.1002/9781118784235.eelt0047.

Schachter, R., & Freeman, D. (2020). Bridging the public and private in the study of teaching: revisiting the research argument. *Harvard Educational Review, 90*(1), 1–25. https://doi.org/10.17763/1943-5045-90.1.1.

Schoenfeld, A. (2019). What makes for powerful classrooms, and how can we support teachers in creating them? A story of research and practice, productively intertwined. In G. Kaiser & N. Presmeg (Eds.), *Compendium for early career researchers in mathematics education* (pp. 495–510). Springer Open.

Shulman, L. (1987). Knowledge and teaching: Foundations of the new reform. *Harvard Educational Review, 57*(1), 1–22. https://doi.org/10.17763/haer.57.1.j463w79r56455411.

Sturmer, K., Konings, K., & Seidel, T. (2013). Declarative knowledge and professional vision in teacher education: Effect of courses in teaching and learning. *British Journal of Educational Psychology, 83*(3), 467–83. https://doi.org/10.1111/j.2044-8279.2012.02075.x.

Swain, M. (2000). The output hypothesis and beyond: Mediating acquisition through collaborative dialogue. *Sociocultural theory and second language learning, 97*, 114.

Yen, S., Lo, Y., Lee, A., & Enriquez, J. (2018). Learning online, offline, and in-between: Comparing student academic outcomes and course satisfaction in face-to-face, online, and blended teaching modalities. *Education and Information Technologies, 23*(5), 2141–53.

Appendix: Preliminary Questionnaire

1. What were your *first thoughts* when you learned that you would be moving your teaching online? Please detail these thoughts and their source(s).
2. Had you had any *experiences* with and/or familiarity with online education prior? Please detail each.
3. How did you feel about these experiences?
4. How did these experiences prepare you for your transition to teaching English online? Please detail these.
5. Can you describe what modifications you made to your classroom teaching practices when you moved online?
6. How do you see your proficiency in online socialization (e.g. online community building, online interaction)? Is this helpful for your teaching practice? How so?
7. How would you describe your proficiency and confidence with managing your online teaching?
8. What best practices are you now implementing in your online English teaching?
9. Are any of these practices based on your online education experiences prior to the pandemic? Please describe.

10. Describe if and how these practices reflect your understanding of language acquisition?
11. Describe if and how these practices reflect what you see as good language pedagogy?
12. Which of these practices do you find the most effective in meeting the needs of your learners? Please detail these.
13. What training/preparation did you have to teach English online? Which of these did you find the most beneficial?
14. Please describe the support you are receiving from your school, other schools and the government?
15. Please describe the resources you find the most helpful. Where and how do you find them? How do you use these?
16. Please describe your biggest challenges teaching English online? How do you handle these challenges?
    1) Materials
    2) Learning activities
    3) Student behavior
    4) Parental involvement
    5) The online venue
    6) Student assessment
    7) Community building
    8) Differing student levels and abilities
17. How would you describe yourself as a language educator?
18. How would you describe yourself as an online teacher?
19. What do you see as the biggest difference (and similarity?) between online and live classroom teaching?
20. Please provide an example of how you use your knowledge of students (in terms of abilities, family background, and interests) to plan and implement your online instruction.
21. What have been some positive responses by students and their parents concerning the move to online English instruction? Negative?
22. What limitations do you see in teaching English online?
23. What do you find particularly attractive about teaching English online?
24. How might you describe the style and flavor of your live classroom English teaching?
25. How might you describe the style and flavor of your online English teaching?
26. How might your students describe your online English instruction?

Part 2

Responses to CALL during the Emergency

5

Anger, Excitement, Shame and Pride: Adult English Learners' Attitudes, Perceptions and Emotional Experiences towards Online Learning

Lisa Cox and Juyoung Song

It is well recognized that school environments impact cognitive, emotional and motivational aspects of learning (Artino, 2012; Stephan et al., 2019). Online contexts have a distinct emotional dynamic, and students' emotions in online environments differ from those in traditional on-campus courses. These emotions impact students' motivation, self-regulation and use and acceptance of learning technologies and, consequently, their learning and academic performance (Stephan et al., 2019). Emotions in this regard are students' reactions to online technologies and lived experiences of emotion that affect their identity and engagement. D'Errico et al. (2016) define emotions as 'multifaceted internal states, encompassing feelings and cognitive, physiological, expressive, and motivational aspects' (p. 11).

Given that researchers are only beginning to understand the relationship between learning and emotion in adult learners, it is not yet well understood how adult students emotionally experience online learning (Marchand & Gutierrez, 2012; Stephan et al., 2019; Zembylas, 2008). Moreover, very little is known about how English learners (ELs) experience online learning, especially ELs with immigrant and refugee backgrounds (Crea & Sparnon, 2017; Halkic & Arnold, 2019; Ku & Lohr, 2003). These students face unique challenges in the online learning environment, including cultural, linguistic and technological challenges, resulting in a 'steep and emotionally difficult learning curve' when interacting with online learning technologies (Conrad, 2002b; see also Hannon & D'Netto, 2007; Zhang & Kenny, 2010). This chapter reports the results from an exploratory cross-case study on the emotional experiences and attitudes of ELs with refugee and immigrant backgrounds in online courses during the Covid-19 pandemic and provides pedagogical implications for online education.

Related Literature

Adult Learners' Emotions in Online Courses

Research on online learning indicates that emotions are pervasive in online environments (Artino, 2012) against the common assumption that online is less emotional. It also suggests that learners' affective experiences online are similar to those in offline learning in that they cover a range of positive and negative emotions that can foster or impede learning (Artino, 2012; D'Mello, 2013). For example, online learners' frustration with educational technology is likely to negatively impact their perceived control and value and, subsequently, bear motivational consequences similar to how frustration with a learning task in the traditional in-person classroom impacts outcomes (Loderer et al., 2020). However, some studies suggest the unique aspects of emotional experiences online (Conrad, 2005; Marchand & Gutierrez, 2012; Stephan et al., 2019; Zembylas, 2008), due to, for example, learners' intensified negative emotions of boredom, anxiety and anger, and lower enjoyment level, are mediated by learners' attitudes and beliefs about the technology used in their learning (Stephan et al., 2019).

Zembylas (2008) and Conrad's (2002b) earlier findings support the conclusions from both camps, indicating that online adult learners experience a range of positive and negative emotions, including fear, anxiety, pride and contentment. However, they attribute these emotions to the very distinct nature of online learning, relating learners' emotions to specific online teaching and learning methodologies and online course expectations. Interestingly, online learners experiencing high levels of anxiety or frustration tend to develop more meaningful learning strategies to assist in understanding difficult course material, whereas their in-person counterparts with high levels of frustration and anxiety do not (Marchand & Gutierrez, 2012). That is, online students seem to develop learning strategies and emotional management skills, taking advantage of what online learning offers (e.g. taking breaks, searching for clarification and working at one's own pace).

Research also indicates that establishing an online community, where students feel a sense of belonging and connection, is integral to a successful online learning experience (Conrad, 2002a; Conrad, 2005; King & So, 2014). Online students 'experience community both cognitively and emotionally', using it to 'enhance their learning and as a comfort' (Conrad, 2005, p. 17). Additionally, research suggests that online educators who embrace the concept of community and create nurturing online spaces are more likely to positively impact students' emotions, increasing their happiness and comfort, and ultimately, their performance (Conrad, 2002a). D'Errico et al. (2016) examined learners' emotions in response to different online activities and found more favourable attitudes to synchronous online activities (e.g. chats with the instructor and classmates) than to asynchronous activities (e.g. forum posts). They conclude that increased participation and eagerness to learn would also likely improve learners' academic performance.

Language Learners' Emotions in Online Courses

As for language learners' emotional experiences, Ushida (2005) explored learners' anxiety levels online and found that they indeed experience high levels of anxiety. Unsurprisingly, learners report high anxiety levels at the start of the semester and waning anxiety levels by its end. Pichette (2009) found that while both online and in-person language learners experience similar levels of anxiety, novice language learners enrolled on online courses feel more anxiety than their counterparts with prior experiences with online courses. Both Ushida (2005) and Pichette (2009) attribute these findings to the very distinct nature of online learning, implying that students might initially be uncomfortable in the new learning context and need more time to adjust.

Research specific to ELs contends that some ELs feel more confident (King & So, 2014; Ku & Lohr, 2003), comfortable (Biesenbach-Lucas, 2003) and relaxed (Zhang & Kenny, 2010) when participating in online discussions compared to face-to-face classes. Students in these studies found that asynchronous forms of communication (e.g. email, forums) provide them with additional time to carefully read and write texts and reflect on course topics before responding, which reduces the listening and speaking demands of the face-to-face classroom (Biesenbach-Lucas, 2003; King & So, 2014; Ku & Lohr, 2003; Zhang & Kenny, 2010). However, some language learners have difficulties understanding the emotion behind their peers' comments without body language and other non-verbal cues available to them in face-to-face courses (Ku & Lohr, 2003; Zhang & Kenny, 2010).

While the existing literature provides an understanding of ELs' emotional experiences in online courses, little is known about how ELs with disrupted educational backgrounds emotionally experience online learning. In particular, refugees – and presumably asylees and immigrants – often come to the learning environment with emotional distress from pre-migration traumas (e.g. war, oppression, loss). In addition, refugees can endure post-migration stress as they settle into their new host country. This stress can also extend into the classroom considering these learners are generally unfamiliar with the new academic system and university culture into which they are entering (Joyce et al., 2010). Indeed, Schlosser (1992) contends that there is an inherent conflict between refugee and immigrant students' home cultures and the US education system, resulting in feelings of isolation, disengagement and inadequacy. These negative emotions are likely intensified among students with disrupted educational backgrounds for whom the demands of formal education can be particularly challenging (Joyce et al., 2010).

Another significant issue is these students' ability to access technology and the internet. A nationwide study found that ELs are less likely to own a personal computer or use the internet compared to their native, English-speaking counterparts (Ono & Zavodny, 2007). However, even when technology is accessible, digital literacy cannot be assumed. Many immigrants and refugees lack the basic skills needed to use computers and the internet for educational purposes (UNESCO, 2018). Russell (2020) reports that ELs are ill-prepared for remote learning, which is likely to result in their negative attitudes towards remote learning, especially at this otherwise stressful time.

Therefore, given the educational crisis caused by Covid-19, which demanded online education, it is timely to explore how ELs with immigrant and refugee backgrounds experience online learning. The primary research questions for this study are: (1) What are adult immigrant and refugee students' perceptions of and attitudes towards online learning? (2) What are these students' emotional experiences with online learning?

Methodology

The research was conducted in an English as a Second Language (ESL) program at a Midwestern US community college in the spring semester of 2021. The college made an abrupt move to remote learning in mid-March 2020 in response to the Covid-19 pandemic. Previously, the ESL program minimally utilized educational technology in the classroom, and many students in the program had limited or no experience with basic technologies, including email, word processors and learning management systems. Therefore, the online courses and related educational technologies were unfamiliar to most study participants.

A total of twenty-five students from two ESL high-intermediate reading courses participated in the study through a survey and follow-up interviews. Participants were recruited from two hybrid courses taught by the first author. Hybrid courses were split equally between online and in-person instruction. Live online sessions occurred via Zoom, and assignments were available in Blackboard. Several participants were also enrolled on 100% asynchronous online courses.

All participants were former immigrants or refugees (twelve male, thirteen female) representing seventeen countries and twenty-two languages (Appendix A). Fourteen students were newcomers to the program and online learning, whereas the rest had enrolled on the program at the start of the pandemic and had taken at least one online course prior to the spring semester of 2021.

Data Collection and Analysis

We utilized surveys and interviews to understand participants' perspectives on and experiences with online education. We sent an electronic survey with forty-two items (Appendix B) to thirty students and received responses from twenty-nine students. However, we used responses from only twenty-five participants after removing extreme or faulty responses to the questionnaire. The survey, adapted from Hannon and D'Netto (2007), Pekrun et al. (2005) and Ku and Lohr (2003), had four sections: attitudes and emotions, online community and socialization, experience with online learning technologies and demographics. The survey text had a readability grade lower than eight to ensure participants comprehended the survey instructions and items.

After removing duplicates and items that indicated intentional response bias, we used an online survey program (Momentive) to generate descriptive statistics of participants' responses through various graphs and tables. We adopted Hannon and D'Netto's (2007) strategy for analysing individual responses, which entailed combining the responses to 'strongly disagree' and 'disagree' and the responses to 'agree' and 'strongly agree' in section one of the questionnaire to indicate either a weak or strong emotional reaction to online learning. This process was repeated for individual responses in the remaining sections relating to online community and online learning technologies, respectively.

As for the interviews, sixteen students participated in individual interviews via Zoom, ranging from thirty to sixty minutes. We selected the interviewees based on their survey responses and willingness to participate. The interview questions focused on the challenges and benefits of remote learning, online community and technology use and acceptance. Member checks were performed with participants to ensure that our interpretation and understanding of the participants' responses were valid.

We analysed the interview data using Braun and Clarke's (2006) thematic analysis procedure. First, the data was transcribed verbatim and checked for accuracy. Second, an initial coding cycle was performed, using a list of researcher-generated codes based on a pilot study we conducted in the autumn semester of 2020. Next, a more elaborative coding cycle was completed, identifying new codes in the data and collating data extracts relevant to each theme into analytical categories in a spreadsheet. Overall, the analysis employed both inductive and deductive approaches, moving between data and analysis and reviewing the data globally and locally to connect major themes regarding participants' emotional experiences and specific aspects of their online learning and participation.

Findings

Students' Perceptions and Attitudes towards Online Learning

Participants were initially resistant to or held negative attitudes towards online learning mainly due to their limited experiences using educational technology or fear of difficulties learning new skills. One student, Vincent,[1] explained, 'Before I start[ed], I said "No, I don't like online class. That's bullshit." It comes too hard for me to figure out.' Despite participants' reluctance to learn online and limited technical competencies, most reported they could easily get started with online English classes (64%). In addition, participants agreed that Zoom (96%) and Blackboard (84%) were effective tools for online learning. Thus, with each successful event, participants' perceptions of their technical readiness improved during the semester. Even Vincent conceded that '[the] impossible is possible for us'.

Nonetheless, for all this improvement, over half of the participants (56%) still considered themselves novice technology users after one or two semesters of online learning, and 54% wanted more support on taking online classes. In the interview, Bibi reflected, 'Every single time you touch [a] computer, you have to learn one thing.' This suggests that participants need more training to develop robust and critical technology literacy regardless of their confidence in using the technological tools.

Participants' impressions of the effectiveness of online learning were also complex. For instance, approximately two-thirds (67%) believed they would learn less online.

One student, Selam, explained, 'We're not really going to "real school." We just going to get [on a] video call. We feel like [we're] just in home and do[ing] nothing.' Another student, Vincent, reiterated this idea: 'I think online nobody care. They say it's online [class], but we didn't care for that like when we are at school.' In other words, participants perceived online learning as less effective than in-person instruction. Students reasoned that online classes did not produce the same 'feeling that we get in person' (Khalid). Even newcomers who had little or no prior experience learning in-person agreed that something critical was missing in online courses: 'I don't feel that I'm a student until I go to the college campus. If I don't feel myself as a student, then I think that is a very big gap [in my] learning' (Niharika).

A veteran student, Hinata, articulated something related:

> When we go to college and see other people, like see the nurse[ing] students, wearing their dress [scrubs], moving around, that encourage us. And when we see the teachers going in and out, holding the papers, they hurry up to catch their class. Yeah, it affects us from inside; We have emotion for that ... And when you see people advance [in front of] you, you say 'Okay, they did it, I can do it.'

Hinata's response indicates the importance of a *shared learning experience* for ELs. This is evident in participants' survey responses regarding their lack of interest in taking another online English course (40%) or willingness to recommend online learning to others (40%). However, despite students' perceptions that online learning is not 'real school', more than half (60%) agreed that it is important to attend online classes, and more than two-thirds of the participants (72%) reported being satisfied with their online learning experience. This contradiction is likely related to their actual experiences taking online courses versus their sentimental impulses towards in-person learning.

Students' Emotional Experiences in Online Courses

Participants reported mixed emotions toward online learning; positive emotions included pride, confidence and excitement, and negative emotions encompassed anger, frustration, shame and loneliness. We divided their emotional experiences into three significant aspects: online technologies, communication and flexibility.

Emotional Experiences with Online Technology

The participants reported feeling frustrated, stressed and angry with educational technology and the internet. This is unsurprising considering most students were new to online learning and had limited exposure to computers and the internet before the pandemic. The following comment is characteristic of students' emotional responses to new technology:

> Online learning when I start, it was hard for me because I don't usually use computer. So, everything we had become hard for me. I don't know how to send the email to my teacher. I was feeling bad, so strong. Sometimes I get mad. (Vincent)

Thus, learning to use computers and the internet for educational purposes presented students with a steep and challenging learning curve. At times, this task was so overwhelming that it impacted students' ability to perform academically:

> The whole system [Blackboard] is new to me. Maybe it will be easy for me later on, but the first term, when I try to find out my assignment, [it] took a lot of time to find out. I had two hours to complete my assignment. I tried almost one and a half-hour to find it, and like after one and a half-hour later, I find it. Now, I only have 30-minute. I thought there is no way I can complete it. Then I shut down the computer, and I slept. I was so mad. (Niharika)

In Niharika's words, we hear his frustration with navigating the college's learning management system, which negatively impacted his motivation to complete an assignment, and ultimately led him to abandon the task. His example suggests that the negative emotion, frustration with the technology, hinders his learning online (Stephan et al., 2019).

What is notable in their emotional experiences with technology is how participants associated feelings of embarrassment/shame (83%) when they faced difficulties. For some students, the embarrassment stemmed from a failure of self-image. They feel incompetent at a task that they think they should be able to complete – in this case, they feel that those issues reflect negatively on their image and ability. For instance, Bibi was critical of himself when he encountered technical problems: 'I keep just ask about myself "What's wrong with Bibi?!"' Other students attributed their embarrassment to a failure to meet others' expectations and, in particular, what their technical problems might communicate to their teachers:

> When I have connection issues, sometimes I feel like maybe the teacher is going to think about like, I just like, don't want to study or anything like that. Because like, maybe she won't think like I don't show up, you know, for no reason. (David)

Despite students' difficulties with online learning, they also reported feeling proud (92%) of learning to use computers and the internet successfully. For instance, Selam explained that she was proud of persisting with online education despite its challenges and acquiring a new skill set, in particular, the ability to use game-based learning platforms:

> I mean, even though [it] is still hard, to be honest, like there is no end, you know, to learning technology ... I think, yeah, I think I know better about technology [now] than I knew before. I even know how to create my own Kahoot! [smiles excitedly] I just tried it myself, and I tried with my friends and we kind of played.

Similarly, Hinata, who said she had 'zero' experience with computers and the internet, also conveyed self-assurance from her progress with online learning technologies:

> [Now,] I know how to Zoom. And how to follow my emails. I didn't [have] that knowledge and confidence to do it [before]. But now, I got confidence to type, to do Zooms. Now, I'm doing Zooms with my family.

In their words, we hear a sense of *emerging* online self-efficacy or the belief that they can handle the technical aspects of an online course. For example, Jenny, who initially struggled to orient to online learning, said, 'I know how to do all the things, so I don't really get worried. Like I know how to deal with the technology.' We found that such digital empowerment was most evident in participants' comments related to constructing new identities for themselves as literate computer users:

> I feel myself is better. You know, before, when I saw the people [college students] who use the computer very well, I thought 'Oh I wish to use it [like] you.' And now, I can use it like other people. (Zana)

Zana's response suggests that ELs' enhanced technological skills could help them build confidence and construct a more positive identity as (online) students and technology users.

Emotional Experiences with Online Communication

Students felt limited in their ability to effectively communicate with their teachers and peers online, negatively impacting their sense of connectedness and motivation. A significant concern conveyed was the lack of sufficient teacher support online. Students learning asynchronously desired real-time support from their teachers. These students reported feeling overwhelmed with managing their learning for the first time in a language they had yet to master. Patrick explained, 'I'm feeling alone because I have to read by myself, explain by myself, and understand by myself. There's no one there to explain to you or to tell you.'

While students enrolled on synchronous courses benefited from contemporaneous support from their teachers, many still found online communication unsatisfactory. Specifically, students found it more difficult to interrupt online lessons to ask questions or attract the instructor's attention: 'When you try to talk to the teacher, the other student talks to her too. She could not hear you very well. She could not answer your question' (Khalid). For synchronous students, the limits of videoconferencing induced negative emotions such as confusion and frustration and a strong desire for individualized (and in-person) attention.

Students considered asynchronous interactions to be inauthentic and forced. For example, regarding a standard point system for posting to the course discussion board, students admitted to posting to earn points, but when the maximum number of points were earned, they promptly withdrew from the discussion. Evidently, these activities were not relevant or meaningful enough to students to prompt authentic engagement.

Similarly, students found it difficult to establish peer relationships online. Students were particularly hesitant to initiate contact with their peers using unfamiliar methods of online communication. Niharika expressed his frustration: 'I even feel shy to send them a message or send them an email because I don't know what they are going to think.' Another student, Vincent, echoed this: 'You feel scared to ask him maybe because he didn't know you really.' Moreover, students learning asynchronously shared that they do not know any of their classmates: 'I didn't talk to anybody over there [asynchronous course]. I just do my work, and that's it' (Bibi). Similarly, Patrick commented, 'I don't have anyone that I know. We don't talk.'

Emotional Experiences with Online Learning's Flexibility

Participants acknowledged that online learning offers flexibility and autonomy. However, students' views of online learning varied depending on their domestic responsibilities. Male students often commented how online learning offered them the ability to accommodate *their* schedules, while female students appreciated that the online medium allowed them to learn without impacting or relying upon *others*.

For instance, one male student said, 'When it comes about online learning, you using your own time. You're not depending on your teacher time or college time. But you depending on your time. That is the good things' (Patrick). Although male students generally agreed that online learning permitted them to manage work, school and leisure activities more effectively, they also conceded that this freedom was insignificant compared to the benefits of in-person instruction.

For female students, the access to education and convenience offered by online learning was often valued more because the requirement to learn in-person could mean learning was altogether unavailable to them. Several female students described the pandemic as a positive event in their lives because it resulted in critical educational access and opportunities. One student, Zana, explained that the pandemic and the subsequent transition to online learning allowed her to return to school after a six-year absence:

> I was the new mom; that's why I just focused on to be a mom and have to take care of my child. That's why I didn't think about the education [at] that time. Now, my life is busy, and that's why online classes is more comfortable for me.

Another student, Rose, disclosed that she was at risk of not graduating due to excessive absences related to her pregnancy. For her, the transition to online learning afforded the opportunity to attend classes consistently and ultimately to graduate. Another female student admitted that online learning permitted her to handle life's responsibilities *while* learning:

> I love the online. I can follow my class when I'm doing some stuff at home, like watching my kids, feeding my kids, or even cooking! [laughs] And I can be on my class doing my laundry. So, I can do two jobs in one time. (Hinata)

Most female participants discussed juggling online learning with domestic duties, which they admitted was challenging but made learning possible in their homes. Thus, more female students expressed positive feelings towards their online experiences than their male counterparts.

Discussion

Participants in the current study did not speak in absolutist terms about online learning but instead 'referred to *specific* emotional responses associated with *certain* aspects' of online learning (Zembylas, 2008, p. 80), similar to results by Ku and Lohr (2003), Zembylas (2008) and Zembylas et al. (2008). However, this study's participants experienced more negative emotions associated with online learning than positive ones, which contrasts with results of other studies (Pekrun et al., 2002; Stephan et al., 2019; Zembylas, 2008; Zembylas et al., 2008). This is likely the result of several factors, including the unique needs of the participants (e.g. support to overcome technology and language barriers), limited use of educational technology before the pandemic and other challenges associated with living and learning during a pandemic (e.g. extreme isolation; no choice in learning remotely).

Technical issues regularly distracted participants from their learning. Participants reported negative feelings (e.g. anger, shame) associated with unfamiliar online learning technologies and unstable internet connections. Although preoccupation with technology is expected among students new to learning online (Conrad, 2005), it was likely exacerbated for the students with refugee and immigrant backgrounds, given their minimal experience with computers and the internet. Halkic and Arnold (2019) maintain that online support structures that address technical, linguistic and cultural problems are 'more crucial for refugees than online education in general' (p. 348).

The impersonal nature of online communication and limited opportunities for social contact caused participants to feel overwhelmed, isolated and lonely, a finding in line with prior research on ELs' emotions in online spaces (Ku & Lohr, 2003; Zhang & Kenny, 2010). Also, similar to other research (Conrad, 2005; Hannon & D'Netto, 2007), the study participants did not perceive online learning as a substitute for in-person instruction but instead preferred organic interactions, such as those that occur during in-person learning. However, participants eventually established and maintained relationships with their peers online, although, and notably, these relationships did not begin to form until their hybrid courses met in person. This finding supports researchers' beliefs that in-person meetings are critical for building community in online spaces (Conrad, 2002b, 2005).

Negative experiences aside, participants were proud of their progress in learning to use computers and the internet for educational purposes. Pride is integral to the learning process as it fosters task orientation, extrinsic and intrinsic motivation, effort and academic achievement (Heckel & Ringeisen, 2019; Vogl et al., 2019). Further, pride has the potential to elicit a positive feedback loop, impacting students' future emotions, attitudes, behaviours and performances (Pekrun, 2006; Pekrun et al., 2002). This effect was evident in participants' discussion of their *emerging* online self-efficacy and integration of educational technologies into their personal lives, suggesting they were constructing new identities as literate computer users. Self-efficacy is critical in online learning; students with high self-efficacy perceive greater control over online learning and technology-related challenges and experience lower levels of anxiety (Heckel & Ringeisen, 2019).

Lastly, the flexibility online learning affords was appealing to all participants, allowing them to better manage conflicts and commitments and exert control over the time, place and pace of their learning. While this flexibility was most attractive to female students burdened with family, work and school responsibilities (Crea & Sparnon, 2017; Zembylas, 2008; Zembylas et al., 2008), schools and educators should consider offering a variety of online learning opportunities post-pandemic to increase all students' access to educational opportunities and positively impact their retention.

Post-Pandemic Lessons

Because ELs' technological literacy and other skills and competencies required for online education might not be fully developed by the time they enrol on an online course, we encourage teachers to address this in their course design and instruction. For example, teachers might apply the following interventions to foster students' digital literacy and, ultimately, a more positive attitude towards online education: (1) offer students early access to online courses, so that they can familiarize themselves with new technologies; (2) scaffold online tasks so that students perceive them as manageable and experience repeated successes in the course; (3) substitute kludgy course technologies with more user-friendly tech designed for ELs or novice technology users; and/or (4) provide individual mentoring or training regarding the use of course technologies.

Further, considering the positive impact pride and self-efficacy can have on student achievement, we recommend that teachers monitor and strengthen students' self-efficacy in the online learning environment. For instance, teachers could survey students at the start of the semester to determine their self-efficacy, routinely check in with students who identify as having low self-efficacy, and provide opportunities for all students to reflect on and celebrate their technological successes.

To address issues of motivation, isolation and loneliness, educators should build 'warm' online spaces that allow for frequent and meaningful opportunities to engage. Online learning can transform into a social environment where interaction thrives if online technologies are used appropriately. We suggest inviting students to assist in designing course activities, so that the interaction is both accessible and meaningful to students. For instance, the technology students enjoy outside of school could be used for school-based communications (e.g. WhatsApp). Importantly, for any community-building interventions to work, schools must train teachers and students to learn and interact in this alternative educational landscape. Teachers cannot assume that students' social skills will automatically transfer to the online environment, especially for ELs new to technology.

Conclusion

This chapter examined the attitudes and emotional experiences of adult immigrant and refugee students learning online, for the first time, during an educational crisis. Gaining a deeper understanding of students' perceptions and emotions related to online learning, especially an under-researched group such as ELs, is critical for designing online learning environments and intervention programs that appropriately respond to their needs, and ultimately, foster academic success. The findings from this study inform schools and teachers of the impact of ELs' emotions and attitudes on their learning, students' technology training needs and methods to cultivate emotionally sound online learning environments.

However, we must be mindful of certain limitations of the present study. Self-report measures of emotions are subject to response bias (Pekrun et al., 2005) because participants' responses were not anonymous (for purposes of awarding extra credit). However, we believe the impact of any response bias is likely minimal because the interview data aligns with the questionnaire responses. The findings in this study are based on a small group of learners undertaking online learning in extreme conditions (i.e. a global pandemic). Thus, the benefits and drawbacks of online learning that were identified might be particularly acute at this time. For this reason, further research is necessary to determine whether participants' attitudes and emotional responses were specific to this study or are indicative of an emotional experience consistent with those of larger groups and under more 'normal' learning conditions.

Note

1. All names are pseudonyms.

References

Artino, A. R. (2012). Emotions in online learning environments: introduction to the special issue. *Internet and Higher Education, 15*(3), 137–40.

Biesenbach-Lucas, S. (2003). Asynchronous discussion groups in teacher training classes: Perceptions of native and non-native students. *JALN, 7*(3), 24–46.

Braun, V., & Clarke, V. (2006). Using thematic analysis in psychology. *Qualitative Research in Psychology, 3*(2), 77–101.

Conrad, D. (2002a). Deep in the hearts of learners: insights into the nature of online community. *Journal of Distance Education, 17*(1), 1–19.

Conrad, D. (2002b). Engagement, excitement, anxiety, and fear: Learners' experiences of starting an online course. *American Journal of Distance Education, 16*(4), 205–26.

Conrad, D. (2005). Building and maintaining community in cohort-based online learning. *Journal of Distance Education, 20*(1), 1–20.

Crea, T. M., & Sparnon, N. (2017). Democratizing education at the margins: Faculty and practitioner perspectives on delivering online tertiary education for refugees. *International Journal of Educational Technology in Higher Education, 14*(43), 1–19.

D'Errico, F., Paciello, M., & Cerniglia, L. (2016). When emotions enhance students' engagement in e-learning processes. *Journal of e-Learning and Knowledge Society, 12*(4), 9–23.

D'Mello, S. (2013). A selective meta-analysis on the relative incidence of discrete affective states during learning with technology. *Journal of Educational Psychology, 105*(4), 1082–99.

Halkic, B., & Arnold, P. (2019). Refugees and online education: Student perspectives on need and support in the context of (online) higher education. *Learning, Media, and Technology, 44*(3), 345–64.

Hannon, J., & D'Netto, B. (2007). Cultural diversity online: student engagement with learning technologies. *International Journal of Educational Management, 21*(5), 418–32.

Heckel, C., & Ringeisen, T. (2019). Pride and anxiety in online learning environments: Achievement emotions as mediators between learners' characteristics and learning outcomes. *Journal of Computer Assisted Learning, 35*, 667–77.

Joyce, A., Earnest, J., De Mori, G., & Silvagni, G. (2010). The experiences of students from refugee backgrounds at universities in Australia: Reflections on the social, emotional, and practical challenges. *Journal of Refugee Studies, 23*(1), 82–97.

King, C., & So, K. K. F. (2014). Creating a virtual learning community to engage international students. *Journal of Hospitality & Tourism Education, 26*(3), 136–46.

Ku, H.-Y., & Lohr, L. L. (2003). A case study of Chinese students' attitudes toward their first online language learning experience. *Educational Technology Research and Development, 51*(3), 94–102.

Loderer, K., Pekrun, R., & Lester, J. C. (2020). Beyond cold technology: a systematic review and meta-analysis on emotions in technology-based learning environments. *Learning and Instruction, 70*, 1–15.

Marchand, G. C., & Gutierrez, A. P. (2012). The role of emotion in the learning process: Comparisons between online and face-to-face learning settings. *The Internet and Higher Education, 15*(3), 150–60.

Ono, H., & Zavodny, M. (2007). *Immigrants, English ability, and the digital divide* [Discussion paper series no. 3124]. Institute for the Study of Labor. Retrieved 27 February 2020, from http://ftp.iza.org/dp3124.pdf.

Pekrun, R. (2006). The control-value theory of achievement emotions: Assumptions, corollaries, and implications for educational research and practice. *Educational Psychology Review, 18*, 315–41.

Pekrun, R., Goetz, T., & Perry, R. P. (2005). *Achievement emotions questionnaire* [User manual]. Retrieved 7 October 2020, from https://www.scribd.com/doc/217451779/2005-AEQ-Manual.

Pekrun, R., Goetz, T., Titz, W., & Perry, R. P. (2002). Academic emotions in students' self-regulated learning and achievement: A program of qualitative and quantitative research. *Educational Psychologist, 37*(2), 91–105.

Pichette, F. (2009). Second language anxiety and distance language learning. *Foreign Language Annals, 42*(1), 77–93.

Russell, V. (2020). Language anxiety and the online learner. *Foreign Language Annals, 53*, 338–52.

Schlosser, L. K. (1992). Teacher distance and student disengagement: School lives on the margin. *Journal of Teacher Education, 43*(2), 128–40.

Stephan, M., Markus, S., & Gläser-Zikuda, M. (2019). Students' achievement emotions and online learning in teacher education. *Frontiers in Education, 4*, Article 109. Retrieved 26 October 2020, from https://doi.org/10.3389/feduc.2019.00109.

United National Educational, Scientific, and Cultural Organization. (2018). *A lifeline to learning: Leveraging technology to support education for refugees* [E-book]. UNESCO. Retrieved 8 September 2020, from https://unesdoc.unesco.org/ark:/48223/pf0000261278.

Ushida, E. (2005). The role of students' attitudes and motivation in second language learning in online language courses. *CALICO Journal, 23*(1), 49–78.

Vogl, E., Pekrun, R., Murayama, K., Loderer, K., & Schubert, S. (2019). Surprise, curiosity, and confusion promote knowledge exploration: Evidence for robust effects of epistemic emotions. *Frontiers in Psychology, 10*, 1–16.

Zembylas, M. (2008). Adult learners' emotions in online learning. *Distance Education, 29*(1), 71–87.

Zembylas, M., Theodorou, M., & Pavlakis, A. (2008). The role of emotions in the experience of online learning: Challenges and opportunities. *Educational Media International, 45*(2), 107–17.

Zhang, Z., & Kenny, R. F. (2010). Learning in an online distance education course: Experiences of three international students. *International Review of Research in Open and Distance Learning, 11*(1), 17–36.

Appendix A

Participant Demographic Data

Table 5.A1 Participants' Countries of Origin

Afghanistan	Bangladesh	Congo	Cuba	Ethiopia	Guinea	Haiti	Kenya	Liberia	Nepal
1	1	4	1	1	1	1	2	1	1
Rwanda	Sudan	Syria	Tanzania	Togo	Turkey	Yemen			
2	3	1	1	2	1	1			

Table 5.A2 Participants' Educational Backgrounds

High school diploma from US institution	14
High school diploma from foreign institution	7
Some college-level coursework	2
A college degree (from outside the US)	1
A graduate degree (from outside the US)	1

Table 5.A3 Participants' US Residency

1–3 years	9
4–6 years	14
7–9 years	1
10 years or more	1

Appendix B

Participant Survey (Sample)

I. Emotions in the Online Language Learning Environment

1. I enjoy being in online English classes.
    - o   Strongly agree
    - o   Agree
    - o   No opinion
    - o   Disagree
    - o   Strongly Disagree
2. I feel frustrated or stressed in online English classes.
3. I feel isolated or alone in online English classes.
4. I am motivated to learn English online.
5. I am proud of myself for learning how to take online English classes.
6. I am confident in using technology to learn English online
7. Online English classes are boring, so I have trouble paying attention.
8. Thinking about the poor quality of my Internet connection makes me angry.
9. I get embarrassed when I have technology problems.
10. I worry that I cannot use the technology to attend online classes.
11. I have lost all hope of understanding how to use technology to learn online.

II. Experience with Online Community & Socialization

1. It is easy to get to know my classmates online.
    - o   Strongly agree
    - o   Agree
    - o   No opinion
    - o   Disagree
    - o   Strongly Disagree
2. I enjoy getting into groups with my classmates in the online class.
3. I would like more time to talk with my classmates online.
4. I feel connected to my online classmates and teachers.

6

Study Abroad from Home: Development of L2 Learner Autonomy in an Unprecedented Online Programme during the Covid-19 Pandemic

Akihiko Sasaki and Osamu Takeuchi

Introduction

Study abroad (SA) programmes have been introduced in language education at colleges and universities worldwide. In Japan, due to the growing demand for English communication skills associated with the rapid advance of globalization, many institutions have developed curricula to send their students overseas. According to the Japan Student Services Organization (2020), more than 100,000 Japanese students were engaged in some form of SA programme in 2018.

However, the outbreak of the Covid-19 pandemic in 2019 had a profound impact on SA programmes around the world. Several SA programmes shifted to remote learning, causing international students to take online classes while confined to their dormitory rooms; some students were even compelled to return to their home countries, as their entire programme was cancelled. Covid-19 also affected students in Japan who were preparing for SA programmes. Due to travel restrictions and campus closures, many students were forced to change their plans for, or even abandon, their SA participation. However, a few programmes promptly switched from face-to-face classes to an online format so that students could participate in the SA programme while remaining in Japan.

Students at the first author's college, Japanese learners of English as a foreign language (EFL), participated in one of those few online SA programmes in 2020, offered by the college's branch school in the United States. Although the students initially expressed frustration and disappointment about not being able to learn English in an on-site, in-person environment, they had positive impressions of online SA after completing the programme, and its novel environment appeared to provide them with a variety of experiences unique to online learning. In this chapter, the authors examine the students' experiences of their online SA and investigate its benefits and drawbacks relative to conventional SA programmes.

Literature Review

A considerable number of studies have investigated the potential effects of conventional (i.e. in-person/on-site) SA on second/foreign language (L2) learners (see Isabelli-García & Isabelli, 2020, for a summary). The focus of past SA research in the second-language acquisition (SLA) field has been mainly on L2 proficiency gains, ranging from modalities of language use such as L2 oral fluency (e.g. Hernández, 2010; Mora & Valls-Ferrer, 2012; Serrano et al., 2012), listening comprehension (e.g. Cubillos et al., 2008; Llanes & Muñoz, 2009), and writing skills (e.g. Sasaki, 2007, 2011) to particular aspects of communicative competence such as lexical (e.g. Briggs, 2016; Tracy-Ventura, 2017), grammatical (e.g. Isabelli, 2004; Issa et al., 2020), phonetic (e.g. Muñoz & Llanes, 2014), pragmatic (e.g. Taguchi, 2011, 2013), and sociolinguistic competence (e.g. Barron, 2006; Regan et al., 2009).

A large portion of these studies has addressed speaking and oral proficiency. According to Isabelli-Garcia et al. (2018), this may reflect 'a bias toward the development of aural/oral skills – at least for SA in FL [foreign language] environments' (p. 451). The L2 learning process in SA is often considered superior to formal classroom learning at home (AH) because its environment 'offers students greater access to NSs [native L2 speakers] and more varied opportunities to use the target language as a tool for exchanging information and participating in social and interpersonal functions' (Hernández, 2010, p. 601). For example, in an investigation of American college participants in an SA programme in China, Du (2013) attributed the improvement in their Mandarin fluency to their exposure to a Chinese-speaking environment both inside and outside the classroom. Masuda (2011) examined Japanese as a foreign language (JFL) learners' ability to use the interactionally significant particle 'ne' and found that interaction with native Japanese speakers during SA enhanced their ability to use 'ne' in pragmatically appropriate ways. Many other studies have discussed the benefits of the linguistic environments of SA for oral communication skills (e.g. Hernández, 2010; Llanes & Muñoz, 2013; Mora & Valls-Ferrer, 2012; Muñoz & Llanes, 2014; Taguchi, 2011).

It is often argued that SA is an ideal environment for cultural learning as well (e.g. Allen et al., 2006), since SA students are immersed not only in the target language but also in the L2 culture, including its clothing, food, housing, media, transportation and how people interact. Direct contact with such cultural properties allows students to learn about an L2 culture in ways that would be impossible in AH classes (e.g. Isabelli-García & Isabelli, 2020).

Such cross-cultural experiences in on-site SA environments often challenge students' preconceptions, stereotypes and values about the L2 culture, which in turn leads to a greater understanding of its products, practices and perspectives, and spurs the development of intercultural competence (IC). According to Bennett et al. (1999), IC is defined as 'the general ability to transcend ethnocentrism, appreciate other cultures, and generate appropriate behavior in one or more different cultures' (p. 13) and is an important outcome of SA (Deardorff, 2006).[1] In her study of American learners of Arabic who completed summer intensive language programmes in Arab countries, Shiri (2015) found that students were able to develop their IC, even in short-term SA, by identifying other cultures and comparing and contrasting them with their own. Yashima (2010) reported that Japanese students who participated in short-term SA developed IC, including an enhancement of open, non-ethnocentric attitudes towards different cultures.

Many recent SLA studies have addressed learners' affective aspects, including motivation (e.g. Du, 2019; Fryer & Roger, 2018), self-efficacy (e.g. Amuzie & Winke, 2009; Cubillos & Ilvento, 2012; Tanaka & Ellis, 2003), autonomy (e.g. Amuzie & Winke, 2009; Kubota, 2017), and agency (e.g. Byker & Putman, 2019; Covert, 2014). Fryer and Roger (2018), for example, examined Japanese SA students' motivation in language learning and found that even short-term SA increased their L2 motivational self-system (i.e. ideal L2 self, ought-to L2 self, L2 learning experiences, as indicated by Dörnyei, 2005) and observed that they maintained a high level of motivation six months after the end of their SA.

Among studies on SA and self-efficacy, Cubillos and Ilvento (2012) found that American college students increased their self-efficacy in L2 skills (i.e. reading, writing, listening, speaking). Tanaka and Ellis (2003) examined Japanese SA students' beliefs about L2 learning and found that their beliefs related to analytic L2 learning, experimental L2 learning and self-efficacy/confidence showed significant changes during the SA experience.

Studies on the impact of SA on learners' autonomy and agency have also produced intriguing results. Amuzie and Winke (2009) studied the beliefs of Asian SA students in the United States and reported that they realized that L2 learning success in SA environments depended on their own efforts outside the classroom and came to believe that learner autonomy was more important in L2 learning than teachers were. Kubota (2017) examined JFL learners' *kanji*[2] knowledge after returning from SA in Japan and found that the sense of learning Japanese through use (rather than through study) they had developed while studying in the Japanese language environment resulted in proactive learning attitudes and continued autonomous learning after their return home.

Agency, defined as 'the capability of individual human beings to make choices and act on these choices in ways that make a difference in their lives' (Martin, 2004, p. 135), is also as important a capacity as autonomy for independent learning. In their study on pre-service teachers' engagement in SA, Byker and Putman (2019) found that SA experiences in an international context enhanced their global competencies, intercultural awareness and cultural responsiveness, while also developing their sense of agency as future educators and citizens. Covert (2014) also reported that SA students built self-efficacy and agency through intentional and purposeful changes in their communication and behaviour that were made to fit the local cultural norms.

Most of these linguistic, cultural and affective benefits for SA learners are generated via conventional forms of SA, in which students are situated in a foreign environment different from their own. However, the outbreak of Covid-19 made it impossible for students to study *abroad*; this highlighted online SA, which allows students to participate in virtual SA programmes from *home*, as an alternative to conventional SA. Then, several questions arise: What are the advantages of online SA? Does online

SA provide students with the same benefits as conventional SA? If it does not, what benefits are lost due to the absence of a foreign environment, and what benefits are gained by having access from home?

This study investigates the characteristics of online SA to identify its advantages and disadvantages relative to conventional SA using interview data obtained from students who experienced this new form of SA.

Methods

Participants

The present study focused on a group of students at a women's college in Japan ($n = 95$, aged nineteen to twenty years) who had completed a four-month online SA programme. Although they were all English majors, their English proficiency at the time of college entrance was relatively low (TOEIC®L&R[3] 400–600; CEFR A2–B1; intermediate–low). In addition, according to the academic advisors who supervised them in the first semester of their first year, they were rather 'other-dependent' learners, in that they performed only their assigned tasks and did not extend the scope of their learning proactively.

All the English majors at this college are required to spend the second semester of their first year participating in an SA programme in the United States as part of the curriculum. In 2020, however, due to the outbreak of the Covid-19 pandemic, their SA programme was transformed into an online format. The students of this study were thus obliged to give up on joining the on-site SA in the United States, but instead took the same SA programme online from Japan.

In this study, 12 students were randomly selected from the entire group and interviewed for qualitative data collection. The authors confirmed with the advisors that none of the selected students was an outlier in terms of either L2 proficiency or autonomy.

The SA Environment

The SA programme of this college is offered by its branch school in Washington State (USA), where more than twenty MATESOL-certified American instructors teach English as a second language (ESL) lessons such as English conversation, writing and reading over a four-month period (fifteen weeks). In the regular SA programme, students live in campus dormitories with other Japanese students supervised by resident assistants (American university students). Following an 'English only' policy, the use of L1 (Japanese) is prohibited on campus, so the students are immersed in English. On weekends, students enjoy outings (e.g. shopping, watching movies) and homestays, where they have opportunities to not only learn authentic English but also experience American culture first-hand.

In 2020, when Japanese citizens' travel to the United States was restricted because of the Covid-19 pandemic, the US branch school immediately shifted its classes online,

Table 6.1 Timetable and Class Format

		JST	PST	Class Format
Morning	1	9:00–10:30	17:00–18:30	Live
	2	10:45–12:15	18:45–20:15	Live
Afternoon	3	12:30 and after	20:30 and after	On demand

Note: JST: Japan Standard Time; PST: Pacific Standard Time.

allowing students to take all ESL lessons from Japan via Zoom videoconference software. Due to the time difference with Japan (which is sixteen hours ahead of Washington State), the classes were offered from Tuesday to Saturday, with the morning classes held in a real-time live format and the afternoon classes held on-demand (see Table 6.1).[4]

During the online SA, the US school took several measures to compensate for the students' insufficient exposure to English. For example, they provided office hours, during which students could meet and talk with each instructor through Zoom. The school faculty also developed extracurricular circles so that students could use English for meaningful communication. However, the real-life experience of American culture, usually gained through regular on-site SA, was not available through the online SA.

Data Collection and Analysis

The interview sessions were held in the semester following the online SA, and the selected twelve students had face-to-face interviews with the first author. Prior to the interview, each student was briefed on the purpose of the study. They were informed that the data would be used only for the purpose of this study and that all information collected during the interviews would be kept anonymous and protected. They were also informed that their participation in the interview was voluntary and that they were free to withdraw at any time. As a result, all twelve students provided written consent and participated in the interview process.

Each interview session lasted fifteen to twenty minutes, was conducted in Japanese and was tape-recorded for later transcription and analysis. The interviews were formatted in a semi-structured manner, with each student being first asked about their general impressions of the online SA programme, followed by specific questions relating to their answers, so that the study could identify both the advantages and disadvantages of online SA and assess how the students enjoyed the advantages, and overcame the disadvantages, of this unique environment.

Findings

Surprisingly, the students' overall impressions of the online SA were mostly positive. The frustration and disappointment voiced prior to the online SA were not mentioned in the interviews, and all the students said that it was 'quite good' or 'better than expected'. An analysis of their comments indicated that online SA had positive effects on their (1) English learning; (2) cultural learning; (3) cost, time and effort; (4) living environment; and (5) motivation to go abroad in the future to learn English more. Each of these is elaborated below.

English Learning

In the online SA, the branch school offered the same classes with the same content using the same textbooks as in the regular SA programme. The difference was that they were delivered through Zoom, and this computer-mediated learning environment generated some unexpected effects on the students' English learning.

First, most students commented that their English listening skills improved through the online SA. Some students suggested that this was due to the absence of classmates:

> Normally, when I do not understand the teacher's words, I can ask my friends, but in online SA, I cannot, because there is no one around me. So, in every class, I tried to listen to the teacher with full concentration, but if I still did not understand, although I felt embarrassed, I asked questions on my own. [S-4][5]
>
> At first, in the on-demand class, I could not understand what the instructor was saying, and I was worried because I did not have any friends to turn to. However, I found out that I could watch on-demand recorded classes repeatedly, and since then I listened to the parts I did not understand until I could fully understand them. In the end, I was able to understand without repeating, so I think my listening skills have improved. [S-7]

Several students mentioned improvements in their speaking skills:

> I would usually be too embarrassed to speak English in class. But with ZOOM, the instructor's face appeared big in the middle of the screen, and only a few classmates were visible on the monitor's edge. So, I could speak without worrying about the gazes of others. I thought it was a good chance to improve my speaking ability, so I actively spoke English. [S-5]
>
> Our instructor recommended that we use office hours, so I did. I was nervous at first, but I found it good practice because in a one-on-one conversation, I could talk slowly and ask what I did not understand without hesitation. Moreover, ZOOM made it easier for me to have access to instructors, so I used it a lot. [S-9]

One student commented on her English writing, saying that she deployed media-based learning strategies to make her writing activities more efficient, which in turn increased her self-efficacy in writing:

> I used to be bad when writing English. First, in the writing class, I opened Google Translate behind ZOOM and used it frequently. But as I used it more, I gradually got the hang of English writing, and then I thought it would be faster to write by myself, so I quit using Google Translate altogether. [S-3]

This study did not measure changes in the participants' L2 proficiency and affective aspects objectively. Therefore, the authors consider it hasty to assume from the aforementioned comments that online SA has the same impact on the development of listening, speaking and self-efficacy as conventional SA does. However, we could at least conclude that the students cultivated autonomous attitudes by taking advantage of this novel online SA environment. For example, the students who mentioned listening (S-4 and S-7), being aware of the unavailability of immediate support from nearby classmates in the Zoom classes, recognized the necessity of listening on their own and began to engage in proactive behaviour such as asking questions and listening to the same recording repeatedly. They might not have developed such autonomous behaviour if the class had been in a face-to-face format, where participants shared the space and relied on each other.

In addition, the use of media created kinds of learning different from those in regular classes. One student (S-5) eliminated her anxiety about speaking by taking advantage of a technical characteristic of Zoom that allowed her to see only a few participants other than the instructor. This enabled her to speak actively in class without fear of being stared at by her fellow classmates. Another student (S-9) made the best of the enhanced accessibility to instructors' office hours and increased opportunities to speak English. For the student who gained confidence in writing (S-3), the multitasking nature of the computer, which makes possible the simultaneous operation of Zoom and a translation application, served as a scaffold for her learning. These results can be regarded as unexpected effects of the online-based SA environment, which might have the potential to resolve students' initial dissatisfaction.

Cultural Learning

The students seemed to have gained cultural experiences unique to online SA, though no direct cultural encounters of the kind that would be possible in regular SA occurred:

> Local high school students [invited by the branch school instructors] frequently participated in the ZOOM classes and shared their American school lives with us. [S-1]
>
> Some relatives of the instructor were invited as guest speakers in the ZOOM class and demonstrated and explained how they prepare for Halloween at home. [S-11]
>
> Instructors' friends from outside the state participated in the ZOOM class, and we were able to learn about their ways of life. [S-6]

Online remote classes are not subject to temporal or spatial constraints and allow a variety of people to participate at any time and from anywhere. Accordingly, the students were able to interact not only with the branch school instructors, but also with local students (S-1), citizens (S-11) and people from outside the state (S-6). In this respect, online SA offers students a chance to encounter a wider range of people and their lives than is possible in regular SA, although these brief encounters might not be enough to transform their cultural perspective and develop their IC.

Cost, Time and Effort

Several comments discussed the benefits of not going to the United States, with cost being mentioned most frequently:

> At first, I was disappointed that I could not go to America, but it was good that I could save on SA expenses. In addition, I did not have to spend time and effort to prepare and travel back and forth. [S-10]

For the regular SA programme, students of this college need to pay about 1,000,000 yen[6] for travel and dormitory expenses, but the online SA programme does not require any of these expenses. It is also an advantage of online SA that students do not need to invest time and effort in preparation and travel. Thus, in online SA, the burden on students and their families in terms of cost, time and effort is much smaller than that of regular SA.

Living Environment

Some students mentioned the advantages of participating in SA from their homes in Japan:

> Since online SA classes were accessible from home and were offered in the same time slots as at Japanese universities, I was able to keep my daily life. [S-8]
>
> I was worried that I would get homesick in the US, so I was relieved to be able to take the online SA program from home for four months. [S-2]
>
> Being in Japan, I took advantage of my free time to take exams, such as MOS [the Microsoft Office Specialist test]. I also took EIKEN[7] to see an improvement in my English ability through SA. [S-11]

Since online SA does not require changes in their living environment, students need not lose the rhythm of their daily lives (S-8), nor worry about the physical and mental problems that international students in conventional SA often experience, such as jet lag, culture shock and homesickness (S-2). Online SA from home also allows students to pursue their academic interests and monitor the progress of their English learning using familiar resources (S-11).

Motivation for Going Abroad in the Future

The two comments below indicate that online SA enhanced the students' motivation to study in the United States in the future to continue their English learning:

> At first, I was mentally and physically insecure about going to an unfamiliar place [the US], but online SA made me feel easy and the classes gave me good impressions about America. Now, I want to go there and learn English. [S-2]
>
> I was negative about going to the US because I thought we could study English in Japan as well. But, while taking online SA classes, I met local people and people

from other states, and I found it enjoyable to directly communicate with them in English. Now, I would like to study in the US in the future. [S-6]

Both students, who had never been abroad, were originally negative about going to the United States. However, their negative feelings were mitigated because online SA reduced their mental and physical burdens (S-2), and the online environment allowed them to communicate with a wider range of people (S-6); they even expressed an intention to participate in SA in the United States in the future.

Discussion

The results suggest that one of the most significant benefits of online SA is that previously other-dependent students developed autonomous attitudes in their learning. The unique environment afforded by the online SA – the absence of classmates, easy access to instructors via Zoom and a continuous availability of domestic resources – served to increase the students' sense of responsibility and proactive attitudes in learning. These goal-oriented, self-initiated/-directed learning attitudes are regarded as self-regulatory behaviours, and Yashima (2013) defined learners who have internalized this self-regulatory capacity as 'agents'. According to Yashima, agents are 'active participants in the learning process … who can make choices regarding their behaviors and who have control over their actions' (p. 1). Yashima also claims that agency involves 'the ability to analyze the situation critically in which the learner is placed and to resist the forces that obstruct making changes in that situation' (p. 2). The autonomous attitudes shown by the students of this study – the choice and implementation of learning behaviours appropriate to the novel online SA environment – seemed to be an initial but important manifestation of their agency. Therefore, an increased sense of agency, a significant psychological attribute that affects learning behaviour, also appears to be one of the benefits of online SA.

Some might argue that online SA without on-site visits lacks some of the advantages of conventional SA and thus regard the former as inferior to the latter. Indeed, online SA lacks some aspects of the cultural learning students can enjoy in conventional SA. The students in this study, for example, did not experience homestays, a part of the regular SA programme, which deprived them of direct exposure to American families and home life. However, it is also true that online SA can create opportunities to encounter people and cultures from wider and more diverse domains, as reported above. Although these brief contacts may not generate the deep reflections required to develop IC, as reported in past studies (e.g. Shiri, 2015; Yashima, 2010), these occasions can still be good avenues for increased cultural awareness. Thus, we argue that online SA has the potential to offer valuable cultural experiences that have qualities different from those of conventional SA.

This study discovered several other advantages of online SA over regular SA. First, online SA significantly reduced the financial, physical and emotional burdens of regular SA. Students and their families could save the expenses of living in and flying to/from the United States and did not have to spend the time and effort required to prepare and go back and forth. They also did not have to worry about jet lag and homesickness, which many international SA students experience. Most importantly, the students in this study, who were negative about SA because of these physical and mental concerns, were able to participate in online SA without anxiety and were eventually motivated to study in the United States in the future.

Post-Covid Lessons

Based on the discussion above, we argue that the distinctive nature of the online SA environment provides types of learning experiences that differ from conventional ones, in that students can develop autonomous learning attitudes while taking advantage of being able to continue their daily lives in Japan. Therefore, the authors maintain that online SA be viewed as a different form of SA rather than an emergency alternative to conventional SA and that both SA types be implemented in the post–Covid-19 era to serve the needs, readiness and concerns of the prospective participants.

The hybrid use of both SA programmes offers another possibility. Participating in an online SA programme prior to a regular one would familiarize students with the class format and the English language used in the classes and would also allow them to build a good rapport with the instructors. In some cases, prior experiences with online SA may increase students' expectations of and motivation for regular SA. Studies have also discussed the effects of pre-SA-departure instruction in reducing culture shock (Goldoni, 2013) and improving language skills (Martinsen, 2010). Thus, online SA could be an effective stepping stone to a full-immersion regular SA and be of great use even in the post–Covid-19 era.

Conclusion

Like any other research, this study has several limitations. First, it examined the interview data of only twelve randomly selected students out of ninety-five students participating in the online SA. A study with a larger sample size might have discovered advantages and disadvantages that were not found in this study. In addition, the students' satisfaction with the online SA was partly due to the ingenious planning and constant efforts of this particular branch school teaching staff as well as advanced technology resources, including the internet environment available in Japan. Therefore, similar research in other institutional environments is needed to enhance the generalizability of the findings of this study.

Despite these limitations, this study revealed that online SA can offer EFL students unique learning experiences that are unavailable in regular SA programmes. Accordingly, online SA should be viewed as a distinctive form of SA and should not be viewed as a crude approximation of conventional SA. The unique elements of online SA will thus still be needed, even in the post–Covid-19 era.

Notes

1. Watson and Wolfel (2015) classified IC into three dimensions: knowledge (e.g. basic facts about a particular place, cultural norms and taboos), skills (e.g. language and negotiation skills) and attitudes (e.g. empathy, self-efficacy, and ambiguity tolerance).
2. *Kanji* is a set of logographic characters in the Japanese writing system. It is considered to be an obstacle in learning Japanese, especially for Western learners.
3. The TOEIC (Test of English for International Communication) is a norm-referenced test designed to evaluate test takers' English proficiency on a standardized scale of 1 to 990. The TOEIC®L&R comprises listening and reading sections.
4. In the on-demand format, the branch school provided video-recorded lessons so that students could watch them at their convenience.
5. English translations in this and subsequent interview quotations were provided by the first author and confirmed by the second author when necessary. The letters and numbers in brackets are confidential identifiers for the students.
6. Approximately US$9,090, as of 20 September 2021.
7. EIKEN (The EIKEN Test in Practical English Proficiency) is the most recognized norm-referenced English proficiency test in Japan. The student (S-11) could not have taken it if she had been in the regular on-site SA because there is no test site in Washington State.

References

Allen, H. W., Dristas, V., & Mills, N. (2006). Cultural learning outcomes and summer study abroad. In M. Mantero (Ed.), *Identity and second language learning: Culture, inquiry, and dialogic activity in educational contexts* (pp. 189–215). Information Age Publishing.

Amuzie, G. L., & Winke, P. (2009). Changes in language learning beliefs as a result of study abroad. *System, 37*(3), 366–79. https://doi.org/10.1016/j.system.2009.02.011.

Barron, A. (2006). Learning to say 'you' in German: The acquisition of sociolinguistic competence in a study abroad context. In M. DuFon & E. Churchill (Eds.), *Language learners in study abroad contexts* (pp. 59–90). Multilingual Matters. https://doi.org/10.21832/9781853598531-007.

Bennett, J. M., Bennett, M. J., & Allen, W. (1999). Developing intercultural competence in the language classroom. In R. M. Paige, D. L. Lange, & Y. A. Yershova (Eds.), *Culture as the core: Integrating culture into the language curriculum. CARLA Working Paper 15* (pp. 13–45). University of Minnesota, Center for Advanced Research on Language Acquisition.

Briggs, J. G. (2016). A mixed-methods study of vocabulary-related strategic behaviour in informal L2 contact. *Study Abroad Research in Second Language Acquisition and International Education, 1*(1), 61–87. https://doi.org/10.1075/sar.1.1.03bri.

Byker, E. J., & Putman, S. M. (2019). Catalyzing cultural and global competencies: Engaging preservice teachers in study abroad to expand the agency of citizenship. *Journal of Studies in International Education, 23*(1), 84–105. https://doi.org/10.1177/1028315318814559.

Covert, H. H. (2014). Stories of personal agency: Undergraduate students' perceptions of developing intercultural competence during a semester abroad in Chile. *Journal of*

Studies in International Education, 18(2), 162–79. https://doi.org/10.1177/1028315313497590.

Cubillos, J. H., & Ilvento, T. (2012). The impact of study abroad on students' self-efficacy perceptions. *Foreign Language Annals, 45*(4), 494–511. https://doi.org/10.1111/j.1944-9720.2013.12002.x.

Cubillos, J. H., Chieffo, L., & Fan, C. (2008). The impact of short-term study abroad programs on L2 listening comprehension skills. *Foreign Language Annals, 41*(1), 157–86. https://doi.org/10.1111/j.1944-9720.2008.tb03284.x.

Deardorff, D. K. (2006). Assessing intercultural competence in study abroad students. In M. Byram & A. Feng (Eds.), *Living and studying abroad: Research and practice* (pp. 232–56). Multilingual Matters. https://doi.org/10.21832/9781853599125-013.

Dörnyei, Z. (2005). *The psychology of the language learner: Individual differences in second language acquisition.* Lawrence Erlbaum Associates. https://doi.org/10.4324/9781410613349.

Du, H. (2013). The development of Chinese fluency during study abroad in China. *The Modern Language Journal, 97*(1), 131–43. https://doi.org/10.1111/j.1540-4781.2013.01434.x.

Du, X. (2019). The impact of semester-abroad experiences on post-sojourn L2 motivation. *Studies in Second Language Learning and Teaching, 9*(1), 117–55. https://doi.org/10.14746/ssllt.2019.9.1.6.

Fryer, M., & Roger, P. (2018). Transformations in the L2 self: Changing motivation in a study abroad context. *System, 78*, 159–72. https://doi.org/10.1016/j.system.2018.08.005.

Goldoni, F. (2013). Students' immersion experiences in study abroad. *Foreign Language Annals, 46*(3), 359–76. https://doi.org/10.1111/flan.12047.

Hernández, T. A. (2010). Promoting speaking proficiency through motivation and interaction: The study abroad and classroom learning contexts. *Foreign Language Annals, 43*(4), 650–70. https://doi.org/10.1111/j.1944-9720.2010.01107.x.

Isabelli, C. A. (2004). The acquisition of the null subject parameter properties in SLA: Some effects of positive evidence in a naturalistic learning context. *Hispania, 87*(1), 150–62. https://doi.org/10.2307/20063017.

Isabelli-García, C. L., & Isabelli, C. A. (2020). *Researching second language acquisition in the study abroad learning environment.* Springer International Publishing. https://doi.org/10.1007/978-3-030-25157-4.

Isabelli-García, C. L., Bown, J., Plews, J. L., & Dewey, D. P. (2018). Language learning and study abroad. *Language Teaching, 51*(4), 439–84. https://doi.org/10.1017/S026144481800023X.

Issa, B. I., Faretta-Stutenberg, M., & Bowden, H. W. (2020). Grammatical and lexical development during short-term study abroad: Exploring L2 contact and initial proficiency. *The Modern Language Journal, 104*(4), 860–79. https://doi.org/10.1111/modl.12677.

Japan Student Services Organization. (2020). *2018 (Heisei 30) nendo nihonjin ryugaku jyokyo chosa kekka* [2018 Report of Japanese students participating in study abroad programs]. Retrieved 10 August 2021, from https://www.studyinjapan.go.jp/ja/_mt/2020/08/date2018n.pdf.

Kubota, M. (2017). Post study abroad investigation of kanji knowledge in Japanese as a second language learners. *System, 69*, 143–52. https://doi.org/10.1016/j.system.2017.07.006.

Llanes, À., & Muñoz, C. (2009). A short stay abroad: Does it make a difference? *System*, *37*(3), 353–65. https://doi.org/10.1016/j.system.2009.03.001.

Llanes, À., & Muñoz, C. (2013). Age effects in a study abroad context: Children and adults studying abroad and at home. *Language Learning*, *63*(1), 63–90. https://doi.org/10.1111/j.1467-9922.2012.00731.x.

Martin, J. (2004). Self-regulated learning, social cognitive theory, and agency. *Educational Psychologist*, *39*(2), 135–45. https://doi.org/10.1207/s15326985ep3902_4.

Martinsen, R. A. (2010). Short-term study abroad: Predicting changes in oral skills. *Foreign Language Annals*, *43*(3), 504–30. https://doi.org/10.1111/j.1944-9720.2010.01095.x.

Masuda, K. (2011). Acquiring interactional competence in a study abroad context: Japanese language learners' use of the interactional particle ne. *The Modern Language Journal*, *95*(4), 519–40. https://doi.org/10.1111/j.1540-4781.2011.01256.x.

Mora, J. C., & Valls-Ferrer, M. (2012). Oral fluency, accuracy, and complexity in formal instruction and study abroad learning contexts. *TESOL Quarterly*, *46*(4), 610–41. https://doi.org/10.1002/tesq.34.

Muñoz, C., & Llanes, À. (2014). Study abroad and changes in degree of foreign accent in children and adults. *The Modern Language Journal*, *98*(1), 432–49. https://doi.org/10.1111/j.1540-4781.2014.12059.x.

Regan, V., Howard, M., & Lemée, I. (2009). *The acquisition of sociolinguistic competence in a study abroad context*. Multilingual Matters.

Sasaki, M. (2007). Effects of study-abroad experiences on EFL writers: A multiple-data analysis. *Modern Language Journal*, *91*(4), 602–20. https://doi.org/10.1111/j.1540-4781.2007.00625.x.

Sasaki, M. (2011). Effects of varying lengths of study-abroad experiences on Japanese EFL students' L2 writing ability and motivation: A longitudinal study. *TESOL Quarterly*, *45*(1), 81–105. https://doi.org/10.5054/tq.2011.240861.

Serrano, R., Tragant, E., & Llanes, À. (2012). A longitudinal analysis of the effects of one year abroad. *Canadian Modern Language Review*, *68*(2), 138–63. https://doi.org/10.3138/cmlr.68.2.138.

Shiri, S. (2015). Intercultural communicative competence development during and after language study abroad: Insights from Arabic. *Foreign Language Annals*, *48*(4), 541–69. https://doi.org/10.1111/flan.12162.

Taguchi, N. (2011). The effect of L2 proficiency and study-abroad experience on pragmatic comprehension. *Language Learning*, *61*(3), 904–39. https://doi.org/10.1111/j.1467-9922.2011.00633.x.

Taguchi, N. (2013). Production of routines in L2 English: Effect of proficiency and study-abroad experience. *System*, *41*(1), 109–21. https://doi.org/10.1016/j.system.2013.01.003.

Tanaka, K., & Ellis, R. (2003). Study-abroad, language proficiency, and learner beliefs about language learning. *JALT Journal*, *25*(1), 63–85.

Tracy-Ventura, N. (2017). Combining corpora and experimental data to investigate language learning during residence abroad: A study of lexical sophistication. *System*, *71*, 35–45. https://doi.org/10.1016/j.system.2017.09.022.

Watson, J. R., & Wolfel, R. L. (2015). The intersection of language and culture in study abroad: Assessment and analysis of study abroad outcomes. *Frontiers: The Interdisciplinary Journal of Study Abroad*, *25*(1), 57–72. https://doi.org/10.36366/frontiers.v25i1.345.

Yashima, T. (2010). The effects of international volunteer work experiences on intercultural competence of Japanese youth. *International Journal of Intercultural Relations, 34*(3), 268–82. https://doi.org/10.1016/j.ijintrel.2009.12.003.

Yashima, T. (2013). Agency in second language acquisition. In C. A. Chapelle (Ed.), *The encyclopedia of applied linguistics* (pp. 1–7). Blackwell Publishing.

7

Technology-Enhanced Out-of-Class Autonomous Language Learning in Times of the Covid-19 Pandemic: A Shifting Perspective for Advanced Learners

Simone Torsani

Introduction

Research on second language values out-of-class learning in that it constitutes the counterpart to formal instruction in foreign-language learning (see e.g. Cumming, 2009; Krashen, 1976; Richards, 2015), and indeed, 'students tend to engage in out-of-class learning activities more frequently than their teachers know' (Benson, 2007, p. 26). Given the importance and weight of out-of-class learning, then, there are good reasons to expect that the digitalization of education during the lockdown following the Covid-19 pandemic might have boosted the recourse to autonomous activities, especially through technology. The aim of the research reported in the present chapter was to assess whether and how such a boosting effect occurred among advanced language learners.

In the late winter of 2020, Italy was the first country to witness an uncontrolled surge in Covid-19 cases. As is well known, the sudden worsening of what was then still an epidemic shortly led to a national lockdown in early March, during which the country's entire educational system abruptly shifted to online working. While the same happened in many other countries (see e.g. Maican & Cocoradă, 2021), the Italian experience lasted longer, especially in the case of higher education and even more so in the case of university education. Despite the support from the country's government, the number of critical voices against distance learning quickly increased among all the actors of the educational system (students, teachers, families and researchers as well). These voices focused on such problems as the feeling of isolation on the learners' part and their difficulty in maintaining participation, two issues that are well known to research in distance language learning (Lamy, 2013), which I will consider as a possible factor towards an increased resorting to autonomy. Alongside these issues, however, many have argued that this experience may constitute an important landmark in the path towards digital innovation of the country's educational system (e.g. Gui &

Morosini, 2020; Molina et al., 2021), which does not involve institutions and teachers alone, but the learners as well.

In the learners' case, one aspect of such innovation may be an increase in the recourse to out-of-class technology-enhanced autonomous learning. However, while easily predictable given the forced lockdown and the digitalization of education, a simple increase in the time devoted to autonomy is not enough for an understanding of the real impact of the pandemic on out-of-class autonomous learning. Indeed, since autonomy is considered as a property of the learner rather than of the situation (Dickinson, 1994; Holec, 1981b), it is less easy to envisage how the experience may have influenced the learners' habits and attitudes.

By comparing data from a survey conducted among advanced language learners in 2021 with the results from a similar one administered before the emergency, this chapter aims at assessing whether the pandemic played a significant role in changing the participants' habits as regards autonomy.

The Covid-19 Pandemic and Technology-Enhanced Out-of-Class Learning

The Ecology of Out-of-Class Autonomous Learning

Autonomy is often defined through Holec's (1981a, p. 3) words as 'the ability to take charge of one's learning'. Such a view is important in a communicative perspective to language teaching, where the learner assumes a more active role with respect to previous approaches (Breen & Candlin, 1980). It is, therefore, not surprising that autonomy has for many years been an important, albeit inevitably complex topic (Godwin-Jones, 2019; Little, 2007; Murray, 2020) in second-language research (see e.g. Benson, 2013; Lai, 2017; Pemberton et al., 1996).

Benson (2007) provides an overview of the different ambits to which autonomy might apply, including out-of-class learning. While seemingly narrower, the notion of out-of-class learning is still broad, since it encompasses a variety of settings and modes of practice (Benson, 2009). Here, however, I will not try to differentiate further and will maintain this broad perspective, according to which out of (or beyond) the classroom simply consists of 'what goes on outside of the classroom' (Richards, 2015, p. 5), in this case through the support of technology. Indeed, the studies quoted in Lai's (2017) overview (pp. 48–53) of out-of-class learning through technology report activities as diverse as enjoying fiction, interacting through social media, using online translators and even structural exercises. Because of this heterogeneity, out-of-class autonomous learning is best interpreted as a complex phenomenon, which explains frameworks such as Benson's (2011) four dimensions (location, formality, pedagogy and locus of control), by which every out-of-class experience may be set, and the number of theoretical models which assume an ecological perspective. Indeed, many frameworks applied by Lai (2017) to learner experience, such as those presented by Barron (2006), Hamilton (2013) and Luckin (2010), revolve around this notion of ecology. The connection between autonomy and ecology is quite straightforward, since autonomy is based on voluntary recourse to tools/activities, which entails the perception of their affordances on the learners' part.

Among such frameworks, that of Barron (2006) stresses the importance of personal interests, which trigger the learner's research of assets and affordances in an ever-changing scenario, where new possibilities may emerge continually. As an example of ecology, we may take one answer (answer no. 2) to a question on how to learn English posted on the now-closed Yahoo! Answers portal.[1] The suggestion provided by a member of that community defines, in its naiveness, a method for language learning, in which different – (often) technology-based – activities are combined: watching movies with subtitles; using the now-closed portal Livemocha to interact with native speakers; doing structural exercises online and so on. The above-mentioned answer is not limited to activities, but also touches upon methodological issues by suggesting, for instance, not to focus too much on grammar. One may interpret this suggestion in terms of ecology, as the various tools and activities are chosen, defined and integrated, based on the respondent's personal experience and beliefs.

What is particularly important, from the viewpoint of this inquiry, is the *dynamic* nature of a learning ecology as defined by Barron (2006), since the changing relationship between individual and context, in the case in question the pandemic, and the transfer of formal language education online, may have changed the learners' attitudes towards out-of-class autonomy. My objective is precisely to capture this shifting perspective. However, Barron's approach, and ecological theories in general, are also important in another respect: namely that, being centred on the person, they force us to investigate and appreciate at an individual level the changes emerging at a macro level, which is precisely what I will try to do in the following analysis.

The Effect of the Pandemic on Technology-Enhanced Out-of-Class Learning

As I have suggested above, there are good reasons to hypothesize that the Covid-19 pandemic might have enhanced the appeal of autonomous out-of-class learning supported by technology for language learners. However, within an ecological approach, such as the one mentioned in the previous section, this enhancement is not limited to the quantity of time devoted to out-of-class learning, but it also implies an adjustment in the learners' attitude towards, and relationship with, activities and tools which are also dependent on the changing of their learning conditions.

First, the relocation online of an entire educational system forced, albeit temporarily, the digitalization of teaching and learning alike. Stated simply, working and studying exclusively online may boost the recourse to online tools, such as dictionaries, or to online communities or sources of recreation. Further, constant online interaction might facilitate the process of content and information sharing.

Second, as suggested in the 'Introduction', distance might imply a perceived decrease in the support on the part of teachers and experts, which may, in turn, lead to a higher recourse to autonomy. Indeed, although teachers may be easier to reach through the same conferencing tools adopted for distance teaching, learners may feel reluctant to contact them. Hence, they may resort to online venues (e.g. forums or other knowledge sharing services) for support, or they may need to resort more to already-known tools, or even learn how to use new ones (e.g. online corpora as a tool for second-language writing; Hyland, 2019).

Third, during the long lockdown imposed by the pandemic, learners simply had more time to devote both to learning and to leisure activities such as watching movies through streaming services. This may involve not only an increase in the time of exposure to the foreign language or the number of tools used for homework, but maybe also more time devoted to exploring the possible integrations of different tools.

The Study

Research Design

Data for this research was collected through a survey conducted during the pandemic among advanced learners enrolled on a 'Foreign Language Teaching' course at the University of Genoa. This group was considered as of interest for two reasons. First, advanced learners and students in linguistics constitute an elite subgroup among language learners and may, due to their expertise and first-hand experience, provide more informed feedback on the different facets of autonomy. Second, as prospective teachers they might, in future, disseminate their experience among their students and/or enhance this important asset. Indeed, as recognized by many (e.g. Sadeghi, Thomas and Ghaderi in this volume), teachers and teaching are pivotal to successful language learning through technology, and this is also true as regards autonomy. Therefore, although this chapter focuses on participants as learners, it is important to remember that they might one day themselves become teachers and support other learners to become autonomous.

The survey was designed and administered in 2021, when education was still at a distance mode for university learners, who had already studied online for about a year and a half. Since it was aimed at assessing whether the pandemic experience had changed the learners' attitudes and habits towards autonomy, its results were compared to those from a previous survey on the same topic, which had been conducted before the pandemic.

The Survey

A fifteen-item anonymous questionnaire was administered through the course's Learning Management System to 115 students, of whom thirty-seven (two male and thirty-five female, aged between nineteen and fifty years) responded (33%). The first set of questions focused on how the pandemic had changed the learners' habits and beliefs regarding autonomy. The second set of questions was aimed at assessing the respondents' recourse to activities which may fall within the spectrum of autonomy – namely, enjoying fiction and music in the language they are learning; frequenting online communities in that language for leisure and entertainment; frequenting online communities for studying; using mobile devices; producing and publishing content in the foreign language; following pages, accounts and channels on social media in the foreign language; resorting to institutional websites for information; resorting to amateur websites; online gaming; and commenting on social media. These activities were chosen so as to provide the broadest perspective on autonomy, and roughly correspond to those quoted in Lai's (2017) overview of learners' habits (pp. 49–55; see also Godwin-Jones, 2019 for an overview of tools and services). Further, since the participants were advanced learners, I also included in this series any tools and information sources which learners autonomously chose to rely on for language study, such as online translators for writing in the foreign language. The third set of questions focused on the skills learners needed to take advantage of autonomy.

Quantitative data from the questionnaire was complemented with qualitative data from semi-structured interviews with six learners from the target group, which were conducted in September 2021. The interviews were based on the questionnaire results and aimed at further exploring through the participants' voices the issues emerging from the questionnaire. This design is referred to as 'sequential explanatory design' and uses qualitative data to triangulate quantitative data, especially unexpected results (Creswell et al., 2003). The interviews were conducted through a videoconferencing app (Microsoft Teams®), lasted about fifteen to twenty minutes each and were recorded; the participating students gave informed consent.

The 2019 Survey

In order to better appreciate how the recourse to autonomy had changed during the pandemic, results from the 2021 survey were compared to those of a similar one, which had been conducted prior to the emergency. A twelve-item anonymous questionnaire was administered in 2019 through the Learning Management System of the same course (Foreign Language Teaching) to 104 learners, thirty-five (three male and thirty-two female, aged between nineteen and twenty-six years) of whom responded (34%). This survey was conceived as a preliminary investigation for a larger project aimed at introducing prospective teachers to out-of-class technology-enhanced autonomous language learning (see Jiménez Raya, 2020, on teacher education for autonomy). The questionnaire was similar to that of 2021, which was actually designed so as to be as comparable as possible to this one. The survey was developed after an extensive review of the literature on the subject, with the aim of connecting the questionnaire to the most relevant issues in the field. The first set of questions, therefore, focused on the participants' habits, which were the same as in the 2021 questionnaire. A second set of questions was aimed at assessing the learners' beliefs (e.g. how much one values autonomy), while a third set of questions focused on their perceived needs (see e.g. Chik, 2018, for an overview of learners' needs in the ambit of technology for autonomy).

Findings

Habits

Most respondents (57%) declared they had resorted to autonomous learning occasionally prior to the pandemic, while only 35% did so on a regular basis. The Covid emergency, however, saw a dramatic increase in autonomy, with 51% of the participants answering that their recourse to autonomy had increased and 35% stating that it had greatly increased (see Figure 7.1). Further, when asked about their recourse to autonomy after the emergency, 68.4% of the respondents stated that it would remain the same, while 10.5% answered that it would increase and 21.1% said that it would decrease.

There was a moderate, although not uniform, consensus ($M = 7.02$ on a ten-point Likert scale,[2] $SD = 2.39$; see Table 7.1 for a summary of the data of this study) that distance had somehow favoured such increase, as later confirmed by Respondent[3] 3: '[During the pandemic] I used the Internet a lot more for seeking information ... since I was at my PC all day, I used the web much more, it was only natural, after all.' However, counter to what was expected, none of the respondents declared that their experience meant for them an increased responsibility for their learning or that it drove them to seek advice or look for help elsewhere.

Despite such an increase, however, no major change can be seen in the participants' habits as regards the activities performed. It emerged from the 2019 survey that three activities were performed on a regular basis by most participants: enjoying fiction/music in the second language (89%), using online language-related tools such as dictionaries (86%) and following informative channels (such as pages on social media) in the foreign language on the web (71%). Other social practices, whether or not learning oriented, were less frequent: 51% of the participants only occasionally actively interacted in social

Table 7.1 Autonomy before and during the Pandemic (Summary of the Most Significant Data in This Study)

	2019	2021
Perceived value of autonomous learning through technology	$M = 7.88$; $SD = 1.43$	$M = 6.58$; $SD = 2.35$** ($d = 0.58$)
Perceived role of the digitalization of education in the recourse to autonomy		$M = 7.02$; $SD = 2.39$
Perceived importance of education for autonomy		$M = 8.44$, $SD = 1.66$
Ideal focus of education for autonomy		Pedagogic/linguistic issues (58%) Technical issues (36%)
Recourse to autonomy	- Regularly (35%) - Occasionally (57%) - Never (8%)[a]	Greatly increased (35%) Increased (51%) Not increased (14%)
Most common activities versus most newly undertaken activities during the pandemic	- Enjoying fiction/music in the foreign language (89%) - Using online language-related tools such as dictionaries (86%) - Following web channels in the foreign language (71%)	- Using digital tools (50%) - Seeking information on the web (50%) - Following web channels in the foreign language (44%)

[a]As declared in the 2021 survey.

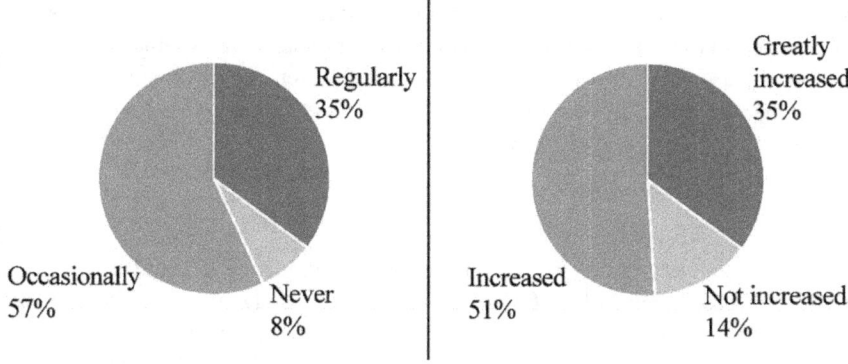

Figure 7.1 The recourse to autonomy before the Covid-19 pandemic (left) and its increase during the pandemic (right).

media using the second language, while 29% never did; there were approximately similar figures for learning-oriented online communities (49% occasionally participated, while 40% never did). The participants were more used to commenting on social media (37%, on a regular basis; 43% occasionally), while online gaming was quite rare, with 69% of participants never engaging in it. Prior to the pandemic, then, the bulk of out-of-class learning through technology was limited to receptive activities, which is in line with the learners' habits reported in the literature (see, for instance, Kuppens, 2010; Toffoli & Sockett, 2010; Wu, 2012), and/or to using digital tools for the study of languages, a practice consistent with the profile of experienced language learners (see e.g. Steel and Levy, 2013, who observe how such tools are used by undergraduate language learners). This trend did not overall change during the pandemic. Among the new activities undertaken during the pandemic period, the participants mentioned using digital tools (50%), seeking information on the web (50%), and following web channels in the foreign language (44%). As regards how they had discovered such activities, 56% had discovered them independently and 33% through teachers, while social media were not a major source of information in this respect (3%), which confirms the non-determinant role of this ambit in their learning ecology.

In this respect, Respondent 4, for instance, plainly stated that he dislikes interacting with people he does not know. A similar position was expressed by Respondent 1, who simply declared herself 'not motivated' to deepen her knowledge of this ambit, which she has never considered a venue for her study. While research has explored and demonstrated the importance of the social aspect in autonomy (see Chik & Breidbach, 2014, and Murray, 2014, for an example), the participants seemed overall to neglect this aspect. When asked about which activities they already used to perform but resorted to more often during this period, the participants declared that watching movies had greatly increased (72%), together with using digital tools (56%) and following web channels in the foreign language (47%).

In conclusion, the participants generally resorted to two broad families of activities – namely, activities that increase exposure to the foreign language (mainly watching movies) and using digital tools for studying. In addition to these two activities, one may notice a heterogeneity of ancillary habits (using social media, online gaming etc.); in other words, personal ecologies of learning can be seen in the responses. However, despite the increase in the recourse to autonomy, this situation has not changed during the pandemic and no other activity emerged.

Beliefs

As regards the learners' beliefs, the survey conducted during the pandemic shows a decrease in the perceived benefits of autonomy for language learning. When asked about the importance of autonomy for their L2 development, respondents to the survey reported a significantly lower value ($M = 6.58$; $SD = 2.35$) with respect to the responses to the same question in the 2019 survey ($M = 7.88$; $SD = 1.43$). If the two responses are compared, we observe a significant decline, with a medium effect size, in the perceived usefulness of autonomous out-of-class learning, as revealed by a one-tailed Mann-Whitney test ($U = 437.5$; $p = 0.009**$;[4] $d = 0.58$). This value might be surprising given the increase in the usage of technology, which would be expected to correspond to a more positive value. However, we may argue that, by having more recourse to autonomy (see above), the learners became more thorough and attentive in their assessment of it. In this respect, Respondent 4 shows how the increased usage of technology for learning caused him to better appreciate some tools:

> [During the pandemic] I resorted more to online translators and databases … and I found new ones. During the pandemic I resorted a lot to [XXX] … which I had not known before, and which I now use more than other tools. Something else I noticed is that I referred much more often to printed materials, because I felt the need not to rely only on digital sources … I always had felt that the [YYY] translator had some flaws, but, yes, during the pandemic I realized this to the full.

Here the respondent suggests that an increase in the usage of digital tools for study actually meant a more profound assessment, which triggered a more informed approach to using them. Such an informed approach involves not only searching for, and eventually switching to, better instruments, but also embedding technology within a wider framework. Recourse to printed dictionaries reveals an inherent lack of full trust in digital tools, but it also signals that autonomy in general and online tools in particular played a more central role in his learning, hence requiring a better integration with other sources, acknowledged as being reliable. This corresponds both to a more proactive attitude and to an approach to ecology in which tools do not operate in a vacuum but, rather, are integrated with one another. Of course, we must remember that the target group is made up of students in linguistics who are arguably more sensitive to issues of quality. However, if they do become language teachers, they will hopefully transmit their beliefs to their pupils.

Benefits and Needs

Two questions of the survey focused on the learners' skills underpinning autonomy. When asked to choose three abilities they felt had helped them in their endeavour (i.e. abilities they felt they already possessed), the most chosen ones were technical competences (58%), knowing the sources where information on the tools can be found (39%), knowing how to integrate different tools (36%) and being able to assess information (36%). As regards the abilities that could have helped them (i.e. abilities they felt they did not possess), the most important ones were being able to assess one's learning (33%), knowing the potential of the available options (31%) and being able to interact online (29%). A large share (24%) of respondents, however, perceived their technical skills to be inadequate.

After their experience with distance learning, the participants found that adequate preparation for autonomy would be helpful ($M = 8.44$; $SD = 1.66$) and, in particular, that such preparation should focus mostly on linguistic issues and abilities (58%), rather than on technical ones (36%). Indeed, the answers as to what competencies learners felt they were missing suggest that it is precisely linguistic and pedagogical issues that constitute a primary concern for learners (for instance, 'knowing the potential of the available options'). This point was confirmed by the interviews: Respondent 4, for instance, concluded that 'although these tools are not always accurate, still they constitute a help learners should not neglect'. Respondent 1 is precise in identifying what learner education should focus on – namely, connecting tools/sources with the different tasks:

> I do not think I need preparation for the technical aspects, nor do I feel I need training as how to use these tools ... what may be of great help, in my view, would simply be a list of resources, trustworthy resources, I could refer to for different tasks. That would be really useful.

Finally, while most learners felt at ease with technology, scarce proficiency in that field may still constitute a serious barrier: Respondent 3 admitted to a lack of adequate knowledge as regards technology for autonomy and therefore considers it as her main need: 'Yes [preparation is useful], because I think my lack of interest in technology for autonomy is a consequence of my scarce technology proficiency, so yes, I'd like to receive proper training.' This is no secondary point, for the lack of suitable technical skills hinders some learners from resorting to autonomy and, consequently, from acting as disseminators, either as expert learners or teachers.

Discussion

The findings of this research reveal that the attitudes and habits of learners in the target group changed during the pandemic. However, such changes are not dramatic and hint at an evolution rather than a revolution. Before attempting any discussion of such changes, I shall define a general profile for autonomy in the target group, which may serve as a backdrop against which to interpret the data from the 2021 survey.

A Profile for Autonomy in Advanced Learners

Learners in the target group are generally aware of the potential of out-of-class autonomous learning through technology. However, while there is a strong heterogeneity in their habits (which can be explained through ecological theories), learners are predominantly oriented towards exposure activities (e.g. watching movies, but also following web channels, reading online, etc.) and using digital tools for studying. While, as seen above, exposure activities are common among most leaners in general, using digital tools such as online translators for studying can be explained by the learners' status as students of linguistics. This makes them more attentive to the importance of tools for language learning and hence, when proficient enough, a potential guidance for other learners or for their future pupils. However, such activities as production and sharing of content or interacting with other people, despite their potential in a communicative perspective, remain peripheral and relegated to niches.

The participants recognize the importance of technology, but generally feel at ease with it, and it does not constitute a problem for most of them. Indeed, when asked about what ability helped them most with autonomy, the majority of respondents to the second survey answered that it was technical expertise. However, it should be kept in mind that when this ability is lacking, as in the case of Respondent 3, it becomes a major hindering factor towards autonomy. Caution, therefore, must be exercised when decisions are taken with respect to the weight of this issue in learner education.

As regards the drawbacks of autonomy, the learners' concerns revolve around the correctness of information (which might explain their scarcely resorting to social media for learning), the ability to understand (and somehow operationalize their own needs) and the need to filter and organize information. Such concerns are in line with those in the existing literature as reported in Lai (2017) and denote a difficult integration between the formal and informal sides of language learning. Such diverse concerns, mainly oriented to the pedagogical/linguistic aspect of autonomy, are represented in their answers, in the second survey, as to what should constitute the bulk of education for autonomy (being able to assess information, knowing their own needs, etc.).

The Covid-19 Pandemic and Its Impact on Autonomy: Lessons Learnt

The main question with respect to the scope of the present chapter is whether the habits and attitudes of the target group towards technology-enhanced autonomy have changed during the pandemic. The answer, as mentioned above, is that they have changed and, scarcely evident as this change may appear at first, especially from a qualitative point of view, the results provide important insight into the matter.

First, there is a quantitative change in the learners' habits. The pandemic has been an opportunity for the participants to increase the time they devote to autonomy in general, which resulted, in particular, in a greater exposure to the second language and in an increase in the number of online tools they used in their work with languages.

A positive outcome of this pandemic and lockdown experience is that many learners who did not resort to autonomy, or did so scantily, had the opportunity to delve more deeply into it. A further important point is that the majority of participants counted on continuing to do so in the future: the pandemic has not only presented the opportunity for an increase in autonomy, but something is expected to remain of this experience.

Second, the experience has not qualitatively changed the participants' habits. The responses to the survey show a relatively static horizon with respect to the participants' general habits for out-of-class learning, where the combination of leisure/exposure activities and study tools maintains its centrality, and even when learners discovered new tools, they were generally limited to these two poles. This is hardly surprising, as the combination of exposure activities and digital tools constitutes the bulk of autonomous learning for the target group (as reported by the 2019 survey), with other activities being variously spread among the learners according to individual preference and beliefs. Also, socially oriented activities remained overall peripheral, and although the participants declare that they spent more time online, they generally neglect social media as a venue for learning.

Third, although during the pandemic the participants quantitatively resorted to a greater amount of autonomy, they were less convinced of its benefits with respect to the first survey. As stated above, while this may at first appear as a negative outcome, it may also indicate that an increase in the recourse to autonomy has been the occasion for a more reflective stance, which is exactly what learner education for autonomy should seek most (see e.g. Dickinson, 1992; Holec, 1981b). Here, the case of Respondent 4 is of great interest. In this case, the situation (distance learning following the pandemic) led to an increased use of study tools, but this caused him to reconsider their affordances (e.g. the flaws he had previously noticed, but overlooked, in a given piece of software were no longer acceptable in the new learning context) and consequently revise his habits, including adding other kinds of tools (here, printed material). This confirms Barron's idea of learning as a dynamic phenomenon, whose changes need to be tracked in order to achieve a fuller understanding of the domain of autonomy.

Finally, during the pandemic experience, learners perceive education for autonomy as being an important asset. Although there is no counterpart from the 2019 survey, the strong figure relating to this point (see above) might be interpreted as a corollary and consequence of the previous points. Indeed, by resorting more to autonomy, the learners have appreciated its potential, but also its (as well as their own) limits, which call for a thorough education and training in this ambit, especially as regards the abilities the participants feel they want more – namely, pedagogical ones (such as self-assessment or the capacity to understand the potential of each tool). This confirms the importance for autonomy of such pedagogical skills as self-regulation (Lai, 2013). Finally, a caveat is in order. While technical and procedural issues are not a concern for the majority of learners, during the pandemic they nonetheless constituted an important barrier for a large share of learners and therefore must not be neglected. Such diversity in profiles and needs, however, is not new to research in learner education for autonomy. The didactic counterpart of an ecological perspective is an individualization of learner training and advising (Mynard, 2020), which these results further endorse.

Conclusions

The premise underpinning the reported research was that the forced shift to distance learning could foster autonomous out-of-class learning through technology. Well, it actually did. However, as seen, this change in the learners' attitudes and habits was more of an evolution than a revolution.

The main finding is that the pandemic, subsequent lockdown and distance learning contributed to making autonomy more present in the participants' ecology of learning, at least quantitatively, but this has implied a more mature and informed consideration of its potential and limitations. The participants, on their part, expressed a strong perception of the importance of education for autonomy, which therefore confirms the former point.

These findings and conclusions should nevertheless be weighed against the limitations of the illustrated research – namely, the small sample and the specificity of the target group, which might reflect the beliefs and habits shared in the survey's site and the rather broad scope of the investigated activities, which make it difficult to understand how each specific activity type has changed in detail. Further research is therefore necessary for a fuller understanding of specific tools, such as, for example, online translators.

However, the main implication of the reported research is that education for autonomy (and, as some respondents argued, technology in general) is all the more important now, since being able to work autonomously means to be better prepared for whatever temporary interruption of normality in education might occur. While learners the world over hope for a return to normality, still experts and governments are preparing for possible future pandemics. Therefore, if, as the findings of the illustrated research seem to suggest, an extraordinary situation involves a more sizeable recourse to autonomy, it follows that learner education for this domain is all the more necessary.

Notes

1. The portal is now closed, and the question is no longer retrievable. However, it was posted in the Italian version of the website, and its id was 20130717162424AAauQTQ; the reported answer is the second.
2. All Likert scales used for this research were on a ten-point basis.
3. Throughout the chapter I use the word 'participants' to refer to those learners who answered the questionnaire, while I use 'respondent' for the participants who were interviewed.
4. Levels of significance: $*p < 0.05$; $**p < 0.01$; $***p < 0.001$.

References

Barron, B. (2006). Interest and self-sustained learning as catalysts of development: A learning ecology perspective. *Human development*, *49*(4), 193–224.

Benson, P. (2007). Autonomy in language teaching and learning. *Language teaching, 40*(1), 21–40.
Benson, P. (2009). Mapping out the world of language learning beyond the classroom. In F. Kjisik, P. Voller, N. Aoki, & Y. Nakata (Eds.), *Mapping the terrain of learner autonomy, learning environments, learning communities and identities* (pp. 217–35). Tampere University Press.
Benson, P. (2011). Language learning and teaching beyond the classroom: An introduction to the field. In P. Benson & H. Reinders (Eds.), *Beyond the language classroom* (pp. 7–16). Palgrave Macmillan.
Benson, P. (2013). *Teaching and researching: Autonomy in language learning*. Routledge.
Breen, M. P., & Candlin, C. N. (1980). The essentials of a communicative curriculum in language teaching. *Applied Linguistics, 1*(2), 89–112.
Chik, A. (2018). Learner autonomy and digital practices. In A. Chik, N. Aoki, & R. Smith (Eds.), *Autonomy in language learning and teaching* (pp. 73–92). Palgrave Pivot.
Chik, A., & Breidbach, S. (2014). 'Facebook Me' within a global community of learners of English: Technologizing learner autonomy. In G. Murray (Ed.), *Social dimensions of autonomy in language learning* (pp. 100–18). Palgrave Macmillan.
Creswell, J. W., Plano Clark, V. L., Gutmann, M. L., & Hanson, W. E. (2003). An expanded typology for classifying mixed methods research into designs. In A. Tashakkori & C. Teddlie (Eds.), *Handbook of mixed methods in social and behavioral research* (pp. 209–40). Sage Publications.
Cumming, A. (2009). Language assessment in education: Tests, curricula, and teaching. *Annual Review of Applied Linguistics, 29*, 90–100.
Dickinson, L. (1992). *Learner training for language learning*. Authentik.
Dickinson, L. (1994). Learner autonomy: What, how and why. In V. J. Leffa (Ed.), *Autonomy in language learning* (pp. 2–12). Editora da Universidade/UFRGS.
Godwin-Jones, R. (2019). Riding the digital wilds: Learner autonomy and informal language learning. *Language Learning & Technology, 23*(1), 8–25.
Gui, M., & Morosini, E. (2020). Didattica a distanza e trasformazione della scuola durante e dopo l'emergenza coronavirus. *Bricks, 2*, 179–83.
Hamilton, M. (2013). *Autonomy and foreign language learning in a virtual learning environment*. Bloomsbury Publishing.
Holec, H. (1981a). *Autonomy and foreign language learning*. Pergamon.
Holec, H. (1981b). A propos de l'autonomie: quelques éléments de réflexion. *Études de Linguistique Appliquée, 41*, 7.
Hyland, K. (2019). *Second language writing*. Cambridge University Press.
Jiménez Raya, M. (2020). Initial teacher education for autonomy: Using possible selves theory to help student teachers construct their professional identity. In M. Jiménez Raya & F. Vieira (Eds.), *Autonomy in language education. Theory, research and practice* (pp. 208–26). Routledge.
Krashen, S. D. (1976). Formal and informal linguistic environments in language acquisition and language learning. *TESOL Quarterly, 10*(2), 157–68.
Kuppens, A. H. (2010). Incidental foreign language acquisition from media exposure. *Learning, Media and Technology, 35*(1), 65–85.
Lai, C. (2013). A framework for developing self-directed technology use for language learning. *Language Learning & Technology, 17*(2), 100–22.
Lai, C. (2017). *Autonomous language learning with technology: Beyond the classroom*. Bloomsbury Publishing.

Lamy, M. N. (2013). Distance CALL online. In M. Thomas, H. Reinders, & M. Warschauer (Eds.), *Contemporary Computer-Assisted Language Learning* (pp. 141–58). Bloomsbury Publishing.

Little, D. (2007). Language learner autonomy: Some fundamental considerations revisited. *International Journal of Innovation in Language Learning and Teaching, 1*(1), 14–29.

Luckin, R. (2010). *Re-designing learning contexts: Technology-rich, learner-centred ecologies*. Routledge.

Maican, M. A., & Cocoradă, E. (2021). Online foreign language learning in higher education and its correlates during the COVID-19 pandemic. *Sustainability, 13*(2), 781.

Molina, A., Michilli, M., & Gaudiello, I. (2021). La spinta della pandemia da Covid-19 alla scuola italiana Dalla Didattica a Distanza alle sfide dell'Educazione personalizzata e dell'Innovazione sistemica. *L'integrazione scolastica e sociale, 20*(1), 47–80.

Murray, G. (2014). Exploring the social dimensions of autonomy in language learning. In G. Murray (Ed.), *Social dimensions of autonomy in language learning* (pp. 3–11). Palgrave Macmillan.

Murray, G. (2020). Learner autonomy and Holec's model: A complexity perspective. In M. Jiménez Raya & F. Vieira (Eds.), *Autonomy in language education. Theory, research and practice* (pp. 89–102). Routledge.

Mynard, J. (2020). Advising for language learner autonomy: Theory, practice, and future directions. In M. Jiménez Raya & F. Vieira (Eds.), *Autonomy in Language Education. Theory, Research and Practice* (pp. 46–62). Routledge.

Pemberton, R., Li, E. S., Or, W. W., & Pierson, H. D. (1996). *Taking control: Autonomy in language learning*. Hong Kong University Press.

Richards, J. C. (2015). The changing face of language learning: Learning beyond the classroom. *Relc Journal, 46*(1), 5–22.

Steel, C. H., & Levy, M. (2013). Language students and their technologies: Charting the evolution 2006–2011. *ReCALL, 25*(3), 306–20.

Toffoli, D., & Sockett, G. (2010). How non-specialist students of English practice informal learning using web 2.0 tools. *ASp. la revue du GERAS, 58*, 125–44.

Wu, M. M. F. (2012). Beliefs and out-of-class language learning of Chinese-speaking ESL learners in Hong Kong. *New Horizons in Education, 60*(1), 35–52.

8

Invisibly Vulnerable: A Corpus-Based Investigation of Media Representations of Australian EAL/D Students in Covid-19 Lockdown

Jessica Morcom and Jianxin Liu

Introduction

The global English language teaching (ELT) community has hailed smart technologies as the saviour in that they not only resurrect mediation and connectivity, but also magnify their power through AI (artificial intelligence) and the IoTs (Internet of things). Thanks to this optimism, after the Covid-19 crisis sent many countries into soft or hard lockdown, technology integration research in ELT has blossomed on many new frontiers, such as video conferencing (e.g. Zoom; Cheung, 2021; Ng, 2020) and virtual reality (e.g. Oculus; Berns et al., 2020; Smith & McCurrach, 2021), as if digitization were an endowment rather than an emergence that should be carefully assessed against the fundamentals. Is the ELT community homogeneous or is it in effect a complex ecology? Since the latter is the consensus by default (Matsuda, 2019), what is the rationale for any umbrella approach?

Throughout the pandemic, unlike their English as a foreign language (EFL) peers, English as a second language (ESL) students often face additional challenges, thanks to sociocultural and linguistic hurdles, but surprisingly, a survey of the literature at the outset of our project found that they had attracted no attention from stakeholders, in respect of policy, curriculum or technology integration research. To understand this contrast, in this chapter, we turn our eyes to Australia, one of the two English-speaking democracies where draconian lockdown measures including school closures were enforced, to report on an analysis of media coverage of EAL/D (English as an additional language or dialect) students. Our analysis aims to highlight widening differences among ELT communities and the need for more situated, nuanced adaptations rather than blind optimism or uniform paradigms. Our investigation centres on a simple question: How have Australian newspapers represented EAL/D students during the Covid-19 pandemic?

In the following, we begin the chapter by detailing Australia's response to the Covid-19 pandemic, the make-up of Australian mass media and the unique ELT situation Australia features. We then outline a corpus curated for investigating the online outlets of six Australian mainstream newspapers and share our analysis of their coverage of EAL/D students. In the last two sections, we discuss the significance and implications of our analysis in tandem with future ELT technology integration in times of global pandemics. We hope that our analysis can help filter out media noises and underscore some more fundamental issues concerning ELT technology integration, such as attendance to vulnerability and care, in response to future public health crises.

EAL/D Students, Australian Covid Lockdown and the Mass Media

Australia is culturally and linguistically diverse: 30% of the population born overseas at the end of 2020, 21% speaking a language other than English at home and 3.3% being Aboriginal and Torres Strait Islander peoples (ABS, 2020). This CALD (cultural and linguistic diversity) make-up sees the term EAL/D used alongside ESL in Australian education to emphasize the presence of 'students whose first language is a language or dialect other than Standard Australian English who require additional support to assist them to develop English language proficiency' (DET, 2020, p. 13). *The EAL/D Advice for Schools* by the state of New South Wales (NSW) further crystallizes Australia's unique EAL/D situation: some students were born in Australia while others recently arrived as permanent or temporary residents, refugees or international students with severely disrupted schooling or no schooling at all due to wars, civil disturbances or first-language literacy (NSW Department of Education, 2020).

The Australian EAL/D landscape has been shaped by historical contingencies. Initially entrenched in assimilation attempted to suppress otherness/difference, it later sought refuge in multiculturalism to promote differences (Oliver et al., 2017). Succeeding policies and practices up to the present day oscillate between fairness and otherness. EAL/D's recent replacement of ESL and other terms (such as LBOTE – language background other than English) evidences such adaptations and implicitly validates the individual's wealth of linguistic ability as an asset, rather than a disadvantage, a deficit or an impairment (Hertzberg, 2012; Oliver et al., 2017). EAL/D teaching and student supports are offered across primary schools, secondary schools, intensive English centres and intensive English high schools, as well as at universities and other private language learning schools. In many of these contexts, 'specialist teachers deliver EAL/D education in a variety of ways to meet the diverse needs of EAL/D students at different phases of learning English' (DET, 2020, pp. 9–10).

Non-native English speaking (NNES) background students constantly face dual tasks of learning ESL and using English as the medium of education (Gibbons, 2001, as cited in Emmitt et al., 2010). In March 2019, 35.9% of students in NSW government schools had a language other than English spoken at home, with 240 different language backgrounds represented (CESE, 2019). The eagerness to integrate EAL/D students into the mainstream often sees a tug of war between one-size-fits-all and diverse/inclusive perspectives. There are concerns about this initiative while mainstream classrooms are plagued by insufficient English proficiency, lacking adequate understanding of EAL/D student needs and a deficit view of ESL (Oliver et al., 2017). For instance, as schools respond to benchmarking exercises imposed by the National Assessment Program – Literacy and Numeracy (or the NAPLAN), a teaching-to-the test craze has been underway, pressuring EAL/D students to catch up to their mainstream peers rather than sharing their knowledge and experiences (Oliver et al., 2017).

A great many students in Australian adult education (including tertiary institutions) are also from EAL/D backgrounds. In 2019, 1,609,798 students were enrolled in thirty-nine Australian public universities, of whom 1,087,850 speak a language other than English at home and 521,948 are international students (Department of Education, 2020). From 2003 to 2008, the number of students attending ESL instruction programmes at a university level doubled (Oliver et al., 2017) and in 2017, 457,243 international students commenced English language programmes in Australia. Approximately 16,085 domestic students came from a NNES background, including 2% Aboriginal and Torres Strait Islander students.

Australia's strategical response to the first wave of the Covid-19 pandemic, shaped by its unique geographical, economic and political configurations, comprised five phases (Stobart & Duckett, 2020): (1) containment, (2) reassurance amid uncertainty, (3) cautious incrementalism, (4) escalated national action, and lastly (5) gradual transition to a new normal. It was assumed that the geography of Australia (e.g. surrounded by water) supported the effectiveness of this response. In March 2020, Australia went into a full lockdown: social distancing, travel bans, interstate and international border closures, testing, contact tracing and quarantine (Furlong & Finnie, 2020; Price et al., 2020). The impact of 'short and long-term consequences of exposure to stress, uncertainty, loss of control, loneliness and isolation' (Furlong & Finnie, 2020, p. 238) on the mental health of individuals did not surface in this phased response until the second wave.

As a federation, Australia had to cope with the inevitable inconsistencies in the message and approach between the federal and state governments. The federal opted for a cautious approach to implementing infection control measures, while states and territories, mainly NSW and Victoria, enforced more comprehensive measures, including school closures (Stobart & Duckett, 2020) and taking care of the safety of returning children to schools (Shaban et al., 2020). State governments were unsure of when to return students to school while the teachers union demanded that online learning continue (Crowe, 2020).

Although some studies suggest that the mental health toll of Covid-19 on Australians may not have been as severe as in other parts of the world (e.g. Rogers & Cruickshank, 2020), the impact of educational closures and online/remote learning on students was significant. It was estimated that during remote learning, 46% of Australian children were vulnerable to the effects on 'educational outcomes, nutrition, physical movement, social, and emotional wellbeing' (Brown et al., 2021, p. 5). Finkel (2020) reported a persistent misconception that remote learning is solely a technical issue rather than orchestration of pedagogy, content and technology (CoSN, 2020) after comparing online learning outcomes and those for in-class education. The report also noticed that ESL students might have a higher risk of experiencing poor learning outcomes. Surprisingly, this was the only mention of ESL students in the report, without any elaboration of the potential risks for this student group.

Amid the pandemic lockdown, media including newspapers have regained influence in connecting people and spreading information (Anwar et al., 2020). The term 'infodemic' that combines the words 'information' and 'epidemic' vividly captures their extensive reach (Anwar et al., 2020; Thomas et al., 2020). An online survey titled *Digital News Report: Australia 2020* (Park et al., 2020) discovered that during the Covid-19 pandemic, hard news consumers rose to 70%, with much higher trust (53%) in news about Covid-19. The use of social media for consuming news also increased, even among older generations: over half of Australians access news on social media.

Such increased reliance on media during the pandemic created not only a space for health- and policy-related information, but also research opportunities for understanding emerging social issues and their impact on vulnerable social groups such as EAL/D students throughout the health crisis. For instance, Furlong and Finnie (2020) highlight that racial microaggressions and xenophobia have increased during the pandemic in media representations of Australian CALD populations, such as inappropriate labelling of the coronavirus as 'Chinese virus pandemonium' by the *Herald Sun* and *The Daily Telegraph*. This revives the idea that there is a 'current social climate of misleading and culturally insensitive media coverage of COVID-19' (Wen et al., 2020, as cited in Furlong & Finnie, 2020, p. 238) and uncovers an inherent limitation in the Australian regulatory approach in terms of ownership and control (Wilding et al., 2018). In this respect, our analysis of EAL/D representations in Australian mainstream newspapers was a timely attempt at remedying this neglect.

A Corpus-Based Newspaper Survey

We developed a corpus-based approach to conduct the media analysis as it allows for investigating media discourse and resulting societal impacts (Biber & Conrad, 2001; Brezina & Gablasova, 2018). In this study, we focus on written textual elements of news articles to thematically survey Australian mainstream newspapers with EAL/D student coverage during the Covid crisis. In our study, we utilized the algorithm of Google's 'News' tab search to collect the most relevant news articles. Google News's Search Engine Optimization is especially significant in that it determines how prominently news web pages are ranked in influencing the number of unique visitors who engage with content (Wilding et al., 2018). It also allows for specific changes in settings to filter and adjust the search results (McEnery & Hardie, 2011). Because our study is focused on EAL/D student representation during the Covid-19 crisis in Australian media, we only collected the most relevant data accessible to the public from 1 March 2020 to 30 June 2021, as illustrated in Figure 8.1.

These news articles were randomly selected to form a selective corpus sample following the corpus procedures, including a frequency list, concordance and thematic analysis pivotal to themes of EAL/D student representation and experiences during the Covid pandemic. Our analysis was to identify major themes of representation in

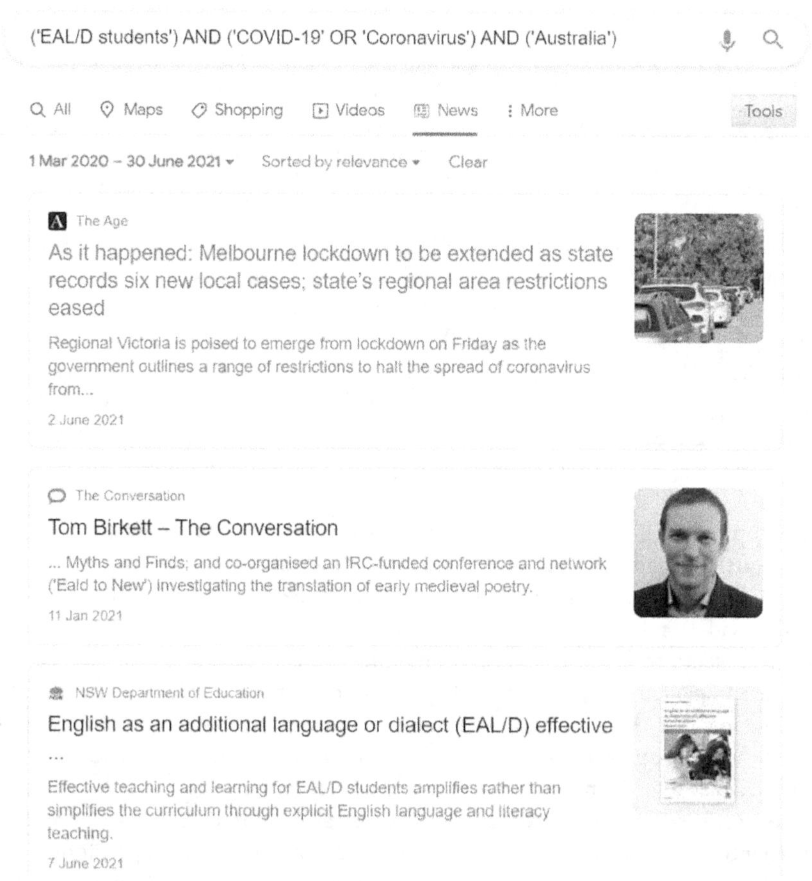

Figure 8.1 Customization of online search settings.

mass media using corpus devices of keyword frequency queries, keyword in context (KWIC) concordances, and thematic analysis. Strings of key search terms (STs) were used to survey and collect news articles following Cain et al. (2020), who conducted a literature review of the public perception of inclusive education in online news media. We used strings of key search words to collect a sample of news articles during the Covid-19 pandemic.

As EAL/D is a term specific to Australian government schools, we expected that it would not be a common term in mass media capable of capturing the range of student groups and educational contexts in Australia. To survey Australian EAL/D populations more broadly, we compiled a list of STs.

The specific representative STs (e.g. multicultural, EAL/D, LOTE) were also inserted in a formulaic string of STs that looked as follows: ('Representative search term') AND ('COVID-19' OR Coronavirus') AND ('Australia'). In total, as Table 8.1 shows, fourteen STs were used within this string to search an online corpus of news articles.

Table 8.1 Key Search Terms

• 'Culturally and Linguistically Diverse' OR 'CALD'	• 'Multicultural'	• 'Minority'	• 'Multicultural'	• 'Minority'
• 'Non-English speaking'	• 'Language Background Other Than English' OR 'LBOTE'	• 'Aboriginal and Torres Strait Islander' OR 'Indigenous'	• 'Language Background Other Than English' OR 'LBOTE'	• 'Aboriginal and Torres Strait Islander' OR 'Indigenous'
• 'Ethnic Communities' OR 'Ethnic Minorities'	• 'English Language Learner' OR 'ELL'	• 'Diversity' OR 'Diverse background'	• 'English Language Learner' OR 'ELL'	• 'Diversity' OR 'Diverse background'
• 'ESL' OR 'English as a second language'	• 'Immigrants' OR 'migrant'	• 'Temporary Residents' OR 'Visa Holders'	• 'Immigrants' OR 'migrant'	• 'Temporary Residents' OR 'Visa Holders'
• 'EAL/D students'	• 'Refugee' OR 'Asylum Seeker'		• 'Refugee' OR 'Asylum Seeker'	

The top results were collected to create a selective corpus based on the following criteria: articles had to (1) be news articles published within the time frame of 1 March 2020 to 30 June 2021, (2) refer to EAL/D students or populations, (3) have a link to Covid-19 related events, and (4) relate to an Australian context. Here 'Covid-19 related events' refer to events that have some connection to, are occurring because of or are impacted by the Covid-19 pandemic such as border closures, online learning, job loss, lockdown, immigration policies, visa issues and many more. We also applied random sampling (i.e. selecting every fifth article) to minimize researcher bias after identifying the original relevant articles and those articles that required a subscription or were from a non-Australian source. Articles that required a subscription, were from a non-Australian source or were repeated previously were skipped. After randomization, the selected articles were compiled into a data set in NVivo to undergo data annotations.

The news sources for the initial 237 relevant articles in the corpus, including non-Australian sources and those requiring subscriptions, and the forty-four articles in the sample were identified and counted to explore which news outlets are representing the experiences of EAL/D populations during the Covid-19 pandemic to the public (see Table 8.2 for details). *The Age* had fourteen (5.91%) articles, the *Sydney Morning Herald* (*SMH*) had thirteen (5.49%), *7NEWS* had five (2.11%) and *9NEWS* had one (0.42%). *The Age* and *SMH* were not included in the sample corpus due to their subscription requirement and the random selection of every fifth article resulted in some other news sources being absent from the sample corpus. Therefore, the quality of representation of EAL/D students or populations by commercial news cannot be efficiently determined in this study. However, the finding of their limited presence in the data collection process is still significant. It is worth noting that *SBS News* and its sub-language services (*SBS Arabic24, SBS Italian, SBS Hindi, SBS Punjabi*) are represented individually. Yet they were counted collectively as *SBS* (total) to represent one news source in the twenty-five total news sources. The same principle was applied to the data about news sources for the corpus samples.

Table 8.2 Sample News Sources

News Sources	No. of Articles	Corpus Sample (%)
SBS Italian	1	2.27
INDAILY	1	2.27
SBS Hindi	2	4.55
The Interpreter	2	4.55
News.com.au	3	6.82
The Guardian	3	6.82
The Conversation	3	6.82
SBS Punjabi	5	11.36
ABC News	11	25
SBS News	13	29.55
SBS (Total)	21	47.73

The Analysis of EAL/D Representations

This section provides a snippet of the patterns of EAL/D representations that have emerged from our analysis of the selected Australian newspaper articles.

Cluster Analysis

Figure 8.2 visualizes with a word cloud the top fifty words from the word frequency query (WFQ) in a cluster analysis. The WFQ reveals that the most commonly occurring word is *government* with 201 counts of the word and a weighted percentage of 0.96% in the corpus. This is followed by frequent occurrences of the words *covid, health, coronavirus, information, community, vaccine, communities, students* and *pandemic*. These top ten most frequently occurring words reveal potential themes of impact on EAL/D populations represented in Australian mass media. The word *students* is among the top ten most frequent, with ninety-five counts and a 0.45% weight. The word *school* is among the top fifty occurring words at number forty-six with thirty-nine counts and a weighted percentage of 0.19%. This cluster analysis also provides insight into themes based on the frequency and occurrence of clusters of words. For example, the light purple cluster shows that the words *students, international, return, minister, Morrison* (the sitting Prime Minister of Australia), and *time* may occur frequently together. This indicates that the return of international students might be a theme of student representation. A light blue cluster of words directly above indicates a theme relating to restrictions, travel, quarantine and India.

Thematic Analysis

From the WFQ list, specific words could be selected to explore the occurrence of these words in more depth. Since our analysis was to explore the representation of EAL/D

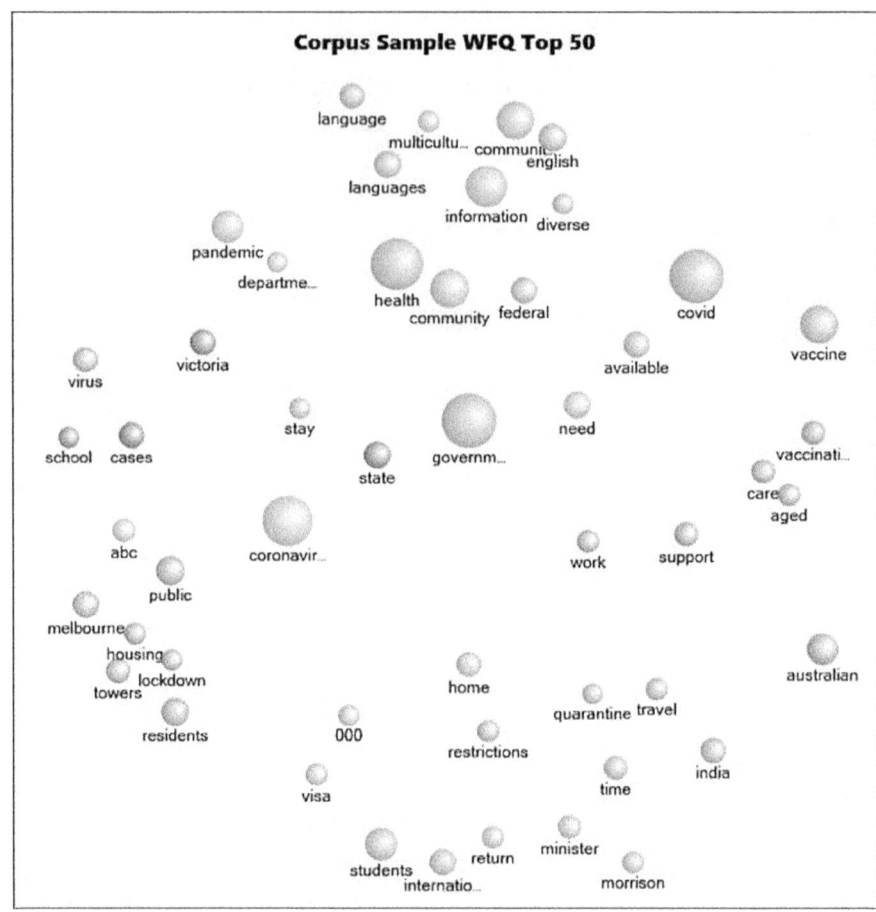

Figure 8.2 Cluster analysis – word frequency query top 50.

students, we conducted a thematic analysis to examine the occurrences of the word *students* in context. A KWIC summary of references to students could be viewed, showing some context before and after each occurrence of the word *students*. This summary listed the references and indicated weighted percentage of coverage for each article as well as a total weighted percentage of coverage of the references combined for each article, as summarized in Table 8.3.

In the article column, the ST (e.g. ST3) together with the article number (e.g. A10) combination indicates which article and STs have occurrences of the word *students*. The references column shows how many times the word *students* is present in that article. The coverage column shows the percentage of coverage that the word *students* makes up in each article. ST2, ST3, ST4, ST6, ST7, ST9 and ST14 retrieved articles that contain references to students. ST14 produced four articles that represent students in some form. The search string for ST14 was ('Temporary Residents' OR 'Visa Holders'). All other STs present only have one article that represents students.

Table 8.3 Summary of 'Students' in the Corpus Sample

Article	References	Coverage (%)
ST3 A10	1	0.06
ST4 A18	1	0.09
ST14 A14	3	0.22
ST9 A13	3	0.21
ST14 A19	4	0.45
ST6 A33	4	0.30
ST2 A6	12	0.44
ST14 A9	16	0.92
ST14 A3	24	1.22
ST7 A9	27	1.43

Note: ST stands for Search Term and A stands for Article.

Although the ST strings can showcase media results that represent students, the number of references and percentage of representation in each article differs. Article nine from ST7 ('Language Background Other Than English' OR 'LBOTE') had the highest count of twenty-seven references to *students* and made up 1.43% of the coverage in the article. This is closely followed by article three from ST14, which had twenty-four references and a coverage of 1.22%. Two articles tie in having just one reference to *students*; however, their coverage slightly differs. Article 10 from ST3 ('Ethnic Communities' OR 'Ethnic Minorities') has 0.06% coverage, while Article 18 from ST4 ('ESL' OR 'English as a second language') has 0.09% coverage.

Each reference to *students* was coded into a *students* node, where it would later be thematically analysed and categorized into themed sub-nodes. Figure 8.3 provides a word cloud that shows some of the most commonly occurring words used regarding *students*. The word cloud provides some preliminary insight into common words which may inform potential themes. The term *students* appears to be the most commonly occurring word, followed by *international* and *return*.

The thematic analysis of student representation in mass media relied heavily on the context surrounding the occurrence of students. The KWIC display sometimes provided insufficient context to determine the theme of the reference. This thematic analysis involved researcher interpretation, which is highly subjective. Examining the references to students in a broader context involved considering the entire sentence where the term *students* appears as well as referring to other evidence within the article. The inspection of the broader context supported the process, except for a few instances where a reference could have fitted into one or more themes.

The thematic analysis revealed that the references to students represented international students and school students. Therefore, references were categorized into *international students* and *school students*. Themes were identified for both groups of students represented in the corpus. We curated the results of the thematic analysis

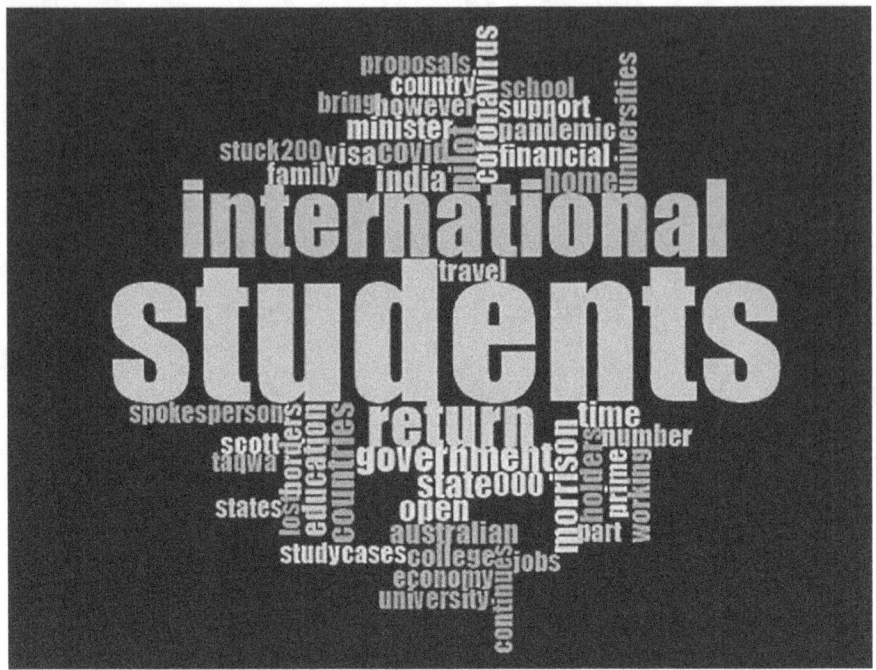

Figure 8.3 The 'students' node word cloud.

for both student groups in Table 8.2 to show the themes, the number of references to students for each theme, the number of articles that had these themes present and the article identifier (made up of the ST and A numbers).

In total, the term *international students* occurs seventy-four times across seven articles. The themes are portrayed across multiple articles, indicating that some articles represent students in relation to multiple themes. Table 8.4 shows the results for themes related to *students* references that are specific to international students. In the following, six of the ten key themes concerning *international students* are further scrutinized in context.

Table 8.5 shows that the word *students* mainly refers to school students, with twelve instances across two articles. Among the five salient themes excluding *Other*, no explicit references are related to EAL/D students or the challenges they may experience during the pandemic, except one article that states that students from two primary schools were included in a Covid case cluster linked to Eid celebrations in the Muslim community. In brief, most themes were about transmission, Covid cases, warnings, and messaging about Covid-19, testing and quarantine, and a return to school after the school was closed for deep cleaning. There were no references to individual student experiences or impact on student learning and well-being.

Table 8.4 'Students' Themes – International Students

Theme	References	Articles	ST & A
Temporary residents	1	1	ST14A19
Not choosing Australia	1	1	ST14A9
Support	2	1	ST14A3
Financial hardship	3	1	ST14A3
Other	4	3	ST14A3, ST14A9, ST7A9
Economy	5	3	ST14A9, ST7A9, ST9A13
Employment	5	1	ST14A3
Travel restrictions	7	4	ST14A19, ST14A3, ST14A9, ST7A9
Disregard	9	2	ST14A10, ST14A3
Return to Australia	32	4	ST14A14, ST14A19, ST14A9, ST7A9

Table 8.5 'Students' Themes – School Students

Theme	No. of References	No. of Articles	ST & A
Transmission	1	1	ST2A6
Return to school	1	1	ST2A6
Covid cases	1	1	ST4A18
Warning/Messaging about Covid	2	1	ST2A6
Testing and quarantine	2	1	ST2A6
Other	5	1	ST2A6

Discussion

Our analysis finds that Australian newspaper stories during the survey period had an exclusive focus on vulnerable international students, with a marked inattention to other EAL/D student groups. While there were potential references to school students from Muslim communities, who may (not) be EAL/D students, the only other representation was of international university students. This is consistent with the extant literature, with prevalent portrayal of international students as vulnerable during the pandemic (Dodd et al., 2021). There is no doubt that their unique needs and isolation during the lockdown can lead to exacerbated vulnerability (Coffey et al., 2021), yet the media representations largely disregard or neglect them rather than being inclusive of them to offer support, especially in relation to the representational themes: employment, financial hardship, disregard and support. One cannot help but wonder: Is this overrepresentation of international students a tactical decision to favour the market while repressing domestic EAL/D student groups? Or is it a scenario noted by Smith and Judd (2020) that the power of privilege in pandemics emphasizes the disproportionate impact on vulnerable groups?

Our analysis further reveals that in the selected survey period, Australian newspapers provided neither explicit references to the term EAL/D, nor representation of other EAL/D student groups, nor the unique vulnerabilities that they may experience during the pandemic. In the coverage with references to EAL/D backgrounds, all the themes were linked to public health issues about Covid-19 such as transmission, Covid-19 cases, warnings, and contact tracing, testing and quarantine, and a return to school, unlike the discussion above that concerns the vulnerabilities of international students during the pandemic (Coffey et al., 2021; Dodd et al., 2021). Even worse, instances with racial or religious inferences cannot be easily dismissed: one article questioned how students from two primary schools are included in a case cluster linked to an Eid celebration in the Muslim community while another article reported on a private Islamic school with Covid-19 cases.

All these instances raise red flags about the power these media representations might have exercised on public opinion and Muslim communities during the pandemic. While such a representation of EAL/D students did not explicitly single out Muslim communities as Covid superspreaders, the discriminatory inferences and the subsequent act of shaming and blaming individuals or groups from diverse backgrounds are unmistakable, corresponding to several recent media representation episodes in Australia (Couch et al., 2020). Given the poor track record of Australian mass media in representing CALD communities and recent racial microaggressions and xenophobia in media representations during Covid-19 (Furlong & Finnie, 2020; Rodrigues & Yin, 2017), this increased reliance on mass media for information can pose a serious threat to public spaces during the ongoing Covid-19 pandemic. In fact, some newspapers had endeavoured to paint low socio-economic suburbs with large CALD recent migrant communities as Covid culprits. Not surprisingly, such incidents as the sudden lockdown of public housing towers in Melbourne played a major role in creating a sense of blame for these communities. The negative media coverage of EAL/D populations during the pandemic might have unwittingly stigmatized public perception of race, ethnicity and even faith.

In a nutshell, our analysis has helped uncover a disturbing absence of EAL/D student representation in Australian mass media in spite of the growing EAL/D student population in schools (CESE, 2019). It is evident that the enduring impacts educational lockdowns may have on vulnerable EAL/D students brings forth an urgent need to advocate for media visibility of EAL/D students during the pandemic. As a nation with a large, growing population of EAL/D students, the education lockdown is a huge social event that may have compounded existing vulnerabilities of these students. The amplification of health- and policy-related news to the masses has overshadowed the coverage of other social issues emerging from Covid-19, including the impacts of the closure of educational institutions.

Implications for the Post-Covid ELT Technology Integration

It is a global trend that NNES have rapidly outnumbered the native English speakers in the past few decades. A World Englishes paradigm built on Kachru's (1990) early work may posit that this disparity is even more conspicuous between NNES in the expanding circles (e.g. EFL or English as an international language) and the inner circles (e.g. ESL, EAL/D; Karmani, 2005; Matsuda, 2019). Strangely, research mainstream and the public still insist on approaching ELT communities as a homogeneous entity (e.g. translating EFL scholarship into other English language learning (ELL) realms, including ESL) with little attention to the fundamental differences between the duo. EFL learners usually see English learning as earning another linguistic currency to attain (elitist) social recognition (e.g. Beard, 2018), while ESL learners must strive for social accommodation variously coded as assimilation, acculturation or gap closing across situated sociopolitical contingencies (Vollmer, 2000), as in the case of Australian EAL/D students. While most EFL learners are in the social mainstream with many entitlements, ESL learners are often fringe social members – immigrants, new arrivals, refugees, or aliens – acutely vulnerable and often in desperate need of support (Flynn, 2015; Liyanage et al., 2016) in times of the pandemic school lockdown examined in the chapter. While mediation (for immersion; Grant, 2020) and motivation (for social recognition; Yashima, 2002) are essential to EFL research and pedagogy, socialization endeavours such as building relationship and intimacy are at the core of ESL practices (Naidoo et al., 2018). It is no wonder that despite full participation in native speaking societies, ESL learners are often linguistically and culturally othered, impaired or displaced in normal times (Oliver et al., 2017) and in times of a public health crisis, neglected and even demonized for achieving the greater social good. The irony is, constituting over 30% of the Australian student population, are EAL/D students not part of the Australian public?

To conclude the chapter, we argue that these fundamental differences such as invisible vulnerability that sets apart the EFL and ESL be foregrounded rather than overlooked by various stakeholders (e.g. language policymakers, curriculum development panels, media corporations) in times of global health crises like Covid-19. The Australian lesson suggests that a utopian narrative championing smart technology at the centre of a pandemic response, chorused by mainstream media and tech-integration paradigms (e.g. SAMR, TPACK; Hilton, 2016), can cause more harm than good not only to various ESL populations, but also to research legitimacy and pedagogical practices. Instead of efficacy craze, future ELT tech-integration in the context of Australian EAL/D should centre on empathy (such as belonging and becoming) to achieve enablement, a term often reserved for learners who are minor, frail or with physical or cognitive impairment (Peters, 2003). In the era of the IoTs when even immersion is virtually at the fingertips (touch), at the glance (facial/eye recognition), or at the tip of the tongue (voice recognition), ELT tech-integration research should strive beyond the narrow confines of technological determinism to foster care, connectivity and interaction. After all, technology is integral to (human) evolution; it is not only a matter of choice, but also a matter of how we manage its emerging capabilities.

References

ABS. (2020). *Migration, Australia. Statistics on Australia's international migration, internal migration (interstate and intrastate), and the population by country of birth.*

https://www.abs.gov.au/statistics/people/population/migration-australia/latest-release. Retrieved on 10 September 2022.

Anwar, A., Malik, M., & Raees, V. (2020). Roles of mass media and public health communications in the COVID-19 pandemic. *Cureus, 12*(9), 1–12. https://doi.org/ https://doi.org/10.7759/cureus.10453.

Beard, M. (2018). Language as currency: Perpetuating and contesting notions of English as power in globalized Korean contexts. *Journal of Comparative and International Higher Education, 10*(1), 19–25. https://doi.org/https://doi.org/10.32674/jcihe.v10iSpring.

Berns, A., Reyes Sánchez, S., & Ruiz Rube, I. (2020). Virtual reality authoring tools for teachers to create novel and immersive learning scenarios. *Eighth International Conference on Technological Ecosystems for Enhancing Multiculturality* (pp. 896–900). Association for Computing Machinery.

Biber, D., & Conrad, S. (2001). Quantitative corpus-based research: Much more than bean counting. *TESOL Quarterly, 35*(2), 331–6. https://doi.org/https://doi.org/10.2307/3587653.

Brezina, V., & Gablasova, D. (2018). The corpus method. In J. Culpeper, P. Kerswill, R. Wodak, T. McEnery, & F. Katamba (Eds.), *English language: Description, variation and context* (2nd ed., pp. 595–609). Palgrave Macmillan.

Brown, N., Te Riele, K., Shelley, B., & Woodroffe, J. (2021). *Learning at home during COVID-19: Effects on vulnerable young Australians* (Independent Rapid Response Report, Issue). https://www.utas.edu.au/__data/assets/pdf_file/0008/1324268/Learning-at-home-during-COVID-19-updated.pdf. Retrieved on 10 September 2022.

Cain, M., Gibbs, K., & McRae, B. (2020). 'Please explain!' public perception of students with diversity in mainstream education as voiced in Australian online news media. *International Journal of Educational Research*. https://doi.org/https://doi.org/10.1016/j.ijedro.2020.100006.

CESE. (2019). *Schools: Language diversity in NSW*. NSW Government. https://education.nsw.gov.au/about-us/educational-data/cese/publications/statistics/language-diversity-bulletin/language-diversity-bulletin-2019. Retrieved on 10 September 2022.

Cheung, A. (2021). Language teaching during a pandemic: A case study of zoom use by a secondary ESL teacher in Hong Kong. *RELC Journal*. https://doi.org/https://doi.org/10.1177/0033688220981784.

Coffey, J., Cook, J., Farrugia, D., Threadgold, S., & Burke, P. J. (2021). Intersecting marginalities: International students' struggles for 'survival' in COVID-19. *Gender, Work & Organization, 28*(4), 1337–51. https://doi.org/https://doi.org/10.1111/gwao.12610.

CoSN. (2020). *COVID-19 response: Preparing to take school online*. https://dpi.wi.gov/sites/default/files/imce/broadband/COVID-19_Member_CoSN.pdf. Retrieved on October 8, 2022.

Couch, J., Liddy, N., & McDougall, J. (2020). 'Our voices aren't in lockdown' – Refugee young people, challenges, and the innovation during COVID-19. *Journal of Applied Youth Studies, 4*, 239–59. https://doi.org/https://doi.org/10.1007/s43151-021-00043-7.

Crowe, D. (2020). Schools safe, say commonwealth medical experts. *Sydney Morning Herald*. https://www.smh.com.au/politics/federal/schools-safe-say-commonwealth-medical-experts-20200424-p54n25.html. Retrieved on 10 September 2022.

Department of Education, S. a. E. (2020). *The higher education statistics collection*. https://www.dese.gov.au/higher-education-statistics. Retrieved on 10 September 2022.

DET. (2020). *EAL/D advice for schools*. https://education.nsw.gov.au/content/dam/main-education/policy-library/associated-documents/eald_advice.pdf. Retrieved on 10 September 2022.

Dodd, R. H., Dadaczynski, K., Okan, O., McCaffery, K. J., & Pickles, K. (2021). Psychological wellbeing and academic experience of university students in Australia during COVID-19. *International Journal of Environmental Research and Public Health*, *18*(3), 1–12. https://doi.org/https://doi.org/10.3390/ijerph18030866.

Emmitt, M., Zbaracki, M., Komesaroff, L., & Pollock, J. (2010). *Language and learning: An introduction for teaching* (5th ed.). Oxford University Press.

Finkel, A. (2020). *Learning outcomes for online versus in-class education*. https://www.science.org.au/covid19/learning-outcomes-online-vs-inclass-education. Retrieved on 10 September 2022.

Flynn, N. (2015). Teachers' habitus for teaching English. *English in Australia*, *50*(1), 21–8.

Furlong, Y., & Finnie, T. (2020). Culture counts: the diverse effects of culture and society on mental health amidst COVID-19 outbreak in Australia. *Irish Journal of Psychological Medicine*, *37*(3), 237–42. https://doi.org/https://doi.org/10.1017/ipm.2020.37.

Grant, S. (2020). Effects of intensive EFL immersion programmes on willingness to communicate. *The Language Learning Journal*, *48*(4), 442–53. https://doi.org/https://doi.org/10.1080/09571736.2017.1422274.

Hertzberg, M. L. (2012). *Teaching English language learners in mainstream classes*. PETTA- Primary English Teaching Association Australia.

Hilton, J. T. (2016). A case study of the application of SAMR and TPACK for reflection on technology integration into two social studies classrooms. *The Social Studies*, *107*(2), 68–73. https://doi.org/10.1080/00377996.2015.1124376.

Kachru, B. B. (1990). World Englishes and applied linguistics. *World Englishes*, *9*(1), 3–20. https://doi.org/10.1111/j.1467-971X.1990.tb00683.x.

Karmani, S. (2005). 'Linguistic imperialism' 10 years on: an interview with Robert Phillipson.(Interview). *ELT Journal*, *59*(3), 244–9. https://doi.org/10.1093/elt/cci045.

Liyanage, I., Singh, P., & Walker, T. (2016). Ethnolinguistic diversity within Australian schools: call for a participant perspective in teacher learning. *International Journal of Pedagogies and Learning*, *11*(3), 211–24. https://doi.org/http://dx.doi.org/10.1080/22040552.2016.1272529.

Matsuda, A. (2019). World Englishes in English language teaching: Kachru's six fallacies and the TEIL paradigm. *World Englishes*, *38*(1–2), 144–54. https://doi.org/https://doi.org/10.1111/weng.12368.

McEnery, T., & Hardie, A. (2011). *Corpus linguistics: Method, theory and practice*. Cambridge University Press.

Naidoo, L., Wilkinson, J., Adoniou, M., & Langat, K. (2018). *Refugee background students transitioning into higher education*. Springer.

Ng, C. H. (2020). Communicative Language Teaching (CLT) through synchronous online teaching in English language preservice teacher education. *International Journal of TESOL Studies*, *2*(2), 62–73. https://doi.org/10.46451/ijts.2020.09.06.

Oliver, R., Rochecouste, J., & Nguyen, B. (2017). ESL in Australia: A chequered history. *TESOL in Context*, *26*(1), 7–26. https://doi.org/https://doi.org/10.21153/tesol2017vo l26no1art700700.

Park, S., Fisher, C., Lee, J. Y., Kieran, M.,Sang, Y., O'Neil, M., Jensen, M., McCallum, K., & Fuller, G. (2020). *Digital News Report: Australia 2020*. https://apo.org.au/sites/default/files/resource-files/2020-06/apo-nid305057_0.pdf. Retrieved on 8 October 2022.

Peters, S. J. (2003). *Inclusive education: Achieving education for all by including those with disabilities and special education needs*. https://documents1.worldbank.org/curated/ar/614161468325299263/pdf/266900WP0English0Inclusive0Education.pdf. Retrieved on 8 October 2022.

Price, D. J., Shearer, F. M., Meehan, M. T., McBryde, E., Moss, R., Golding, N., Conway. E. J., Dawson, P., Cromer, D., Wood, J., Abbott, S., McVernon, J., & McCaw, J. M. (2020). Early analysis of the Australian COVID-19 epidemic. *Epidemiology and Global Health*. https://doi.org/https://doi.org/10.7554/eLife.58785.

Rodrigues, U. M., & Yin, P. (2017). *Transnational news and multicultural Australia: Cultural diversity and news in Australia*. https://static1.squarespace.com/static/5b0fd5e6710699c630b269b1/t/5bfe334e562fa75285375c0d/15433https://static1.squarespace.com/static/5b0fd5e6710699c630b269b1/t/5bfe334e562fa752853 75c0d/1543385963184/altman-transnational-news-and-multicultural-australia.pdf. Retrieved on 8 October 2022.

Rogers, S., & Cruickshank, T. (2020). Change in mental health during highly restrictive lockdown in the COVID-19 pandemic: Evidence from Australia. *PeerJ, 9*, e11767. https://doi.org/https://doi.org/10.7717/peerj.11767.

Shaban, R. Z., Li, C., O'Sullivan, M. V. N., Gerrard, J., Stuart, R. L., Teh, J., Gilroy, N., Sorrell, T. C., White, E., Bag, S., Hackett, K., Chen, S. C. A., Kok, J., Dwyer, D. E., Iredell, J. R., Maddocks, S., Ferguson, P., Varshney, K., Carter, I., & Shaw, D. (2020). COVID-19 in Australia: Our national response to the first cases of SARS-CoV-2 infection during the early biocontainment phase. *International Medicine Journal, 51*(1), 42–51. https://doi.org/https://doi.org/10.1111/imj.15105.

Smith, J. A., & Judd, J. (2020). COVID-19: Vulnerability and the power of privilege in a pandemic. *Health Promotion Journal of Australia, 31*(2), 158–60. https://doi.org/https://doi.org/10.1002/hpja.333.

Smith, M., & McCurrach, D. (2021). The usage of virtual reality in task-based language teaching. *Proceedings of the 28th Korea TESOL International Conference: Re-envisioning ELT altogether, all together* (pp. 153–65). KOTESOL.

Stobart, A., & Duckett, S. (2020). *Australia's COVID-19 response: The story so far.* https://grattan.edu.au/news/australias-covid-19-response-the-story-so-far/. Retrieved on 10 September 2022.

Thomas, T., Wilson, A., Tonkin, E., Miller, E. R., & Ward, P. R. (2020). How the media places responsibility for the COVID-19 pandemic – An Australian media analysis. *Frontiers in Public Health*, 483. https://doi.org/https://doi.org/10.3389/fpubh.2020.00483.

Vollmer, G. (2000). Praise and stigma: Teachers' constructions of the 'typical ESL student'. *Journal of Intercultural Studies, 21*(1), 53–66. https://doi.org/10.1080/07256860050000795.

Wen, J., Aston, J., Liu, X., & Ying, T. (2020). Effects of misleading media coverage on public health crisis: A case study of the 2019 novel coronavirus outbreak in China. *Anatolia, 31*(2), 331–6. https://doi.org/doi:https://doi.org/10.1080/13032917.2020.1730621. Retrieved on 10 September 2022.

Wilding, D., Fray, P., Molitorisz, S., & McKewon, E. (2018). *The impact of digital platforms on news and journalistic content.* https://www.accc.gov.au/system/files/ACCC+commissioned+report+-+The+impact+of+digital+platforms+on+news+and+journalistic+content,+Centre+for+Media+Transition+(2).pdf. Retrieved on 8 October 2022.

Yashima, T. (2002). Willingness to communicate in a second language: The Japanese EFL context. *The Modern Language Journal, 86*(1), 54–66. https://doi.org/https://doi.org/10.1111/1540-4781.00136.

Part 3

Technology Integration into Teaching at the Time of the Pandemic

Lockdown with *La Casa de Papel*: From Social Isolation to Social Engagement with Language

Antonie Alm

On 25 March 2020, New Zealand declared a state of national emergency to curtail the spread of the Covid-19 pandemic. At 11:59 pm, the entire nation went into self-isolation. The following six weeks under lockdown had a deep impact on people's daily routines. The psychological effects of life in quarantine are well documented (Brooks et al., 2020; Medeiros et al., 2020; Pfefferbaum & North, 2020). According to Brooks et al. (2020), emotional distress during confinement is triggered by several factors: loss of usual routine, reduced social and physical contact with others, concerns for inadequate basic supplies, fear of infection and confusion due to insufficient information. Anderson et al. (2020) forecast that 'many of the psychosocial impacts are likely to manifest in the medium and long term' (p. 6). University students were equally affected. Early studies, exploring the different attitudes and perspectives towards lockdown provide insights into the impact of the pandemic on students' mental well-being around the world. In Switzerland, Elmer et al. (2020) noted a rise in stress, anxiety, loneliness and depression symptoms among undergraduate students. In New Zealand, Gerritsen (2020) found that university students were affected by increased living costs due to higher bills for power and the internet, while income from part-time jobs disappeared. Medeiros et al. (2020) recommended adopting a positive attitude towards challenging situations, such as taking more time to read, as a way of overcoming the stress of social isolation.

The surge in the number of Netflix subscriptions during the first months of lockdown (Rushe & Lee, 2020) suggests that many turned to digital entertainment to cope with life under lockdown. When Netflix released the fourth season of *La Casa de Papel* in April 2020, the show topped the charts, becoming the most in-demand title in the world (Katz, 2020). Made accessible through synchronization and subtitling, the popular Spanish TV show not only entertained locked-down people around the globe, but it also provided a special treat to those who discovered the subscription-based streaming service for language learning. The potential of Netflix (and similar providers) for digital language immersion has been described as game-changing for language education (Tapper, 2019). With over fifty Spanish language series on Netflix (netflix.com), learners of Spanish are currently the main beneficiaries of this trend.

A small but growing field of academic inquiry, the use of Netflix for language learning has been investigated in both formal (Alm, 2021a; Dizon, 2016; Dizon &

Thanyawatpokin, 2021) and informal (Dizon, 2018; Fievez et al., 2021) learning environments, mostly focusing on the effect of the subtitling option on language development. Subtitles (L1 subtitles, captions, dual subtitles) have made L2 Netflix series accessible to language learners; in the words of Vanderplank (2016), 'subtitles have made video educational' (p. 168). The positive effect of multimodal input on comprehension and language development is well documented in Peters and Muñoz's (2020) recent special issue on the topic. This chapter takes a different perspective, discussing the potential of L2 Netflix viewing for meaningful engagement with language.

Engagement

The psychological concept of engagement describes the quality of a student's active involvement in a learning context. Widely used in educational research (Fredricks et al., 2004; Linnenbrink & Pintrich, 2003; Matos et al., 2018, Reeve & Tseng, 2011; Reschly & Christenson, 2012; Skinner et al. 2009) and second-language acquisition (Baralt et al., 2016; Mercer, 2019; Philp & Duchesne, 2016; Svalberg, 2009), engagement is conceptualized as a multidimensional construct that describes how learners *act*, *think* and *feel* when involved in formal learning activities. *Behavioural engagement* refers to observable actions performed by learners in the classroom: the degree of effort, persistence and the amount and quality of learners' in-class participation (Philp & Duchesne, 2016). Matos et al. (2018) sum up the involvement in learning activities in terms of on-task attention and effort as 'working hard' (p. 580). *Cognitive engagement* relates to mental processes such as strategy use, metacognitive knowledge and self-regulation (Linnenbrink & Pintrich, 2003), and in a language learning context, 'focused attention to form' (Baralt et al., 2016, p. 213). The ability to employ sophisticated learning strategies has been described by Matos et al. (2018) as 'working smart' (p. 580). Positive emotions, such as enthusiasm, interest and enjoyment, are critical indicators for *emotional engagement* (Skinner et al., 2009), also described as 'task-facilitating', as opposed to 'task-withdrawing' (Reeve, 2012, p. 150) emotions such as anxiety, boredom or frustration, which can lead to disengagement. In the words of Matos et al. (2018), emotionally engaged learners are 'working enthusiastically' (p. 580). Some models include *agentic engagement*, described by Reeve and Tseng (2011) as the learner's 'proactive, intentional and constructive contribution into the flow of the learning activity' (Reeve, 2012, p. 151). When learners get actively involved in the learning process by expressing learning preferences, they are 'working proactively' (Matos et al., 2018, p. 580).

The four engagement components can be operationalized for L2 viewing. Behavioural engagement refers to the time spent on the viewing activity. Time spent alone, however, is, as pointed out by Mercer (2019), no indicator for learning engagement. A learner-viewer might be 'watching hard' yet not paying much attention to the L2, focusing instead on the L1 subtitles (or even letting the show run in the background, a habit known as background binging). Similarly, they might be 'watching enthusiastically' and greatly enjoying the show but making little effort to understand or learn from the L2 input. Both dimensions are clearly interrelated, as enjoyment is likely to result in more viewing time. A positive L2 viewing experience can also trigger cognitive involvement and encourage learners to 'watch smart' by applying comprehension and learning strategies such as using captions instead of subtitles, pausing and replaying sequences, looking up and writing down words and phrases, or even to 'watch proactively' by developing regular viewing routines and making viewing choices that correspond to learning goals.

The social dimension of engagement is recognized in all models, even in those who do not include it as a distinct category. Mercer (2019) stresses that all learning is socially situated, and Reeve (2012) points out that engagement 'cannot be separated or disentangled from the social context in which it occurs' (p. 152). This applies to students in the social context of the classroom, as well as to the social conditions that affect out-of-class L2 engagement. In relation to L2 viewing, aspects such as existing Netflix L1 viewing habits or L2 viewing in one's social circles can affect a learner's willingness to engage in L2 viewing. More specifically, relating to the context of the learning activity, *social engagement* concerns the relationship among learners, enabling social interaction for language practice. According to Philp and Duchesne (2016), learners are socially engaged when they 'listen to one another, draw from one another's expertise and ideas, and provide feedback to one another' (p. 57). Similarly, Svalberg (2018) argues that 'learners who have established a social relationship with their peers are more likely to engage with and deploy attentional resources to a language task than those who have not' (p. 23). While Svalberg conceptualizes engagement in the context of language awareness, focusing on the development of declarative L2 knowledge, it relates in most other models to L2 practice.

Drawing on previous operationalizations of engagement in a language learning context, the concept is applied in this study to out-of-class learning during lockdown. Participants viewed Spanish Netflix series and shared their experiences through regular blog posts and comments. The research questions are as follows:

1. To what extent did the experience of lockdown affect learners' willingness to engage with learning?
2. How did learners engage with L2 viewing?
3. To what extent did L2 blogging support engagement with language?

Methodology

Participants and Task

The data used in this study is drawn from a larger project. For this investigation, thirteen profiles were selected from twenty-two participants, which included nine German students. The students (six male and seven female) had an intermediate level of Spanish and were aged between nineteen and thirty-seven years. The pseudonyms are inspired by the Spanish TV series *La Casa de Papel*.

During the seven-week project, students watched a minimum of two weekly episodes of a self-selected Spanish Netflix series. In addition, they shared their viewing and learning experiences in personal blogs. Weekly instructions guided students in their written responses: (1) prior experiences with Netflix, (2) choosing a series, (3) using *Language Learning with Netflix* (LLN), (4) developing a viewing routine, (5) focus on vocabulary, (6) approaches to Netflix viewing, (7) evaluation. Those with no access to Netflix were provided with an account. In addition, they received free access to the chrome extension LLN, which offers a range of language features, such as dual subtitles (for more information on the use of LLN in this project, see Alm, 2021b; Alm & Watanabe, 2021). Students were introduced to the task prior to the 2020 lockdown. During lockdown, students viewed their episodes from their homes, communicating with each other through their blogs. The blogs provided the qualitative data for this study. Errors in the learners' text have not been corrected.

Data Collection and Data Analysis

The larger study utilized a mixed-methods research design and collected qualitative and quantitative data. NVivo was used for the thematic analysis of the blogs. The data was analysed for specific themes and the topics of the research question (Ellis & Barkhuizen, 2005). The questionnaire data was analysed through SPSS. The sixteen items were measured using a five-point Likert scale. The Cronbach's alpha reliability coefficient for the questionnaire was 0.808, indicating that the questionnaire had good internal consistency. Excel was used to visualize the responses using averages. In the text, agreement percentage refers to the combined percentage of *strongly agree* and *somewhat agree*.

Findings and Discussion

Experiencing Lockdown

Blog and questionnaire data provided a cohesive picture of the impact of lockdown on learners' willingness to engage with learning (Research Question 1). The effects were immediate for many students. As soon as the New Zealand government announced provisions for lockdown, almost half (46%) of the participants left the university to stay with their parents in other parts of the country. The physical relocation and the change in teaching mode (zoom classes or recorded lectures) impacted on study habits. Significantly, 85% agreed that lockdown affected their psychological well-being. All agreed that their study routine changed, and 92% found it difficult to motivate themselves to study, with 77% struggling to get their work done (see Figure 9.1).

Many students wrote about their experiences of lockdown, worries and personal struggles which affected their ability to focus on their studies. The suddenness of change is articulated by Helsinki, who expressed in her fourth blog entry (Helsinki 4) a sense of disorientation: '¡Qué una semana loca! El mundo se está volviendo loco, los residentes en mi Universitaria Residencial se están volviendo locos, y yo también me estoy volviendo loca. Todo el mundo tiene muchas preguntas sobre el virus y yo no tengo ninguna respuesta' [What a crazy week! The world is going crazy, the residents in my dorm are going crazy, and I'm going crazy too. Everyone has so many questions

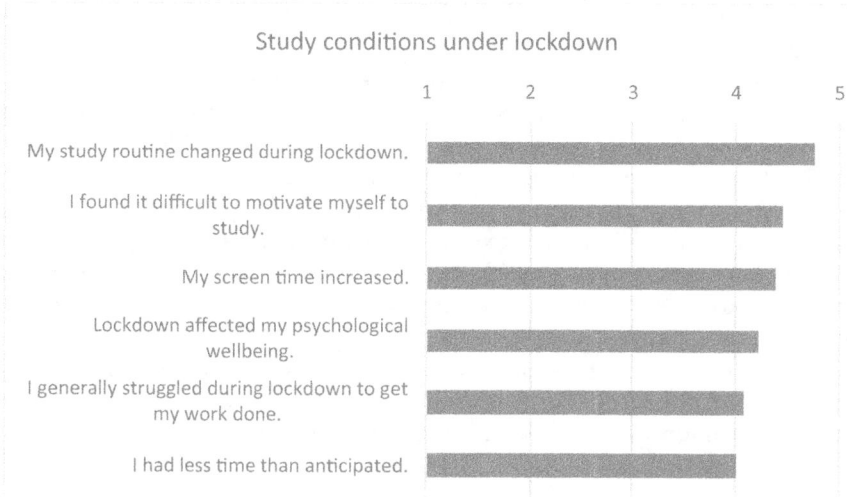

Figure 9.1 Study conditions under lockdown.

Note: 1, *strongly disagree* to 5, *strongly agree.*

about the virus, and I don't have any answers]. Similarly, Madagascar (5) described the transition into lockdown as 'chaos': '¡qué caos! Ha sido una transición completa de la vida antes, uno que, aunque debemos ajustar, no es fácil, y para mi, es una lucha' [What a chaos! It has been a complete transition from life before, one that, although we must adjust, is not easy, and for me, it is a struggle]. Alaska (4) worried about the consequences of lockdown on employment: 'Todos están preocupados por el desempleo' [Everyone is worried about unemployment]. A week later, she describes a feeling of social isolation: 'quiero terminar este aislamiento ya. ¡Me vuelve loca porque extraño a mis amigos demasiado!' [I want to end this isolation now. It drives me crazy because I miss my friends too much!]. Lockdown significantly affected these students' well-being. Facing uncertainty, worries and struggle, they described the changes in emotional terms, *loco, caos, lucha*. Studying under these conditions represented a challenge for many. Helsinki (6) reported, 'La semana pasada fue mucho más difícil que una semana normal de universidad. Las clases que solían tomarme una hora para asistir ahora me llevan casi dos' [Last week was a lot harder than a normal week of university. Classes that used to take me an hour to attend now take me almost two]. Outside of their usual study context and faced with often unexpected issues related to lockdown, many lost their motivation to study. A few weeks into lockdown, Madrid (6) reported, 'He encontrado la vida en cuarentena bastante difícil y aburrida. Parece que me falta la motivación para hacer los deberes escolares. Me ha sido difícil crear una rutina saludable porque la verdad es que ir a la universidad era mi rutina' [I have found life in quarantine to be quite difficult and boring. I seem to lack the motivation to do my homework. It's been hard for me to create a healthy routine because the truth is that going to university was my routine]. Similarly, Alaska (7) wrote, 'Falta la motivación de hacer muchas cosas ... mi cerebro está casi muerto' [The motivation to do many things is missing ... my brain is almost dead].

The experiences of lockdown expressed by these students – uncertainty, personal worries and struggles, loneliness, fear of unemployment, workload issue and lack of motivation – align with the observations of Anderson et al. (2020), Elmer et al. (2020) and Gerritsen (2020) about the psychological effects of lockdown. The changes in the students' social environments at home, at university or at work affected the emotional well-being of many and their ability to focus on their studies. Their experiences further reflect the interconnectedness of engagement and the social context in which learning takes place (Reeve, 2012). The loss of control over external circumstances appeared to affect students' ability or willingness to engage in learning. To an extent, the Netflix assignment enabled students of this class to engage in an activity that related to an established routine (for most) or to accessible activity that was met with curiosity. The option of selecting a series of personal interest allowed them to exercise some agency and immerse themselves in a Spanish environment.

Engaging with L2 Viewing

The second research question focused on the forms of engagement involved in L2 viewing, as expressed by participants in their blogs.

La Casa de Papel was the most popular Netflix series, watched by five students, followed by *Elite*, watched by three. Both shows released new seasons during the lockdown period, indicating that many were influenced in their choices by the popularity of the series.

Once in lockdown, more than half (54%) of the students increased their viewing times, and 77% indicated that the Netflix assignment gave them a sense of continuity (see Figure 9.2). Frankfurt (commenting on Alaska 4) described her regular L2 viewing as the only positive thing about Covid-19. It enabled many to focus on something they enjoyed, and made them feel productive, as pointed out by Madagascar (6): 'La tarea de mirar la serie me ha ofrecido la oportunidad de enfocarme en algo – algo que no toma mucha capacidad de mente, sino que ocupa mi mente por algun tiempo, y en una manera que me hace sentir productiva' [The task of watching the series has offered me the opportunity to focus on something – something that doesn't take much of my mind but occupies my mind for some time, and in a way that makes me feel productive]. While the nature of many other assignments changed since lockdown, with classes shifting online, the Netflix task remained the same as before lockdown. Edimburgo (5) remarked, 'Seguro que tenemos suerte con esta clase porque pudimos hacer mucho desde la casa antes del confinamiento, entonces podemos seguir con estas maneras' [Surely, we are lucky with this class because we could do a lot from home before confinement so that we can continue with these ways].

An established social pastime of most students, 85% changed their Netflix routines to Spanish during the intervention, giving their recreational activity an educational purpose. Cairo's (3) tendency to binge watch resulted in strong behavioural engagement. She was already into the second season of *La Casa de Papel* in the second week of lockdown: 'No puedo dejar de ver, es tan adictivo' [I can't stop watching, it's so

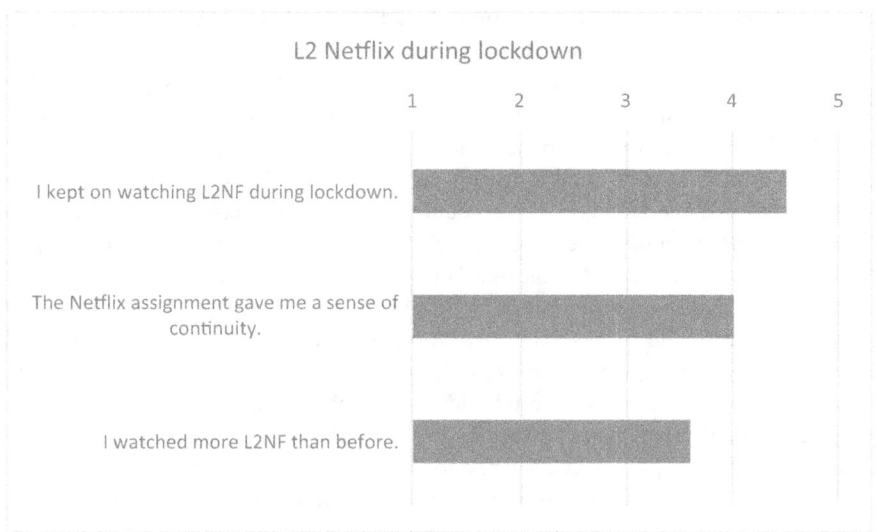

Figure 9.2 L2 Netflix viewing during lockdown.

Note: 1, *strongly disagree* to 5, *strongly agree*.

addictive]. Watching their series 'hard' and 'enthusiastically', the blog extracts suggest that the viewing activity fulfilled an emotional need for structure and continuity, enabling students to feel productive and good about themselves, when control over many other areas in their lives was restricted.

They also engaged socially, by sharing their experiences in their blogs. Cairo's blog about *La Casa de Papel* was followed by four fellow watchers. She was thinking of them when she inserted 'Atención: ¡spoiler!' in her text. Dakar (in Cairo 3) reacted to the spoiler alert: 'También estoy viendo Casa de Papel pero estoy un poco atrasado, así que tuve que dejar de leer hasta la alerta de spoiler jajaja' [I'm also watching Casa de Papel, but I'm a little behind, so I had to stop reading until the spoiler alert hahaha]. Similarly, Madrid was thrilled to find a fellow *Elite* watcher in Madagascar, who, having watched five episodes in one week, called herself 'adicta' [addicted]. Madrid (in Cairo 3) left a comment on her blog: 'me encanta que veamos el mismo programa. ¡Qué asombroso!' [I love that we watch the same show. How amazing!]. Viewers of other programmes also joined in the conversation. Cairo (in Madagascar 4) seemed to line up *Elite* for her next binge watch: ' Parece que Élite es una serie muy buena, creo que voy a verlo después de terminar la Casa del Papel' [It seems that Elite is a very good series, I think I'll watch it after I finish Casa de Papel]. Alaska (in Madagascar 4), who had watched *Elite* previously, followed with a recommendation of the show, affirming its binge worthiness, claiming, 'No podía parar' [I couldn't stop].

The comments illustrate that students related to each other's viewing experiences by sharing their enthusiasm for their shows. Some of them were able to watch their series together with someone in their bubble, the small group of people allowed in their physical surroundings. Edimburgo (5) made use of the dual English and

Spanish subtitles of the LLN extension to enable her boyfriend to watch *La Casa de Papel* with her, two episodes every night: 'Usando LLN podemos pasar tiempo juntos relajándonos, puedo hacer mis deberes y el puede motivarse más para aprender español. Sería cool si él pudiera hablar conmigo y practicar el idioma … como couple goals???' [Using LLN we can spend time together relaxing; I can do my homework and he can be more motivated to learn Spanish. It would be cool if he could talk to me and practice the language … as couple goals???]. The set-up allowed them to engage together with the series, each at their level. Alaska commented enviously, '¡¡¡A Ahhhh couple goals siiiii!!! Me encantaría tener un novio que habla español conmigo. ¡Espero que pueden aprender juntos!' [Ahhhh couple goals yesssss!!! I would love to have a boyfriend who speaks Spanish with me. I hope you can learn together!], and Katmandú announced her plan to watch *La Casa de Papel* with her dad. Cherishing these opportunities for relationship building through the L2 viewing activity, Alaska and Katmandú finished their comments with 'Un abrazo x' [A hug x] and 'cuídense <3' [take care, <3], nurturing the virtual relationships with their readers.

The blog interactions between these learners reinforced their positive viewing experiences, building connections and coming together as a community of viewers. The social function of the blog will be explored in the next section.

Engaging through L2 Blogging

The third research question addresses the forms of engagement supported by the blogging activity. The blogs provided learners with a communication tool during lockdown: 85% agreed that blogging allowed them to interact with their classmates during lockdown and that it gave them a feeling of togetherness, and 77% enjoyed talking with others in their blogs about the series. The commenting component made the writing activity more personal (92%; Figure 9.3).

Most students were familiar with the practice of commenting on social media. Yet commenting in an educational context was a new experience. Once participants found commonalities in their viewing experiences, it developed into an enjoyable practice. The analysis of the questionnaire shows strong positive correlations between the item 'Commenting made the writing activity more personal' and items relating to peer relationships and the social cohesion of the class (items 1–3 in Table 9.1).

Some students proactively interacted with their peers by providing support and advice, such as Edimburgo (in Frankfurt 4), who, reading about Frankfurt's time management issues, suggested that she sets an alarm, a technique that worked for herself. She finished her comment with an encouraging, '¡tal vez debes probar esto!' [maybe you should give this a try!]. To engage their readers and to elicit comments, some ended their posts with a question. Jabalpur (5) wrote about the advantages of breakout rooms on Zoom, asking her readers about their view on this new practice: '¿Qué creen?' [What do you think?]. Similarly, she frequently asked questions in her comments (in Madagascar 5), '¿Recomiendas Elite? ¡He terminado mi programa de televisión y quiero ver otro!' [You recommend Elite? I've finished my TV show and I want to watch another one!] or tagged others to get their attention (in Jabalpur 4), '@Edimburgo ¡Espero que se sienta mejor desde el martes!' [@Edimburgo, I hope

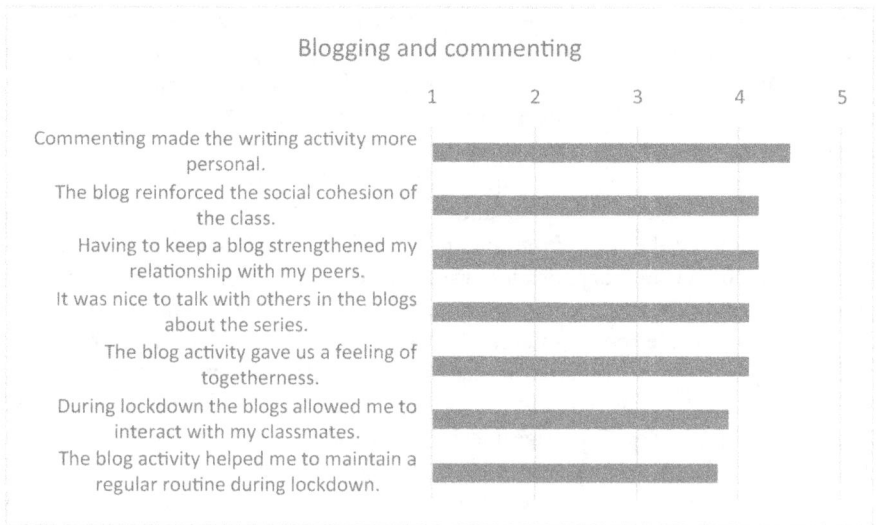

Figure 9.3 Blogging and commenting.

Note: 1, *strongly disagree* to 5, *strongly agree.*

Table 9.1 Correlations between Commenting and Social Engagement

Commenting Made the Writing Activity More Personal	p	Effect Size (Pearson's r)
1. It was nice to talk with others in the blogs about the series.	0.005	0.72
2. Having to keep a blog strengthened my relationship with my peers.	0.010	0.68
3. The blog reinforced the social cohesion of the class.	0.035	0.58

you feel better since Tuesday!]. Creating interesting titles was a technique Helsinki adopted to attract readers: '¿Es Sara una asesina?' [Is Sara a murderer?]. However, the announcement of spoilers, 'Spoilers de la temporada 4 La Casa de Papel', might have had the opposite effect.

The blogging activity enabled students to communicate with each other and engage cognitively with language as they constructed their texts to convey their viewing experiences and engage their readers. For example, words relating to the viewing activity such as 'temporada' [season], 'episodios' [episode] and 'atraco' [heist] might have been picked up incidentally, but it is likely that they have been looked up to report on the viewing. Interestingly, the word 'spoiler' was kept in English – with inverted exclamation marks by Cairo to give it a Spanish appearance – suggesting a form of translanguaging, the integration of two language systems in one (Wei, 2018). However, the word 'spoiler' is an Anglicism in Spanish, and some students might have been aware of the customary use of the English term. Other words which might have been assumed to be Anglicisms, like 'cool', were used in English. 'Couple goals', on the other hand, was followed by three question marks by Edimburgo, signalling that she did not know the Spanish translation. Alaska, however, engages in translanguaging by integrating the English word in her response, '¡¡¡A Ahhhh couple goals siiiii!!!', with exaggerated but appropriate Spanish punctuation and prolonged interjections to emphasize the emotional tone of her reaction.

Learners also wrote *about* the language they used. They used their blogs to try out new words and language structures and share them with their peers. Cairo (5), for example, presented the word, 'tontería' [nonsense], leading to an exchange between participants about uses for application, with Amsterdam (in Cairo 5) thanking her for teaching them a new word, '¡Gracias por ensenarnos!'. Learners commented in their blogs about the perceived usefulness of colloquial and even vulgar language for its authenticity and value for everyday interactions. Madrid (5) reflected on the use of text language in *Elite*, which was made salient through the display on a phone screen. He provided a long list of text language, including 'Genial = gnl, Ok = okas, También = tb, Espero = spro, Te quiero mucho = tqm', deducing that words starting in 'es-' omit the first letters, '*si una palabra comienza con es, se omiten'. Encouraging his readers to use these abbreviations in their communications to come across as more authentic, he signed off with 'okas'. 'La próxima vez que envíe un mensaje de texto a un amigo, intente usar el idioma de texto común en español. Te hará sonar como un local e impresionará a los hispanohablantes. ¡Eso es un plus! ¿¡Okas!?' [Next time you send a text message to a friend, try using the common Spanish text language. It will make you sound like a local and impress Spanish speakers. That's a plus! Ok!?].

His experimentation with *vosotros*, the second-person plural pronoun used in Spain but not in other Spanish-speaking countries, provides another interesting example of engagement with language. Watching a programme from Spain, he was exposed to a form he did not encounter in class, as his teachers were from Venezuela and Chile, using the pronoun in the third person plural, *ustedes*. Addressing his classmates with the informal plural *vosotros*, he wrote an uplifting message, encouraging his classmates to engage in positive activities to lessen the burden of lockdown, '¡Necesitas os llenáis tu cara con muchos chocolates y relajad! Disfruta mientras puedas, porque la vida es breve. Pase tiempo con su familia y lo más importante, encuentre tiempo por vos mismos. Cread, escribid, leed, cocinad, hornead, aprended, cantad, bailad y reíd. Hay todas las medicinas para perseverar los retos de permanecer dentro de nuestras casas' [You need to fill your face with lots of chocolates and relax! Enjoy it while you can because life is short. Spend time with your family and most importantly, find time for yourself. Create, write, read, cook, bake, learn, sing, dance and laugh. These are all the medicines to persevere in the challenges of staying in our homes]. Using *os* and the *-áis* ending in the first sentences, he used the right forms, but not in the right sequence, which should have been 'necesitáis llenaros'. Yet he finished the sentence with 'relajad', which is the correct plural imperative. He continued with the informal form in the singular, 'disfruta', and then in the following sentences switched to the formal form with 'pase'. His use of 'vos' (second-person singular pronoun used in Argentina) demonstrates his familiarity with a range of Spanish address pronouns, creating an interesting linguistically syncretic sentence. In other words, cognitively engaged, he drew on his linguistic resources to construct his L2 knowledge. The iteration of activities in the following sentence – 'cread, escribid' and so on – are all correct forms of the plural imperative. Apologetic about this excessive use of the *vosotros* form, indicating the predominant use of *ustedes* in the class, he finished his entry explaining his ultimate motives for acquainting himself with the Spanish conjugations, 'Perdón por la forma de "vosotros". Estoy experimentando más con esta conjugación, así puedo estar más seguro de hablar español desde España. Algún día espero ser embajador en España para Nueva Zelanda' [Sorry about the 'you' part. I am experimenting more with this conjugation, so I can be more confident in speaking Spanish from Spain. Someday I hope to be ambassador in Spain for New Zealand] (Madrid 6).

These examples illustrate how learners engaged cognitively with language, constructing texts with a social and communicative orientation. The dialogic structure of the blog supported the interactive orientation of the texts. Writing with an audience in mind, real or imagined, students constructed their texts to elicit reactions and comments from their readers. In that sense, the blog also provided an authentic environment for using the informal plural form, as opposed to class situations where students often work in pairs, using the singular form *tú*.

Engaging with L2 Viewing through L2 Blogging

The combined viewing and writing activities enabled participants to engage at different levels with the L2. They engaged predominantly emotionally with the series during their viewing and cognitively in their written interactions. Through the construction of reader-oriented texts, learners expressed their social engagement. The extracts illustrate how engagement dimensions overlap and interact with each other. As learners became more familiar with each other, learning from other blogs and finding comfort in reading about similar experiences during lockdown, their willingness to engage in interactions developed, triggering new levels of engagement. The interconnectedness of the engagement dimensions, backing Mercer's (2019) claim that 'true engagement' (p. 646) necessitates multiple dimensions of engagement, can also be explained through the lens of self-determination theory (SDT; Deci & Ryan, 2002). This theory identifies the three basic psychological human needs of autonomy, competence and relatedness as the source of a person's state of well-being. In an educational context, autonomy relates to the learners' need to regulate learning experiences and the ability to make decisions that match personal interests. In this task, learners were able to choose their viewing content. Further, the structure of the activity allowed learners to develop their writing in areas of personal interest and maintain relationships with classmates during lockdown. The assignment also made students feel effective in completing the activity, addressing the basic human need of competence. A subjective quality, competence relates to the need of feeling capable of managing a task. Assisted by Spanish or dual subtitles through the LLN extension, students felt confident in their viewing and in reporting about their viewing experiences in their blogs at their level of understanding. The third component of SDT, relatedness, encapsulates the social dimension. The blog activity enabled students to share their experiences and construct and develop their language simultaneously. Just as the three basic human needs do not operate in isolation, engagement is multidimensional, and its components are interconnected.

Emotional engagement, triggered by choice, precedes cognitive engagement, and satisfying cognitive engagement can reinforce emotional engagement. Similarly, the ability to share emotional and cognitive engagement can strengthen these forms of engagement and further support the social connections between members of the learning community.

Conclusion and Post-Pandemic Lessons

The experiences of these students demonstrate the relevance of the social dimension in language learning at a number of levels, providing valuable lessons for language learning beyond lockdown.

The temporary disconnection of students from the social structure of their educational environment has highlighted the need for relatedness for engagement. The inability to maintain informal and formal social interactions with their peers and teachers created unease and a sense of disorientation in many students. Their blog testimonies show that the lack of social connectedness negatively affected students' well-being and willingness to study. Supporting learners to develop a sense of belonging in a learning community will be more important than ever, as the psychological impact of the pandemic is likely to be ongoing (Anderson et al., 2020).

The learners' experiences further demonstrate the interconnectedness between engagement and the social context in which learning occurs (Reeve, 2012). The shift from classroom-based learning to online learning required learners to use new communication tools (e.g. Zoom, breakout rooms) which changed the social dynamic of the class. The familiar blog communication structure was used for informal interactions between learners in Spanish during lockdown. Students engaged in blog interactions because they were perceived as socially relevant, which is an important element to remember for post-pandemic design of language learning environments.

For most of the students of this cohort, Netflix was an established pastime. The viewing of L2 series enabled students to relate the L2 activity to a familiar social activity. The lockdown situation has shown that most learners are able to access L2 resources in their own space. While the idea of drawing on learners' informal digital L2 activities is not new (e.g. the concept of bridging activities proposed by Thorne and Reinhardt, 2008), the positive experiences of these learners demonstrate the benefits of making out-of-class L2 engagement a shared experience.

References

Alm, A. (2021a). *Language Learning with Netflix*: From extensive to intra-formal learning. *The EuroCALL Review, 29*(1), 81–92.

Alm, A. (2021b). *Language Learning with Netflix*: Extending out-of-class L2 viewing. *International Conference on Advanced Learning Technologies (ICALT)*, 260–2. https://doi.org/10.1109/ICALT52272.2021.00084.

Alm, A., & Watanabe, Y. (2021). Functional caption literacy development through intra-formal L2 viewing. *Aula Abierta*, *50*(2), 635–42. https://doi.org/10.17811/rifie.50.2.2021.635-642 .

Anderson, D., Dominick, C., Langley, E., Painuthara, K., & Palmer, S. (2020). *Rapid Evidence Review – The immediate and medium-term social and psychosocial impacts of COVID-19 in New Zealand*. Retrieved 16 September 2022, from https://www.msd.govt.nz/documents/about-msd-and-our-work/publications-resources/statistics/covid-19/social-impacts-of-covid-19.pdf.

Baralt, M., Gurzynski-Weiss, L., & Kim, Y. (2016). Engagement with the language: How examining learner's affective and social engagement explains successful learner-generated attention to form. In M. Sato & S. Ballinger (Eds.), *Language learning & language teaching. Peer interaction and second language learning. Pedagogical potential and research agenda* (pp. 209–40). John Benjamins Publishing Company.

Brooks, S. K., Webster, R. K., Smith, L. E., Woodland, L., Wessely, S., Greenberg, N., & Rubin, G. J. (2020). The psychological impact of quarantine and how to reduce it: Rapid review of the evidence. *The Lancet*, *395*(10227), 912–20. https://doi.org/10.1016/S0140-6736(20)30460-8.

Deci, E. L., & Ryan, R. M. (Eds.). (2002). *Handbook of self-determination Research*. University of Rochester Press.

Dizon, G. (2016). Online video streaming in the L2 classroom: Japanese students' opinions towards Netflix and subtitles. *OSAKA JALT Journal*, *3*, 70–87.

Dizon, G. (2018). Netflix and L2 learning: A case study. *The EuroCALL Review*, *26*(2), 30–40. https://doi.org/10.4995/eurocall.2018.9080.

Dizon, G., & Thanyawatpokin, B. (2021). *Language Learning with Netflix*: Exploring the effects of dual subtitles on vocabulary learning and listening comprehension. *Computer Assisted Language Learning Electronic Journal*, *22*(3), 52–65.

Ellis, R., & Barkhuizen, G. (2005). *Analysing learner language*. Oxford University Press.

Elmer, T., Mepham, K., & Stadtfeld, C. (2020). Students under lockdown: Comparisons of students' social networks and mental health before and during the COVID-19 crisis in Switzerland. *PLOS One*, *15*(7), e0236337. https://doi.org/10.1371/journal.pone.0236337.

Fievez, I., Montero Perez, M., Cornillie, F., & Desmet, P. (2021). Promoting incidental vocabulary learning through watching a French Netflix series with glossed captions. *Computer Assisted Language Learning*, 1–26. https://doi.org/10.1080/09588221.2021.1899244.

Fredricks, J. A., Blumenfeld, P. C., & Paris, A. H. (2004). School engagement: Potential of the concept, state of the evidence. *Review of Educational Research*, *74*(1), 59–109.

Gerritsen, J. (2020, 14 April). Students struggling during Covid-19 lockdown 'ringing up in panic'. *RNZ*. Retrieved 16 September 2022, from https://www.rnz.co.nz/news/national/414161/students-struggling-during-covid-19-lockdown-ringing-up-in-panic.

Katz, B. (2020, 4 April). Why Netflix's 'Money Heist' is the most in-demand show in the world. *Observer*. Retrieved 16 September 2022, from https://observer.com/2020/04/.

Linnenbrink, E. A., & Pintrich, P. R. (2003). The role of self-efficacy beliefs in student engagement and learning in the classroom. *Reading & Writing Quarterly*, *19*(2), 119–37.

Matos, L., Herrera, D., & Claux, M. (2018). Students' agentic engagement predicts longitudinal increases in perceived autonomy-supportive teaching: The squeaky wheel gets the grease. *The Journal of Experimental Education*, *86*(4), 579–96.

Medeiros, A. de, Pereira, E., Silva, R., & Dias, F. (2020). Psychological phases and meaning of life in times of social isolation due the COVID-19 pandemic a reflection in the light of Viktor Frankl. *Research, Society and Development*, *9*(5), e122953331. https://doi.org/10.33448/rsd-v9i5.3331.

Mercer, S. (2019). Language learner engagement: Setting the scene. In X. Gao (Ed.), *Second handbook of English language teaching* (pp. 643–60). Springer. https://doi.org/10.1007/978-3-030-02899-2_40.

Peters, E., & Muñoz, C. (2020). Introduction to special issue language learning from multimodal input. *Studies in Second Language Acquisition*, *42*(3), 489–97.

Pfefferbaum, B., & North, C. S. (2020). Mental health and the Covid-19 pandemic. *New England Journal of Medicine*, *383*(6), 510–12.

Philp, J., & Duchesne, S. (2016). Exploring engagement in tasks in the language classroom. *Annual Review of Applied Linguistics*, *36*, 50–72. https://doi.org/10.1017/S0267190515000094.

Reeve, J. (2012). A self-determination theory perspective on student engagement. In S. L. Christenson, A. L. Reschly, & C. Wylie (Eds.), *Handbook of research on student engagement* (pp. 149–72). Springer. https://doi.org/10.1007/978-1-4614-2018-7_7.

Reeve, J., & Tseng, C. M. (2011). Agency as a fourth aspect of students' engagement during learning activities. *Contemporary Educational Psychology*, *36*(4), 257–67.

Reschly, A. L., & Christenson, S. L. (2012). Jingle, jangle, and conceptual haziness: Evolution and future directions of the engagement construct. In S. L. Christenson, A. L. Reschly, & C. Wylie (Eds.), *Handbook of research on student engagement* (pp. 3–19). Springer.

Rushe, D., & Lee, B. (2020, 21 April). Netflix doubles expected tally of new subscribers amid Covid-19 lockdown. *The Guardian*. Retrieved 16 September 2022, from http://www.theguardian.com/media/2020/apr/21/netflix-new-subscribers-covid-19-lockdown.

Skinner, E. A., Kindermann, T. A., Connell, J. P., & Wellborn, J. G. (2009). Engagement and disaffection as orgorganisationalnstructs in the dynamics of motivational development. In K. R. Wentzel & A. Wigfield (Eds.), *Handbook of motivation at school*. (pp. 223–45). Routledge.

Svalberg, A. M. L. (2009). Engagement with language: Interrogating a construct. *Language Awareness*, *18*(3–4), 242–58.

Svalberg, A. M.-L. (2018). Researching language engagement; current trends and future directions. *Language Awareness*, *27*(1–2), 21–39.

Tapper, J. (2019, 2 March). No habla español? How Netflix could transform the way we learn languages. *The Guardian*. Retrieved 16 September 2022, from http://www.theguardian.com/education/2019/mar/02/netflix-languages-education.

Thorne, S. L., & Reinhardt, J. (2008). 'Bridging activities', new media literacies, and advanced foreign language proficiency. *Calico Journal*, *25*(3), 558–72.

Vanderplank, R. (2016). *Captioned media in foreign language learning and teaching: Subtitles for the deaf and hard-of-hearing as tools for language learning*. Springer.

Wei, L. (2018). Translanguaging as a practical theory of language. *Applied Linguistics*, *39*(1), 9–30.

10

Online Learning in the Time of Coronavirus: Paradigmatic Lessons Learnt through Critical Participatory Action Research

John I. Liontas

Introduction

On 30 January 2020, the World Health Organization (WHO) declared Covid-19 a global health emergency. Forty-one days later, on 11 March 2020, the WHO declared Covid-19 a global pandemic. Alarm bells were set off in nearly every corner of the world. Everything was in a state of flux. An ever-changing list of decrees and directives ruled the day. To reduce the impact and spread of the Covid-19 pandemic, institutions worldwide were forced to adjust the mode of delivery from face-to-face learning to online learning almost overnight. Transferring courses online became a Herculean task not many felt competent to undertake. For those who teach online regularly, the transition was of no significant consequence. But for those who teach face-to-face in physical spaces, the transition from in-person learning to distance learning presented a mountain of worries – a mountain only a few were able to climb successfully. Transitioning to (a)synchronous online mode of instruction led to great anxiety and frustration among those who were unaccustomed to online teaching.

Against the landscape of such global events and rapid change, this chapter paints a picture of the trials and tribulations my students and I endured together when the University of South Florida (USF) first informed all faculty and students during Spring Break 2020 to hold classes online henceforth. The aftermath of that consequential decision is presented in a rich narrative analysis (Toledano & Anderson, 2020) on teaching and learning online. Befitting the parameters of a defined action research plan, the nexus of said analysis is located in the context of the evolving experiences of those involved in the pedagogical process reported herein (Burns, 2010a). Accordingly, this chapter presents action research from a narrative point of view that is anchored in the quality principles of *historical continuity, reflexivity, dialectics, workability,* and *evocativeness* (Heikkinen et al., 2012). The theory, practice and transformation of the relationship and interaction among the people involved in the pedagogical process are given particular weight herein. I begin by first acknowledging the past course of events that shaped the present pedagogical practices. Doing so contextualizes the historical continuum of the practice development, the logical sequence of the events and the causal relations underlying the transition to online learning.

Understanding the Transition to Online Learning

The Day the Dam Broke – a Local Perspective

In mid-March 2020, the Florida Board of Governors ruled that all State University System of Florida students should not return to campus for two weeks after spring break.[1] A clarification soon followed by the Provost of USF that we were not cancelling classes, but instead transitioning to a variety of delivery options to continue courses. The move to online was to prevent the 'mixing of people' following spring break. Containing the spread of the coronavirus was of paramount importance.

An avalanche of information soon followed. University guidance and mitigation protocols in response to Covid-19 were made quickly available. Faculty were asked to practice social distancing. Departments were instructed to create a communication plan with faculty to maintain the continuity of learning. An *Academic continuity resources* page with links to a Faculty Toolkit and a Student Toolkit, including several training sessions during spring break on available software (e.g. Faculty Information Sessions, Module X, Comprehensive Training of Canvas Basics, Live Online Support Sessions and One-on-One Consultations and Support), was put up by the USF Administration. This page was to provide faculty and students with the information and resources necessary to support (a)synchronous course delivery should the university pivot to temporary remote instruction (Singh & Thurman, 2019; Starkey, 2020).

23 March 2020 – the Day Critical Participatory Action Research Was Unveiled

Despite having a range of digital resources and platforms available to use, accessibility to the two synchronous doctoral classes I was now offering online (on Mondays and Wednesdays) was the first registered calamity I experienced as several students had pronounced difficulties signing in remotely. For some, either the audio or the video feed was not working properly. For others, the course link was inoperable even though the instructions I had carefully prepared for them in a special two-page handout did indicate how to navigate the key features of our *Canvas* course management system. A video link to Canvas Primer for USF students was also available for them to peruse. Needless to say, on 23 March 2020, class did not begin at the appointed time – 5:00 pm ETD – and some students were 'missing in action' for about forty minutes.

Pushing feelings of frustration aside, I opened the class with a frank discussion of the urgency of transitioning instruction from face-to-face to distance learning. Said urgency, I informed students, necessitated a critical participatory approach that would quickly address our institutional directive at the local level. I invited all course participants to join me in exploring the transition to online learning as the overarching research problem to be solved quickly under the guiding principles of action research given that we only had about eight more such three-hour meetings per course. Students were reminded of the pedagogical process envisioned henceforth: creating viable research centred on their own online lived experiences that would help them broaden critical consciousness while creating meaningful change that could inform and support our glocal learned communities and organizations (Niemi, 2019). The creation and co-creation of knowledge constructs and meaning-making processes exemplifying the essential mediating role of technology in online instruction was singled out as the most desired learning outcome of this entire research enterprise.

Research Design and Methodology

Research steps conducive to shared principles embedded in critical participatory action research (CPAR) models were subsequently developed and implemented in short order. Data collected was thematically analysed employing descriptive (What happened?), diagnostic (Why did it happen?), predictive (What is likely to happen in the future?) and prescriptive analytics (What is the best course of action to take?). Findings (themes or patterns of meaning within data) were successively subjected to a final hermeneutic analysis – the *hermeneutic circle* – to elicit an in-depth understanding of meanings produced through systematic interpretation processes (e.g. Gadamer, 1975; Heidegger, 1962; Schön, 1983). In the end, interpretations reached in the formation of new knowledge via hermeneutic phenomenology were communicated to everyone involved in this study. As needed, issues emerging from those overarching analytic themes supporting novel concepts or explanations were jointly resolved and corrective action taken prior to applying findings to the reality on the ground: our online environment in which diverse perspectives are included to create one cohesive community of learners concerned with the efficacy of online instruction in general and learning to learn with online technologies in particular. In all, ten different research steps were assigned to three different stages. In Stage 1, *Planning for Research and Problem Solving*, it was important to diagnose the problem, generate alternatives and design an action plan. These three initial steps provided the needed foundation upon which the next three consecutive steps could be taken in Stage 2, *Implementing Actions and Assessing Results*: implement action plan, collect and analyse data and dialogue about process. The next four steps comprised the steps involved in the third and final stage, Stage 3, *Evaluating and Reflecting on Results*. These included evaluating outcomes, reflecting on results, deciding on next steps and communicating results to stakeholders.

Applying an informal, qualitative, interpretive and reflective methodology, the CPAR undertaken involved twelve doctoral students (two international male students, both from Saudi Arabia, and ten female students, seven of whom were international students from China, Egypt, Indonesia, Saudi Arabia, Turkey and Venezuela) studying the broader fields of second language acquisition and instructional technology. The conceptualization of research in action and the operationalization of the various steps involved in carrying out an effective CPAR study formed the nucleus of the classroom-based research pursued post–mid-March 2020. Three overarching questions guided the conceptual framework of this research:

1. What are the most critical mitigation plans likely to ensure a seamless transition from face-to-face instruction to synchronous online instruction?
2. Which e-learning technologies best support online learning and teaching?
3. What effect do e-learning technologies have on the process of online learning and teaching?

In carrying out the CPAR, these doctoral students (hereafter research-practitioners) were expected to work together as a collaborative research team (i.e. *community*) who not only recognize a problem or limitation (i.e. *domain*) in their workplace situation (nearly half of them were practicing teachers/instructors at the time of the study), but who together are also able to devise a receptive plan to counteract the problem, implement the plan, observe what happens, reflect on the outcomes, revise the plan as needed, implement it, reflect anew, revise and the like (i.e. *practice*). In effect, embracing the features of *community*, *domain* and *practice*, they were expected to build an online Community of Practice while developing competence with the e-learning technology practices of their community (Wenger, 1998; Wenger-Trayner & Wenger-Trayner, 2015).

From the outset, the CPAR envisaged was to be a joint partnership with the course instructor, the author of this chapter, who also served during the Covid-19 pandemic period as the director of the Technology in Education and Second Language Acquisition doctoral program at the USF. The emphasis of the classroom-based study reported here was on ongoing improvement of practice by the research-practitioners themselves. All involved in this research were tasked to systematically reflect on their teaching or other work and collect data and representative samples that will answer the questions this study posed.

Iterative Problem-Solving Process: Formulation, Testing, Evaluation

From inception to completion, neither the *action* nor the *research* included a formal design, execution or assessment of one or more problem-solving cycles as an integral part of the research effort reported here. When taken apart, at least initially, both 'action' and 'research' necessitate understanding of philosophical assumptions (the act of taking something for granted or supposing something, even without proof) or presumptions (a belief on reasonable grounds or probable evidence). Such assumptions/presumptions, in turn, are more likely than not to influence a great many of the decisions we were prepared to make in a short space of time (six weeks in all) regarding our research design process and subsequent data analysis (Carr, 2006, 2007; Denzin & Lincoln, 2003, 2005; Fox et al., 2007).

These ideas and practices, often taken for granted within a specific school of thought, whether explicitly or implicitly stated, included *ontological* (nature of reality or realities guiding the research design), *epistemological* (knowledge of what can be known through apperception of lived realities, experiences and understandings), *axiological* (role of values of what is important and valuable in data interpretation) and *methodological* (methods, procedures and strategies allowable within the research paradigm) assumptions. Additional insights are derived from the specialization (e.g.

the school of thought, the field of study) itself, the extant literature of the topic under investigation and the theoretical frameworks/premises (select theories/commitments from within the specialization to which the research must adhere). In short, they required much advanced planning and reflective thinking concerning action *conceived* and research *initiated* (Heikkinen et al., 2007; Johnson, 2005; Kemmis & McTaggar, 2005; Lofthouse et al., 2016).

Advanced planning thus becomes, metaphorically speaking, the linchpin that keeps a wheel securely on its axle. Reflecting on how a pin placed transversely through an axle can keep a wheel in position is not enough. Reflective thinking only lends weight to the notion of awareness of one's own knowledge, assumptions and past experiences and the conditions that shaped those experiences. Simply put, it is thinking that reflects or redirects back to the source. Conversely, reflexive thinking involves thinking from within experiences to become ever more conscious, open-minded and self-critical – that is, reflexivity as the process of reflecting on yourself, the researcher. The research process itself can thus become a point of analysis. It guards against inappropriate assumptions and preconceived ideas or patterns of thought and behaviour that inherently influence research decisions and the (re)interpretation of data. How the implications of learning can impact the broader context research-practitioners work in further underscores the process of critical self-reflection impacting self-practice. Such reflective/reflexive thinking is pivotal in interpretivistic research in that multiple realities can be and are socially constructed and reconstructed by the individuals who collaboratively toil to gain knowledge through understanding the meaning of the process or the experience itself (Chen et al., 2018; Merriam & Tisdell, 2016; Niemi et al., 2010; Patton, 2002; Poon, 2008).

So contextualized, the action research shepherded here did involve, and was mainly based on, a practical, iterative problem-solving process (plan-act-observe-reflect-revise- …) involving the ten steps noted in the previous section. By applying an iterative design process, we were thus able to practice, refine and improve our initial research initiative – a trial-and-error methodology of sorts in which the nth approximation of the procedure is derived from the previous ones. With each new iteration, we had to clearly define what we were trying to accomplish. Knowledge constructs befitting online learning thus had to be created and tested quickly. Those constructs that showed promise were iterated rapidly until they took satisfactory structure to be more fully developed; those that failed to show promise were perfunctorily abandoned. This iterative approach allowed us to put *user experience* at the heart of the CPAR design process. As such, it required us to rehearse the instructional practices that optimize online learning, to anticipate challenges (and opportunities) closely associated with the use of specific digital technologies and to propose solutions that remedy the limitations of remote learning while, concurrently, exploring more deeply the theoretical and technology-enhanced details of the issues resulting from having to implement a synchronous online pedagogy that responds to the institutional demands resulting from the compulsory transition from in-person learning to online learning (Adedoyin & Soykan, 2020; Bailey & Lee, 2020; Moorhouse, 2020).

In addition, by reviewing and discussing the evolving issues in open dialogic forums, we were also able to isolate the affordances and constraints of each technology considered for immediate use. Consequently, information and data collected had to be specific to the digital platform, tool or resource investigated and, moreover, purposefully focused on the growth and qualitative change noted within each new iteration. Within such a continuous cycle, the progression of each iterative sampling involving specific modes of instructional delivery was subject to renewed formulation, responsive testing and agile evaluation. Insights gleaned from each iterative cycle were then used as the basis for the next cycle – the requisite mechanism of iteration to produce a consistent result that is reliable and valid for developing a more formal research agenda (Meraz et al., 2019).

Exactly what this entails will remain context dependent as each new iteration cycle – typically better than the last – allows investigative teams to continue to probe, revise, test, repair and evaluate areas for improvement and, even more importantly, perhaps, to implement the lessons they learnt while engaging in meaningful action research on the effectiveness of e-learning technologies in online learning. From cycle to cycle then, the actual process of engaging in CPAR thus impels new constructs of knowledge, which, in turn, feed back into the data collection and analysis stage. In short, the CPAR process reported here is iterative in that it is systematic and progressively recursive until the outcomes attained also profusely apprehend the course goals pursued. In what follows next, I present answers to the questions this research probed.

Results and Discussion

Question 1: What are the most critical mitigation plans likely to ensure a seamless transition from face-to-face instruction to synchronous online instruction?

During the transition from in-person learning to online learning, the most critical mitigation plans are always those that centre on understanding the challenges and opportunities e-learning technologies present either individually or collectively. But to gain insight into these, both a critical evaluation of those technologies and an introspective account of one's own perception and sensory experiences with those technologies must occur if viable solutions to common problems are to be found in quick succession. Just the web of instructions or configuration options that one needs to navigate ever so charily, only to replace one tool with another, at times confounds even the most seasoned practitioners and technology enthusiasts among us. For example, BigBlueButton – a free software web conferencing system – provides real-time sharing of audio, video, slides, whiteboard, chat and screen, all important features in an open-source web conferencing and social collaboration software solution for online learning for sure. But the default Canvas Conferences provider also has a horrible tendency to freeze up and distort video, sometimes even audio, at the most inopportune times. The ability for students to see each other's webcam feeds without distortions was more often than not a hit-and-miss proposition. Having to switch browsers, either from Chrome to Firefox or from Firefox to Chrome, not to mention Safari for Mac computers or Bing for Windows PC computers here, to rejoin the audio or share the camera was a troubleshooting technique employed way too often. 'ICE Error 1007' appearing on the screen was yet another tech hiccup that caused much consternation among users who were asked to either switch to a different internet provider or restart their computers or mobile devices to resolve connection problems due to network or firewall issues.

Investigating virtual classroom software alternatives to BigBlueButton to find the best user-friendly solution with survey tools, markup tools and session recording is therefore a must. But given the variety of e-learning platforms available, including Online/Web-based, Windows, Mac, iPhone and Android, to name but a few, it is prudent to note that not all platforms, whether software application or web-based technology, are created equal. Some are free and open-source software (or FOSS, where code is open to developers; see Audacity, Jitsi Meet, YakYak), others free and proprietary (sometimes referred to as closed-source software; code is closed, and copyrighted, and use is limited to distribution or modification; see Google Meet) and still others 'freemium' (a portmanteau of the words 'free' and 'premium'; basic product or service is free of charge, but charges are added for advanced features, services and goods; see Skype, Zoom, Microsoft Teams, Whereby) and proprietary or paid and proprietary. Other alternatives to BigBlueButton include Adobe Connect, Blackboard Collaborate, BrainCert, LearnCube, Schoology, TutorRoom and Whereby.

Whether hosted as a stand-alone product on the company server or as a cloud-based platform hosted by the software firm, they all endeavour to deliver a high-quality experience to remote users in a digital learning environment. And they all do it in their own distinct ways, enabling instructors to plan, implement and assess specific learning processes. Having a keen understanding of the unique features these learning management systems (LMSs) support, not to mention those asserted in course management systems or student information systems, is key to the types of activities students are asked to engage in and the types of assignments, tasks and/or projects (Williams et al., 2012) they are expected to complete on their own or collaboratively in groups. Beyond that, LMSs also provide the digital space where e-learning materials and resources can be stored and organized, assessments and quizzes can be given and progress tracked and recorded, and instructors and students can interact using blogs, forums and the like (Rimmer, 2020; Turnbull et al., 2019). More to the point, knowing the types of links a platform permits – for example, Google Classroom links easily with other Google tools like Gmail, Google Drive or Google Sheets, whereas Microsoft Teams integrates easily with Office 365 applications (Access, Excel, One Note, Outlook, PowerPoint, Publisher, Skype for Business, Teams and Word) – helps the overall facilitation of remote learning and the digital culture instructors and students seek to create to manage, among them, engagement, communication, interactivity, functionality, collaboration and discussion.

Finally, experiencing the apps that allow users to send and receive messages, photos and more, and even start cross-platform video-voice calls one-to-one or with a group on iOS or Android (Google Meet, Google Duo) can increase engagement and efficacy. Students can have productive user-friendly video meetings with agendas, collaborative notes and emoji responses (Team.video). Well-organized and thoughtfully designed high-quality digital learning experiences enable students to partake in group video calls and chats for the web sans signups or downloads (Talk, VideoMeeting, Whereby) or videoconferencing, online meetings, chat and mobile collaboration (Zoom). Moreover, those apps that aid users in creating information and general presentations, online training materials, web conferencing, learning modules, webinars and user desktop sharing (Adobe Connect) – especially those that help lead group communication and collaboration, including presenting, web conferencing, whiteboard drawing, document sharing, and user desktop sharing (Apache OpenMeetings), or those that generate unique links with one click, share it with participants and enjoy unlimited meetings (Skype Meet Now) – either individually or collectively, are certain to fuse related content, tools and resources into a cohesive whole worthy of future research efforts and a more streamlined online pedagogy.

Table 10.1 presents a comprehensive listing of the most common platforms available to date and the features commonly found in them. Where practical, the alphabetical order of platforms and features is thematically grouped.

Question 2: Which e-learning technologies best support online learning and teaching?

Not to be overly hyperbolic, but there are, both literally and figuratively, myriad educational technology tools, social media platforms, language learning apps and podcasts as well as YouTube (an American online video-music sharing and social media platform owned by Google) and Spotify (a Swedish audio streaming and media services provider and one of the world's largest music streaming service provider) channels and other digital resources online that can be used to ensure effective and efficient learning. For example, to embed video content and auto-captioning capabilities into a course, Stream – a media hosting platform – may be intentionally used. Similarly, to increase creativity and student engagement, Flipgrid (a video discussion platform: instructors post topics, students respond with short videos) and Padlet (a digital bulletin board: students create and share digital content) can be used. Alternatively, Camtasia can be used for screen recording and presentation creation while Audacity is best employed for recording and editing audio files. How best to navigate the depth and breadth of these e-learning technologies alone remains a formidable challenge, even under the most favourable conditions of exploration and discovery, respectively.

Fortunately, most students today are well adapted to online interactions via a host of applications, tools and devices. Applications such as WhatsUp Messenger, or simply WhatsUp (an American cross-platform centralized instant messaging and voice-over-IP service owned by Facebook, Inc., allowing users to send text and voice messages, make voice and video calls, and share images, documents, user locations and other content), WeChat (a Chinese multipurpose instant messaging, social media, and mobile payment app developed by Tencent), Line (mobile messenger app) and Telegram (cross-platform, cloud-based messaging system) are but four applications students readily utilize to communicate, not to mention iMessage (an instant messaging service developed by Apple Inc.), Facebook Messenger (an American instant messaging app and platform developed by Facebook, Inc.) or InstaMessage-Instagram Chat (an instant messaging tool allowing private communication with friends, acquaintances and contacts from the photo social network, Instagram) – three additional applications that facilitate a private messaging function between two or more people who are able to send and receive information in direct messages and group chats, similar to chat rooms, using their phone's internet connection (Liontas, 2021b).

Table 10.1 Digital Platforms and Their Features

Platforms
- Android
- Android Tablet
- Blackberry
- Chrome OS
- Google Chrome
- iOS
- iPad
- iPhone

- Java
- Java Mobile
- KaiOS
- Linux
- Mac
- Microsoft Edge
- Microsoft Stream
- Microsoft Office Outlook

- Moodle
- Online
- Self-Hosted
- Slack
- Software as a Service (SaaS)
- Windows
- Windows Mobile
- Windows S

Features
- Ad Free
- Agenda
- Anonymity
- Asynchronous
- Audio Calling
- Video Calling
- Audio/Video Calling
- Audio Chat
- Encrypted Chat
- Secure Chat
- Team Chat
- Team Work
- Video Chat
- Blur Filter
- Brainstorming
- Browser Based
- Java Based
- Web Based
- Call Recording
- Meeting Recording
- Screen Recording
- Record Videos
- Collaborative Whiteboard
- Interactive Whiteboard
- Shared Whiteboard
- Crypto
- End-to-End Encryption
- Privacy Focused

- Desktop Sharing
- Document Sharing
- File Sharing
- Integrated File Sharing
- Photo Sharing
- Facebook Integration
- Gmail Integration
- Google Classroom Integration
- Google Docs Integration
- Google Chrome Extensions
- Microsoft Office Integration
- Sharepoint Integration
- Twitter Integration
- Wikipedia Integration
- Group Collaboration
- Real-time Collaboration
- Real-time Analytics
- Team Collaboration
- Live Broadcasting
- Live Meeting
- Meeting
- Meeting Notes
- Messaging
- Team Messaging
- Voice Messages
- No Download
- No Registration Required
- Online Training
- Peer-to-Peer

- Remote Desktop
- Remote Work
- Educational
- School
- Student
- Share Videos
- Share Your Screen
- Mind Mapping
- Speech to Text
- Planner
- Polling
- Surveys
- Synchronization
- Syncs with Gmail
- Timed Sessions
- PDF Annotation
- Video Annotation
- Video Conferencing
- Video Interviews
- Video Streaming
- Movie Streaming
- Watch Videos
- Watch Videos Together
- Webinar
- WebRTC
- WordPress

Our own findings confirm the efficacy of such digital resources for enabling communication between and among course participants and instructor, a two-way personal communication highway of sort. In addition, game-based learning tools like Quizlet, Kahoot, Plickers, and Quizizz help teachers assess students while engaging them in anxiety-free learning environments. Game-based learning tools have been demonstrated to improve students' learning processes (Wang & Tahir, 2020; Yürük,

2019). Again, the judicious use of such tools to informally assess learning was found to exert a positive effect on the overall climate of the online environment. A select few of these resources can be profitably used in class and shared with students to help support and validate their online learning experience in these trying times and long after the pandemic becomes, hopefully soon, a distant memory. More importantly, these are all e-learning applications our students are familiar with and use almost hourly, at times even inconspicuously during class. Redirecting such familiar behaviours towards content and language learning is an area of research worth examining more closely in the near future. In the meantime, capitalizing on the availability of these digital resources for learning purposes – that is, apps, devices, programs, software, tools, videos, websites and much more – is a necessary and a very prudent step to take.

Question 3: What effect do e-learning technologies have on the process of online learning and teaching?

While navigating extant e-learning technologies remains a formidable challenge still, accessing them is as easy as clicking on a link. The technologies heretofore cited had a lasting effect on the macro-culture of learning and teaching. Some, more than others, left an enduring impression upon the ways we as research-practitioners experienced online learning. Difficult as making a choice may be, the correct choice always depends on the learning objectives of the tasks students are asked to engage in, the students' technical proficiency in using a range of digital tools effectively, the availability of such tools for purposeful personalized and group work exemplifying innovative projects and, finally, the students' overall experience with content-driven activities and planned online interactions that create renewed opportunities for self-expression and identity agency (Liontas, 2020, 2021a, 2021b; Wharton, 2007). Through consequential dialogic interactions, I can firmly attest, learners can be motivated to solve problems they were not even aware were problems until now, model correct academic language use and digital citizenship in their individual or collaborative work and, notably, become aware of second-language acquisition and instructional technology knowledge gaps that will require sustained research and analysis efforts in the days ahead. Such assertion is easily discernible in the findings our CPAR efforts revealed.

Among the several choices we tested in our iterative problem-solving process, videoconferencing emerged as the most popular communication channel, with email being the electronic means that was least used. Being able to see and hear everyone via video became the modus operandi students employed freely to express their perceptions of and attitudes towards learning in general and the nature of the subject itself in particular (Kozar, 2016; Todd, 2020). Despite occasional glitches at first with BigBlueButton and Zoom, the transition over to Microsoft Teams soon became second nature to us all. Additionally, the advanced LMS functionality of the cloud-based education technology platform Canvas provided the needed e-learning interface that secured instructor innovation and student success. Best used on a desktop, content creation such as weekly modules, readings, course materials, handouts, assignments, tests, quizzes, discussions and videoconferences did much to customize students' dynamic learning experience (Bailey & Lee, 2020; Kolb, 1984).

Furthermore, awareness of knowledge gaps was particularly evident in the weekly online discussion forums students were asked to engage in. Therein, they found their own voice to restructure old routines and recognize new ones. The breakout rooms (where much collaborative group work took place) created one such dynamic learning space that consistently promoted improved student empowerment and agency par excellence. Other popular communication choices included webinar-style presentations, paragraph or essay-type writing activities, online notice boards, digital Post-it notes, multimedia and video recording activities and open- or closed-ended quizzes, principally gamified quizzes and competitive games.

The productive use of these e-learning technologies positively impacted student learning. Using them in class transformed conventional modes of learning into dynamic and motivating learning environments. Ostensibly, they encouraged social interaction between instructor and learners, learners and their peers, and learners and other practitioners. They also enhanced learners' analytical and critical thinking skills, and previous research on Web 2.0 technologies and CALL in particular support such assertions (Wang & Vásquez, 2012; Yang & Kuo, 2020). Above all, the flexibility, openness and purposeful access to resources promoted autonomy of learning and ownership of thoughts and ideas, views and interests. The use of such resources then, from tools to applications to devices, has the potential to positively impact the development of specific skills, knowledge, convictions, beliefs and attitudes, thereby further influencing students' construction and reconstruction of knowledge and (meta)cognition. Our findings confirm the positive impact these collectively had on learning the specific content my courses covered in Spring 2020, especially when research-practitioners were given the dialogic freedom and the responsibility to self-determine the selection of e-learning technologies for their own learning.

Consequently, creating an inquiry learning community – a *Community of Practice* in Wenger's (1998) notion – is not only a construct to be endeavoured in theoretical terms, but the actualization of an educational experience in pragmatic terms (Wenger-Trayner & Wenger-Trayner, 2015), wherein teaching presence, cognitive presence and social presence combine purposefully with *reflexivity* and *dialectics* to produce learning and training environments that mediate *workability* and *evocativeness*, respectively. Expressed differently, through dialogic videoconferencing interactions, online discussion forums and collaborative exchanges in the breakout rooms facilitating de facto *reflexivity* (i.e. reflecting deeply on the learning experience itself) more broadly, the principle of *dialectics* flourished, right from the start, in that research-practitioners were given the space needed to voice their opinions, thoughts and ideas, and, importantly, the conditions of learning and training that empowered them to express freely their concerns about and interpretation of the perceived effects e-learning technologies had on the process of online learning and teaching that mattered to them (Hartshorn & McMurry, 2020). Through such targeted interpersonal discussions, these research-practitioners were able to concertedly construct and co-construct the reality of events affecting their learning online and the diversity of interpretation of data that was hitherto subjected to renewed analysis and meaning creation. These rational, synergistic expressions of reality mediated the ensuing communication of perceived and apperceived learning believed to spearhead the improvement of the praxis itself. As previously disclosed, the principle of *workability* was given high priority in that the action-research design framework which this study was theoretically and conceptually built on had to inform and support our glocal learned communities and organizations; that is, the study's research ethics (i.e. autonomy, justice, beneficence, nonmaleficence and fidelity) and applied precepts on the broader community had to have a defined outcome validity, not only process/ecological validity. And because the nature of CPAR was certain to educe research-practitioners' (unwanted, repressed, suppressed) emotions and feelings, the creation and co-creation of understanding and meaning, of knowing reality as a function of the passage of time, had to allow for the transference of affective states among instructor and research-practitioners, especially during hermeneutic cycles of knowledge construction (Flessner, 2014; Leuverink & Aarts, 2019; Martí & Villasante, 2009; Newton & Burgess, 2008; Stephens & Margey, 2015). Open and candid discussions of psychosomatic health and well-being, warning signs and management strategies of practising mindfulness included, revealed ever so nakedly the impact the principle of *evocativity* had on the community of these learners. Empathy and community-support mechanisms shared environmental insights that further actualized the said principle.

Lessons Learnt and Future Directions

In this section, I review three paradigmatic lessons this CPAR study revealed. These lessons, I assert with complete confidence, can help us view this pandemic (and others likely to come still) as a springboard from which future investigations could be marshalled to better appreciate the dynamic enterprise of teaching and learning while taking into account cognitive, affective and behavioural dimensions.

The first lesson, 'Understanding e-Learning Technologies', is a lesson that need not be learnt the hard way. Having apposite contingency plans ready to mitigate potential glitches, from access to information and communication technology denied to equipment failure – not to mention here unfamiliarity of e-learning applications, slow internet connection, internet bandwidth and zoom fatigue, especially eye strain – is half the battle. Sagacity and shrewdness in executing e-learning technologies understanding are the other half of the battle. Cutting corners with e-learning technologies is therefore most impolitic, as more often than not, the integration of any new digital technology will reveal itself to be more of a perplexing phenomenon to understand than an afterthought to be sidelined post-haste.

The second lesson, 'Understanding Choice and (Cognitive) Flexibility', is key to online learning, bar none. It entails exercising reflective thought in the selection of platforms, tools, applications, devices and resources making learning experiences real and meaningful, not only imaginative. Equally important, it involves implementing innovative instructional practices, strategies and activities that foster high-value collaborative learning. Such learning is best observed when students are empowered to discover their own identity and self-agency in purposeful technology-driven tasks and projects befitting their intellectual capacity to construct and reconstruct knowledge and (meta)cognition. Indeed, choice and flexibility to choose the type of student-centred learning spaces created – that is, spaces where interest in the subject material is ignited, curiosity stimulated and creativity nurtured – is, simply stated, one of the most valued benefits derived from synchronous online learning and, perhaps, one of the most critical lessons we learnt to date from the Covid-19 global pandemic.

The third lesson, 'Understanding and Prioritizing Psychosomatic Health and Well-Being', brought the pandemic to the forefront of the online experience. Covid-19 affected everyone, myself included. Stress, anxiety, uncertainty, frustration and, yes, even acute cases of xenophobia (fear of the unknown) at times, were all biologically basic emotions we had and/or experienced during the pandemic, some of us more than others. How we cope with these emotions and ailments impacts our ability to function as a community of learners who meet online on a weekly basis to discuss the theories and practices figuring prominently in the research arena of second- and foreign-language acquisition around the world. But they also increase the risk factor for rising mental health problems impacting one's emotional, social and physical life if unaddressed, from anxiety disorders to depression to post-traumatic stress disorder. Faced with such realities, conversations with students about psychosomatic health (the state of being healthy) and well-being (the state of living a healthy spiritual, emotional, physical, environmental, occupational, social and intellectual lifestyle) became the opening salvo of nearly every online class meeting I had in the second half of the 2020 spring semester. I have continued those 'breaking the coronavirus ice' discussions ever since. The goal of such transparent discussions was to help students process pandemic-related trauma and adjust to the 'new normal' of attending classes remotely through careful reflection and dialogue with others.

In closing, applying the lessons learnt from the Covid-19 pandemic to promote positive outcomes for all learners is a worthwhile pursuit indeed and, importantly, a renewed opportunity to rethink the ways we teach and the ways our students learn (Burns, 2010b). The means by which my students and I had to manage and renegotiate our respective roles in the lived experiences reported herein provide fertile ground for scientific advancement whose paradigm characteristics go beyond fact-findings that improve the quality of the action(s) already taken. Whether fundamental or applied (quantitative, qualitative or mixed research), such research could well involve different types of research (e.g. exploratory, descriptive, explanatory, longitudinal, cross-sectional, policy-oriented, classification, comparative, causal, theory testing, theory building) pending objectives pursued, variables tested and hypotheses proven or refuted based on clearly defined parameters, assumptions and environments. Synchronous online learning is one such context that can make, for example, longitudinal investigations possible. Varied and distinct as these research paradigms all are, in them, nonetheless, solutions to problems and answers to questions will be found because of the opportunities that the challenges of the Covid-19 pandemic created. Categorically so surmised here, the complexities and challenges of e-learning abound. But so are the opportunities to answer the bell at a time when everything else around us seems to come apart at the seams. Debating both the challenges and the opportunities thrust upon us by the pandemic in the digital public square of ideas is the ultimate act of cognition and metacognition, of knowing and of knowing about our knowing, of understanding the voice deep inside our mind – the inexorable path to attaining a higher level of introspective self-consciousness. In short, it is the silver lining in the clouds of worry that fill our days still. Everything else is pleonastic cacophony – plain and simple.

Note

1. 'Statement on the Status of the State University System', 15 March 2020, https://www.flbog.edu/2020/03/15/statement-on-the-status-of-the-state-university-system/.

References

Adedoyin, O. B., & Soykan, E. (2020). COVID-19 pandemic and online learning: The challenges and opportunities. *Interactive Learning Environments*, 1–13. https://doi.org/10.1080/10494820.2020.1813180.

Bailey, D. R., & Lee, A. R. (2020). Learning from experience in the midst of COVID-19: Benefits, challenges, and strategies in online teaching. *Computer-Assisted Language Learning Electronic Journal*, 21(2), 178–98.

Burns, A. (2010a). *Doing action research in English language teaching: A guide for practitioners*. Routledge.

Burns, A. (2010b). Action research: Contributions and future directions in ELT. In J. Cummins & C. Davison (Eds.), *International handbook of English language teaching. Part II* (pp. 987–1002). Springer.

Carr, W. (2006). Philosophy, methodology and action research. *Journal of Philosophy of Education*, 40(4), 421–35.

Carr, W. (2007). Educational research as practical science. *International Journal of Research & Method in Education*, 30(3), 271–86.

Chen, S., Huang, F., & Zeng, W. (2018). Comments on systematic methodologies of action research in the new millennium: A review of publications 2000–2014. *Action Research*, 16(4), 341–60.

Denzin, N. K., & Lincoln, Y. S. (2003). *The landscape of qualitative research: Theories and issues* (2nd ed.). Sage.

Denzin, N. K., & Lincoln, Y. S. (2005). *The Sage handbook of qualitative research* (3rd ed.). Sage.

Flessner, R. (2014). Revisiting reflection: Utilizing third spaces in teacher education. *The Educational Forum*, 78(3), 231–47.

Fox, M., Martin, P., & Green, G. (2007). *Doing practitioner research*. Sage.

Gadamer, H. (1975). Hermeneutics and social science. *Cultural Hermeneutics*, 2(4), 307–16.

Hartshorn, K. J., & McMurry, B. L. (2020). The effects of the COVID-19 pandemic on ESL learners and TESOL practitioners in the United States. *International Journal of TESOL Studies*, 2(2), 140–57.

Heidegger, M. (1962). *Being and time*. Harper & Row (Original work published 1927).

Heikkinen, H. L. T., Huttunen, R., & Syrjälä, L. (2007). Action research as narrative: Five principles for validation. *Educational Action Research*, 15(1), 5–19.

Heikkinen, H. L. T., Huttunen, R., Syrjälä, L., & Pesonen, J. (2012). Action research and narrative inquiry: Five principles for validation revisited. *Educational Action Research*, 20(1), 5–21.

Johnson, A. (2005). *A short guide to action research* (2nd ed.). Pearson Education Inc.

Kemmis, S., & McTaggar, R. (2005). Participatory action research: Communicative action and the public sphere. In N. K. Denzin & Y. S. Lincoln (Eds.), *The Sage handbook of qualitative research* (3rd ed., pp. 559–603). Sage.

Kolb, D. A. (1984). *Experiential learning: Experience as the source of learning and development*. Prentice Hall.

Kozar, O. (2016). Perceptions of webcam use by experienced online teachers and learners: A seeming disconnect between research and practice. *Computer Assisted Language Learning, 29*(4), 779–89.

Leuverink, K. R., & Aarts, A. M. L. (2019). A quality assessment of teacher research. *Educational Action Research, 27*(5), 758–77.

Liontas, J. I. (2020). Understanding language teacher identity: Digital discursive spaces in English teacher education and development. In B. Yazan & K. Lindahl (Eds.), *Language teacher identity in TESOL: Teacher education and practice as identity work* (pp. 65–82). Routledge.

Liontas, J. I. (2021a). The dialogic circles of digital pedagogy: Reconceptualizing research and teaching practices in ELT. *SPELT ELT Research Journal, Special Issue: Engaging Research in ELT, 1*(1), 17–31.

Liontas, J. I. (2021b). Attaining knowledge of idiomatics in the age of Corona and beyond. In K. Kelch, P. Byun, S. Safavi, & S. Cervantes (Eds.), *CALL theory applications for online TESOL education* (pp. 1–34). IGI Global Publishing.

Lofthouse, R., Flanagan, J., & Wigley, B. (2016). A new model of collaborative action research: Theorising from inter-professional practice development. *Educational Action Research, 24*(4), 519–34.

Martí, J., & Villasante, T. R. (2009). Quality in action research: Reflections for second-order inquiry. *Systemic Practice and Action Research, 22*(5), 383–96.

Meraz, R. L., Osteen, K., & McGee, J. (2019). Applying multiple methods of systematic evaluation in narrative analysis for greater validity and deeper meaning. *International Journal of Qualitative Methods, 18*, 1–6.

Merriam, S. B., & Tisdell, E. (2016). *Qualitative research: A guide to design and implementation* (4th ed.). Jossey-Bass.

Moorhouse, B. L. (2020). Adaptations to a face-to-face initial teacher education course 'forced' online due to the COVID-19 pandemic. *Journal of Education for Teaching, 46*(4), 609–11.

Newton, P., & Burgess, D. (2008). Exploring types of educational action research: Implications for research validity. *International Journal of Qualitative Methods, 7*(4), 18–30.

Niemi, R. (2019). Five approaches to pedagogical action research. *Educational Action Research, 27*(5), 651–66.

Niemi, R., Heikkinen, H. L. T., & Kannas, L. (2010). Polyphony in the classroom: Reporting narrative action research reflexively. *Educational Action Research, 18*(2), 137–49.

Patton, M. Q. (2002). *Qualitative research and evaluation methods* (3rd ed.). Sage.

Poon, A. Y. K. (2008). How action research can complement formal language teacher education. *The Asia-Pacific Education Researcher, 17*(1), 43–62.

Rimmer, W. (2020). Responding to the coronavirus with open educational resources. *International Journal of TESOL Studies, 2*(2), 17–32.

Schön, D. A. (1983). *The reflective practitioner: How professionals think in action*. Basic Books.

Singh, V., & Thurman, A. (2019). How many ways can we define online learning? A systematic literature review of definitions of online learning (1988–2018). *American Journal of Distance Education, 33*(4), 289–306.

Starkey, L. (2020). A review of research exploring teacher preparation for the digital age. *Cambridge Journal of Education, 50*(1), 37–56.

Stephens, S., & Margey, M. (2015). Action learning and executive education: Achieving credible personal, practitioner and organisational learning. *Action Learning: Research and Practice, 12*(1), 37–51.

Todd, R. W. (2020). Teachers' perceptions of the shift from the classroom to online teaching. *International Journal of TESOL Studies, 2*(2), 4–17.

Toledano, N., & Anderson, A. R. (2020). Theoretical reflections on narrative in action research. *Action Research, 18*(3), 302–18.

Turnbull, D., Chugh, R., & Luck, J. (2019). Learning management systems: An Overview. In A. Tatnall (Ed.), *Encyclopedia of education and information technologies* (pp. 1–7). Springer Nature.

Wang, A. I., & Tahir, R. (2020). The effect of using Kahoot! for learning – A literature review. *Computers & Education, 149*, 1–22.

Wang, S., & Vásquez, C. (2012). Web 2.0 and second language learning: What does the research tell us? *CALICO Journal, 29*(3), 412–30.

Wenger, E. (1998). *Communities of practice: Learning, meaning, and identity*. Cambridge University Press.

Wenger-Trayner, E., & Wenger-Trayner, B. (2015). *Communities of practice: A brief introduction*. Wenger-Trayner. http://wenger-trayner.com/introduction-to-communities-of-practice/.

Wharton, S. (2007). Social identity and parallel text dynamics in the reporting of educational action research. *English for Specific Purposes Journal, 26*(4), 485–501.

Williams, K. C., Cameron, B. A., & Morgan, K. (2012). Supporting online group projects. *NACTA Journal, 56*(2), 15–20.

Yang, Y. F., & Kuo, N. C. (2020). New teaching strategies from student teachers' pedagogical conceptual change in CALL. *System, 90*, 1–13.

Yürük, N. (2019). Edutainment: Using Kahoot! as a review activity in foreign language classrooms. *Journal of Educational Technology and Online Learning, 2*(2), 89–101.

11

Technology-Mediated Writing Tasks in the Online English Classroom: Focus on Form via Synchronous Videoconferencing

Valentina Morgana and Michael Thomas

Introduction

While the Covid-19 emergency occurred at a moment when digital tools had already been playing a key role in second-language education, both within and outside of formal contexts, the pivot to remote online teaching during 2020 identified the need for more research on how secondary schools were adjusting to their new online world (Bailey & Lee, 2020). Education in Italy was significantly affected during the pandemic, and it became the first European country to enter a period of sustained lockdown lasting for several months. A closer examination of how the pandemic has impacted on teaching and communicating with students in the language classroom suggests that several aspects warrant further reflection in the context of research on CALL (Moorhouse, 2020).

First, what are the implications of the widespread use of videoconferencing tools and the consequent move from the classroom into a personal workspace? Secondly, how can we understand the complete sense of responsibility that students now bear for their engagement in lessons, whether they are actively involved in a digital task or easily distracted behind a screen? Finally, given the urgency which accompanied the move online, in what ways do language educators understand the potential risks and affordances of digital pedagogy? All of these aspects have contributed to building a virtual form of language teaching in which the integration of tasks and technology is no longer simply advocated but has become a firm expectation, if not a requirement. Whether the education strategies employed during the Covid-19 pandemic to date will remain in use in the future is difficult to predict in a constantly shifting digital landscape, but there are, without a doubt, lessons language educators need to reflect on for the future, particularly in the school sector.

Over the past twenty years, task-based language teaching (TBLT) has attracted an increasing amount of research from the field of CALL and second-language acquisition (SLA; Ellis et al., 2019b; Hubbard & Levy, 2016; Thomas & Reinders,

2012) as it offers mutually beneficial opportunities to both fields. However, there are still concerns about the efficacy of the approach in second- and foreign-language learning. One of the main concerns about TBLT is the perception that there is no explicit focus on grammatical rules, and this could negatively impact students' language learning (Sato, 2010). In fact, even if there is no explicit focus on form, TBLT enables attention to form through implicit meaning-related activities (Ellis, 2009; Long, 2015).

Moreover, in the TBLT cycle outlined by Willis (1996), students follow three steps: they complete pre-task activities; they then perform the main task, and finally close the cycle with some (optional) post-task activities. Various strategies have been used to draw attention to form at the pre-task stage. In particular, researchers have focused on modelling (Van de Guchte et al., 2019), planning (Ziegler, 2018) and visual input modification (Lee & Huang, 2008). Arising from this context, this chapter reports preliminary results on the effects of pre-task modelling and planning on students' learning of narrative tenses (the past simple and past continuous) through a study that was also designed to respond to English as a foreign language (EFL) teachers' concerns about not teaching grammar rules explicitly, especially via online learning. Although coursebooks are designed to follow a communicative approach, most secondary EFL teachers in Italy prefer to teach grammar rules during the pre-task phase. Given this context, the main aims of this study were (a) to investigate whether explicit attention on form at the pre-task stage would lead to a more accurate use of the narrative tenses being taught and (b) to explore the implications for secondary school teachers and learners of attempting this type of approach online.

Review of the Literature

Explicit Focus on Form in the Pre-Task

The choice of task type and the conditions under which it is performed are not neutral. As the tasks will have an impact on students' language proficiency in terms of accuracy, fluency and/or complexity (Skehan, 2003), they should be carefully selected by the teacher. In this respect, pre-task activities play a key role in drawing attention to target language features and encouraging learners' engagement with the content of the task (Van de Guchte et al., 2016). The question of whether explicit grammar teaching in the pre-task is useful has proved quite controversial in previous research studies of the topic. Some researchers support the idea that an explicit focus on form can lead to improved accuracy, especially in EFL contexts (Littlewood, 2007).

On the other hand, other researchers (see, e.g. Ellis, 2016) have demonstrated how a focus on grammar at the pre-task stage risks directing the student's attention to form, negatively affecting the communicative purpose of the task – that is, students are more focused on producing accurate language than on fluency and meaning making. However, an explicit focus on form in the pre-task may lead to more frequent use of the target feature in the task performance and even in the post-task stage (Ellis et al., 2019b). In line with this view, the study examined in this chapter incorporates explicit grammar instructions in the pre-task and compares the effects on EFL learners' accurate use of language with and without grammar instructions.

Planning

Several studies have investigated changes in planning at the pre-task stage and the effects on students' language learning (Foster & Skehan, 1999; Ortega, 1999). Planning is a key component of the pre-task stage, and researchers have largely investigated its potential. Both guided and unguided planning have resulted in improved performance of oral tasks, demonstrating positive results leading to improved fluency. Research also shows positive effects on complexity. However, the results demonstrating the effects of pre-task planning on accuracy are mixed. Some studies have observed that different planning conditions produce no specific effect on accuracy. Foster and Skehan (1996, 1999), for instance, investigated the impact of guided and unguided pre-task planning on a subsequent oral task performance. Results revealed that students from the guided group (the detailed group, as defined by the authors) produced more complex utterances, but no significant difference was found in terms of accuracy. A further study by Foster and Skehan (1999) conducted with L2 learners produced similar results: students were exposed to different sources of planning (teacher-led, individual and group planning), with each planning group focused on different aspects (language vs content). As expected, results showed different effects based on the source of planning, but not as a result of the focus-on-language versus focus-on-content distinction.

On the other hand, more recent studies have shown pre-task planning to have a positive influence on accuracy (Ellis, 2009, 2016; Mochizuki & Ortega, 2008). In his review of the impact of pre-task planning on fluency, complexity and accuracy, Ellis (2009) demonstrated that thirteen out of nineteen studies included in the review reported a positive effect on accuracy. For example, Mochizuki and Ortega (2008) conducted a study with fifty-six secondary school EFL students in Japan to investigate whether pre-task guided planning conditions with a focus on grammar (relative clauses) would impact learners' fluency, complexity and accuracy in the performance of an oral storytelling task. Students were assigned to different conditions (guided planning, unguided planning and no planning). Results showed that pre-task guided planning promoted a more accurate use of relativization compared to the other two groups. Thus, the findings of the study confirmed that beginner-level L2 students may need additional grammar resources during planning time to achieve language goals.

Van de Guchte et al. (2016) examined the effects of pre-task modelling on learners' task performance. As in Mochizuki and Ortega (2008), the pre-task planning had a specific focus on form (locative prepositions), in particular aiming to measure the effects on accuracy and complexity of two different foci (focus-on-language vs focus-on-content) at the pre-task stage. Forty-eight secondary school students of German as a foreign language participated in the study. They were randomly assigned to two different planning conditions (focus-on-language or focus-on-content). As part of the guided planning time, all students completed a modelling task. The aim of the modelling video was to provide learners with an example of how to perform the main task. Results showed that pre-task planning had an influence on students' oral task performance. In particular, in the immediate post-test activity, students in the focus-on-language group outperformed students in the focus-on-content group in the accurate use of the target structure, using it more often and more accurately. However, when the post-test was delayed, no significant difference was found. A possible explanation for this is that the focus-on-language group did not receive explicit focus-on-form instructions and grammar explanations, which probably impacted their long-term acquisition processes.

Ellis et al.'s (2019a) experimental study involving seventy-two eighth-grade EFL learners, also examined the impact of pre-task explicit instruction in relation to an oral focused task. Two groups, an explicit instruction task group, which received a short grammar lesson followed by practice activities, and the task-only group, which completed the same task without pre-instruction, completed two oral dictogloss tasks enabling learners to produce past passives. Findings indicated that the explicit instruction group produced more frequent but less accurate and complex target language, which calls into question the efficacy of focusing on linguistic form prior to task performance.

Kim's (2012) experimental research explored pre-task modelling as a type of planning strategy in relation to Korean junior high school students' attention to question structures. Two groups, a pre-task modelling group and a no modelling group, completed a pre-test involving three tasks in dyads as well as two post-tests during a period of five weeks. The modelling group undertook guided planning by watching pre-task videos, whereas the other group did not, and data was collected from students via think-aloud protocols and analysed based on language-related episodes. Findings suggested that students from the pre-task modelling group had positive implications for focus-on-form and learners' question development.

Planning in Technology-Mediated Writing Tasks

So far, research on pre-task planning and focus-on-form has mainly examined oral narrative tasks. Very few studies have been conducted on the effect of pre-task planning on L2 written performance (Ellis & Yuan, 2004). Additionally, as far as we know, only one study has investigated the role of planning on written production in computer-mediated contexts (Adams et al., 2014). Ellis and Yuan's (2004) study examined different types of planning and their effects on fluency, complexity and accuracy. In particular, they investigated whether forty-two EFL undergraduate learners produced more accurate and complex texts with pre-task planning or careful online planning activities. Similar to the study presented here, students were asked to write a narrative based on a set of related pictures. The three planning conditions were as follows: no planning, pre-task planning and online planning. Participants in the online planning group had no pre-task planning time but were given unlimited online planning time. Participants in the pre-task planning group had ten minutes to plan before the task and limited online planning time (seventy-five minutes). There was no explicit focus-on-form in the pre-task or online planning phase. Results showed that learners in the online planning group, who were unpressured by time constraints, produced more accurate texts than the pre-task planning group. However, the pre-task planning group outperformed the other groups in syntactic variety and fluency.

The study conducted by Adams et al. (2014) investigated planning in task-based computer-mediated writing with forty-five EFL learners at a university in Malaysia. Participants were assigned to different experimental conditions (planning, online planning and no planning) and had to work on an English for specific purposes task, which was to write a wiki page on an engineering project. Accuracy measures revealed that students in the unlimited online planning group produced more accurate language compared to the other groups, confirming the results of Ellis and Yuan (2004).

Based on this review, technology offers opportunities to design and implement various types of writing tasks, whether synchronous or asynchronous, and could facilitate SLA processes. Further studies are needed to understand what type of language learning tasks could offer opportunities for the development of writing skills, both in formal and informal contexts.

Methodology

Context of the Study

This study examined the effects of modelling and guided planning on students' written task performance with an explicit focus-on-form (narrative tenses) in a pre-task activity in an online teaching context. Students were asked to perform a subsequent writing task similar to the one presented in the pre-task (a crime story). The independent variable considered was planning under two different conditions: ten minutes of unguided planning (with no grammar focus) and guided planning (with an explicit focus on grammar). The correct use of the target structures – the past simple and past continuous – constituted accuracy in this context. In addition to the integration of both complexity and accuracy from previous research, and similar to Van de Guchte et al. (2016), this study also featured the concept of modelling. As part of their planning time, learners read and listened to a crime story similar to the one they were asked to produce in the main task. One group ($n = 12$) focused on the use of narrative tenses in the story (the guided planning group), while the others ($n = 12$) did not have a specific focus (unguided planning). The study investigated the following research questions:

1. How do modelling and planning with and without an explicit focus on form impact learners' knowledge of a specific language feature?
2. What are students' perceptions of the efficacy of technology-mediated writing tasks and pre-task work?

Based on the positive results of previous studies, it was hypothesized that the guided planning group (with a focus-on-form) would outperform the unguided planning group in the post-test as they had been guided towards the noticing and use of target language features in the pre-task activity. Additionally, we hypothesized that learners would not perceive any significant differences in planning and performing their task in a technology-mediated environment as their focus would be mainly on the task rather than on the technology used.

Participants

The participants were twenty-four thirteen- and fourteen-year-old EFL learners (at the A2 level of the Common European Framework of Reference for Languages (CEFR)) from a lower secondary state school in Italy. There were thirteen girls and eleven boys. Most of the students were Italian L1 speakers; two students had a Chinese language background and two were bilingual (Italian/Spanish). The teacher (one of the researchers) assigned them to two different groups: a guided planning group ($n = 12$) and an unguided planning group ($n = 12$). To ensure balance and homogeneity between the two groups, students were assigned to their group based on their results in the Oxford placement test which they had taken at the beginning of the school year. The groups included the same number of students at A1, A2 and A2+ levels of the CEFR. Normally, according to the Italian secondary school curriculum, students have three hours of English lessons per week. During the first phase of the lockdown, the learners involved in the study had only two hours per week.

Due to the Covid-19 health emergency, all lessons took place remotely using the Google for Education workspace – namely, Google Classroom. The platform included a bundle of applications that students could use synchronously during the lessons such as a word processor (Google Docs), a videoconferencing tool (Google Meet) and a presentation tool (Google Presentation).

Research Design and Procedure

This study followed a pre- and post-test research design carried out over a period of three weeks (see Table 11.1). Qualitative evidence was also collected through student questionnaires. Learners took a pre-test on the use of the target structure (the past simple and past continuous) one week prior to the beginning of the study (Phase 1), and the same test was administered one week after the experiment had finished as a post-test

Table 11.1 Research Design

Timing	Stage	
Phase 1	Pre-test	Cloze grammar test on a crime story
Phase 2	Pre-task (modelling)	Two task conditions: guided and unguided planning
Phase 3	Pre-task (planning) – story outline	Two task conditions: guided and unguided planning
Phase 4	Main task (story writing)	Writing task performance
Phase 5	Post-test	Cloze grammar test on a crime story
One week later	Qualitative data collection	Questionnaire on attitudes and perceptions

(Phase 5). The two-phase pre-task on the crime story (Phase 2 and 3 – modelling and planning) was carried out under two conditions: guided and unguided planning.

The Crime Story

The main task (Phase 4) involved a crime story writing task. This type of task was chosen as it could be used to focus learners' attention on the target grammatical structures (the past simple and past continuous) and also because learners were familiar with this type of story as they were working on the same genre in their Italian literature lessons. As the first phase of the pre-task (modelling), all participants read and listened to a picture-based crime story taken from their digital course book (Bowen & Delaney, 2019). The story was 1,943 words long and featured multimodal input, including pictures, sounds and an actor narrator. The language used in the story was positioned at the A2 level of the CEFR and included the use of coordinate and subordinate clauses, time expressions relating to the past simple and past continuous tenses (e.g. when, while, then) and key vocabulary items relating to crime and mystery.

Pre-Task Modelling

For the pre-task modelling phase (Phase 2), learners in the guided planning group were instructed to focus on the use of the verbs in the past simple and past continuous forms. A brief description of the grammar rules was also provided on an observation sheet. Students were required to produce ten written examples of the use of the past simple and past continuous from the story. The teacher shared the digital handout with instructions via Google Classroom and was able to read students' answers synchronously. Students from the unguided planning group received no instructions on language but were informed that they could take notes while reading and listening to the story. At the end of the story, students were given five minutes for general comprehension questions before they were required to submit their notes to the teacher. Overall, the duration of the pre-task modelling phase was about one hour. Before reading and listening to the story, all participants were informed that they were going to rewrite the crime story as their main task (Phase 4).

Pre-Task Planning

Following the reading-while-listening modelling task (Phase 2), learners were split into two breakout rooms on Google Meet. All students received the main writing task instructions. Before performing the main task, all students were given fifteen minutes as planning time (Phase 3: pre-task planning). Learners were asked to write an outline of the crime story. Those in the unguided planning group did not receive any specific instructions on the target language to be used to perform the task. Learners in the guided planning group received the same instructions and had the same planning time but in addition received a grammar bank handout in English with a series of explanations on how to use the past simple and past continuous to tell a story, including examples of time expressions. The teacher strongly encouraged them to make use of the handout while planning the story. They were also informed that they would not be able to use the grammar bank handout during the main task performance (Motchizuki & Ortega, 2008). Students were required to plan the task in English (L2), and during the planning time, neither student group was allowed to use any other resources such as the internet or dictionaries, although due to the online conditions it was not possible to monitor this activity. The teacher/researcher was, however, able to monitor the planning time via Google Docs, and all students used the full fifteen-minute time period provided. Four students (three from the unguided planning group and one from the guided planning group) asked for extra time, but this was not granted. On completion of the planning time, learners submitted their outlines on Google Classroom. On account of the distance learning context in which the study took place, learners were only informed that they would not be able to use their notes during the main task after they had submitted their outlines.

The Main Task

Students performed the main task during the following lesson (Phase 4). They were all shown a series of pictures from the story and were required to rewrite it by providing as many details as they could remember. They had sixty minutes to perform the task. A week later, all students completed a post-test activity on the use of narrative tenses (Phase 5).

Data Collection

Two types of instruments were used to collect the main data for this study. The first was a pre- and post-test consisting of forty cloze items on the use of narrative tenses (past simple and past continuous). The test was designed by the teacher/researcher and validated by two native English teachers who answered the test. When more than one answer was possible, the test was modified using more restrictive options.

The second instrument was a questionnaire consisting of four main questions (three Likert-scale items and one open-ended question). The questionnaire was designed to offer both quantitative and qualitative evidence of learners' attitudes to and perceptions of written digital tasks in distance learning. For example, students were asked how the pre-task planning phase performed online contributed to their ability to write crime stories. The open-ended question required students to describe their experience using adjectives and short phrases. It was designed to better understand students' perceptions of what and how they learnt during the treatment. Ethical procedures were conducted in line with the BERA framework (British Educational Research Association) by ensuring the anonymity and confidentiality of data. The parents of the school students provided written informed consent, and the children assented to their participation.

Findings and Discussion

Pre- and Post-Tests

The pre- and post-tests were administered one week before and one week after the main task. The main aim was to measure students' proficiency in the target language features (narrative tenses) before and after the treatment. The test was administered using Google Modules and automatically assessed by the system on the basis of the rules set by the teacher. To ensure the validity of the results, all tests were double-checked by the teacher/researcher.

Table 11.2 shows the results of the grammar test, revealing that both groups performed at a similar level in the pre-test, with the unguided planning group performing slightly better than the guided planning group. As confirmed by the data, both groups reached a higher level in the post-test, demonstrating that the written task had had an impact on their gain in knowledge of narrative tenses. The Shapiro-Wilk test confirmed that the data was normally distributed, so the t tests were conducted to measure between-group differences.

The t test on pre-test scores revealed no significant difference between the groups in the pre-test ($t = 0.710$; $p = 0.2492$), indicating that the two groups' overall competence in narrative tenses appeared to be quite balanced. Interestingly, the difference between the groups on the grammar test scores decreased even more in the post-test ($t = -1.269$; $p = 0.231$), confirming a similar competence level between the two groups. Additionally, an intra-group analysis of the scores was conducted to reveal any significant differences in scores within each group (Table 11.3). The data revealed a more significant difference in the performance of the guided planning group between the pre- and post-tests ($t = -3.773$; $p = 0.003$) compared to the unguided planning group ($t = -1.648$; $p = 0.128$).

To summarize, both groups seemed to have started the project with similar competence in the use of narrative tenses in stories. In addition, as measured by the pre- and post-tests, all students had improved their competence in the targeted language features after the intervention. However, a greater improvement was observed in students from the guided planning group. Thus, results confirmed our first hypothesis that a focus on form would increase the accurate use of the language structure. These findings support those of Mochizuki and Ortega (2008), Van de Guchte et al. (2016) and Adams et al. (2014), but conflict with those of Foster and Skehan (1999) and Ellis et al. (2019a), who did not find any particular difference between the guided and unguided groups in terms of accuracy.

Table 11.2 Intergroup Analysis – t Test

Measure 1	Measure 2	t	p
Pre-test – unguided planning	Pre-test – guided planning	0.710	0.492
Post-test – unguided planning	Post-test – guided planning	-1.269	0.231

Table 11.3 Intragroup Analysis – *t* Test

Pre-Test	Post-Test	t	p
Unguided planning	Unguided planning	-1.648	0.128
Guided planning	Guided planning	-3.773	0.003

Table 11.4 Results and Descriptive Statistics of the Grammar Pre- and Post-Test

	Unguided Planning, Pre-Test	Unguided Planning, Post-Test	Guided Planning, Pre-Test	Guided Planning, Post-Test
Number of students	12	12	12	12
Mean	26.250	30.583	24.167	31.500
SD	6.369	3.579	6.753	4.815
Shapiro-Wilk	0.936	0.947	0.953	0.963
p Value of Shapiro-Wilk	0.452	0.600	0.683	0.828

Note: Maximum possible score 40/40.

Student Questionnaires

The questionnaire included four Likert-scale questions: three questions focused on students' perceptions of the modelling and planning task and one question asked about their perceived achievements. Results from the Likert-scale questions were tabulated and compared using descriptive statistics (see Table 11.4).

Questions 1, 2 and 3 asked about how the pre-task planning (Q1), the modelling task (Q2) and the technological tools used (Q3) contributed to students' ability to rewrite a story using narrative tenses (past simple and continuous). For each of these aspects, students had four options to choose from (0 = did not contribute; 1 = contributed partially; 2 = contributed; 3 = contributed significantly).

As can be seen from the results, students' perceptions of the contribution of the three variables, planning, modelling and digital tools, were very similar (see Table 11.5). Overall, it appeared that students perceived the modelling task as the most relevant to the development of their ability to rewrite a story using narrative tenses. The last Likert-scale question focused on the perceived proficiency in the use of the targeted language structures (past simple and continuous). The question asked to what extent students felt able to use the past simple and continuous correctly. Answers ranged from 0 (objective not reached) to 3 (objective fully reached). Results showed that learners from group A (guided planning) perceived that they fully achieved the language objectives compared to the students from the unguided planning group (ten out of twelve students in group A chose Answer 3 (fully reached), while only six from group B gave the same answer).

Table 11.5 Results for the Students' Perception Questionnaire

	Q1 – Planning		Q2 – Modelling		Q3 – Digital Tools	
	Guided Planning	Unguided Planning	Guided Planning	Unguided Planning	Guided Planning	Unguided Planning
Number of students	12	12	12	12	12	12
Mean	2.000	2.083	2.333	2.333	1.917	2.083
SD	0.739	0.669	0.778	0.651	0.793	0.669

The questionnaire also included an open-ended question about students' general perception of the digital writing task. The responses were first delivered in Italian and then translated into English for research purposes. Students were asked to use adjectives and short expressions to describe their experiences. From the qualitative analysis of students' answers, most of them seemed to have benefitted from the modelling and planning work on narrative tenses regardless of their group. 75% used positive adjectives to refer to the type of task (e.g. 'enjoyable', 'engaging', 'not dull', 'relaxing').

Moreover, 64% of the students positively evaluated the organization of the pre-task work and made explicit reference to time management (e.g. they felt they had been given the correct amount of time to perform the task) and modelling and planning. Students from the guided planning group also mentioned that they found the digital handout very useful in their story planning. The modelling story and the use of pictures were perceived as the most significant activities to successfully perform the subsequent writing task (78% of the students mentioned them). Interestingly, technology was only mentioned as a support tool (e.g. classroom was easy to use; faster writing, spelling correction). Students appeared to be more focused on the type of tasks (e.g. modelling, planning) than on the technology they were using to perform it. Similar findings were reported in Solares (2014).

As the findings of this study indicate, pre-task planning is one of the areas that could potentially benefit from online teaching because of the more engaged nature of the task approach (Ellis et al., 2019a; Mochizuki & Ortega, 2008). Furthermore, the affordances offered by the technology fostered language awareness as the digital writing tool enabled students to correct and reorganize the text (and consequently, their ideas) effortlessly. Students felt at ease with the use of the videoconferencing tool, particularly when using the breakout rooms, as observed in other studies (Van de Guchte et al., 2019).

Post-pandemic Lessons

While the widespread use of videoconferencing tools can be innovative for language education, as indicated by this study, it also presents new challenges for teachers and learners, particularly in school contexts. Videoconferencing and digital classrooms are, in fact, just online tools, and it is essential that teachers and educators adapt their teaching to use these digital tools effectively. During the pandemic to date, reshaping the way standard EFL classes have been delivered has required significant time for teachers to plan and design their lessons. It is particularly evident in large classes – as is frequently the case in secondary schools – that videoconferencing can be distracting as not all participants are visible at the same time and/or on one screen. Moreover, the way teachers and students communicate in these online environments can lead to significant technical and linguistic challenges (Bailey & Lee, 2020). Computer-mediated interactions, filtered through a webcam and an unstable internet connection, can make communication less natural for school-age participants. In addition, the move from face-to-face presence-based classrooms to personal workspaces has often led to frustration as students usually like to keep their personal life and online presence separated from their school identity. As was the case for participants in this study, having everything in the same space provided a constant opportunity for multitasking, which served to move learners' attention away from the lesson.

The Covid-19 pandemic has been influencing school education in unprecedented ways in Italy and around the world, with many children experiencing disruptions to their school life. Remote forms of online learning present teachers and learners with greater opportunities to develop flexible pedagogical practices (Bailey & Lee, 2020). The emergency has forced educators and researchers to rethink the primary purpose of online teaching as children, teens and pre-teens cannot be fully responsible for their own learning. Remote learning impacted various areas of the standard learning processes, from time management to communication patterns, so the mere translation of tasks to the online environment was not sufficient. Exploring how tasks can be modified and adapted to online contexts should be the first step towards a more effective technology-mediated curriculum (Ziegler, 2018). This requires adequate training and commitment from all stakeholders involved in the process of online education, from curriculum designers, to teachers, educators and school principals, as well as managing the expectations of students and their parents and carers (Moorhouse, 2020).

Conclusion

The purpose of this study was to investigate the effects of pre-task guided planning on learners' knowledge of a target structure (narrative tenses – past simple and past continuous). This chapter has focused on the first part of the study, presenting and discussing the results from the pre- and post-tests together with the student questionnaires. Students' written productions and measures of accuracy, fluency and complexity will be the focus of the second phase of the study. Results showed that technology-mediated tasks seemed to have an influence on students' learning, but it was the task, rather than technology, that guided learning, thus, confirming results of previous studies (see e.g. Solares, 2014). A range of opportunities for innovative learning has been identified. The study demonstrated that carefully designed digital tasks could be successfully implemented in the context of remote education. Moreover, the use of videoconferencing tools (e.g. use of breakout rooms) and a shared digital platform adapted easily to both groups' pre-task work. While promising in the context of this study, the urgency that accompanied the wider implementation of distance EFL classes has led to other examples in which language educators have not had the time or expertise to translate tasks into online environments effectively. This still represents one of the major challenges hindering the successful integration of tasks and digital technologies. For this reason, more research on how to design specific training for teachers to help them overcome these challenges and take advantage of the opportunities presented by technology-mediated TBLT curriculum implementation via distance learning is required in the future.

References

Adams, R., Amani, S., Newton, J., & Alwi, N. (2014). Planning and production in computer-mediated communication (CMC) writing. In H. Brynes & R. M. Manchón (Eds.), *Language learning insights from and for L2 learning* (pp. 137–62). John Benjamins Publishing Co.

Bailey, D. R., & Lee, A. R. (2020). Learning from experience in the midst of COVID-19: Benefits, challenges, and strategies in online teaching. *Computer-Assisted Language Learning Electronic Journal, 21*(2), 178–98.

Bowen, P., & Delaney, D. (2019). *Step up gold 2*. Oxford University Press.

Ellis, R. (2009). The differential effects of three types of task planning on the fluency, complexity, and accuracy in L2 oral production. *Applied Linguistics, 30*, 474–509. https://doi.org/10.1093/applin/amp042.

Ellis, R. (2016). Focus on form: A critical review. *Language Teaching Research, 20*(3), 405–28.

Ellis, R., Li, S., & Zhu, Y. (2019a). The effects of pre-task explicit instruction on the performance of a focused task. *System, 80*, 38–47.

Ellis, R., Skehan, P., Li, S., Shintani, N., & Lambert, C. (2019b). *Task-based language teaching: Theory and practice*. Cambridge University Press.

Ellis, R., & Yuan, F. (2004). The effects of planning on fluency, complexity, and accuracy in second language narrative writing. *Studies in Second Language Acquisition, 26*(1), 59–84.

Foster, P., & Skehan, P. (1996). The influence of planning and task type on second language performance. *Studies in Second Language Acquisition, 18*(3), 299–323.

Foster, P., & Skehan, P. (1999). The influence of source of planning and focus of planning on task-based performance. *Language Teaching Research, 3*(3), 215–47.

Hubbard, P., & Levy, M. (2016). Theory in computer-assisted language learning research and practice. In F. Farr & L. Murray (Eds.), *The Routledge handbook of language learning and technology* (pp. 24–38). Routledge.

Kim, Y. (2012). Effects of pretask modeling on attention to form and question development. *Tesol Quarterly, 47*(1), 8–35.

Lee, S.-K., & Huang, H.-T. (2008). Visual input enhancement and grammar learning: A meta-analytic review. *Studies in Second Language Acquisition, 30*(3), 307–31.

Littlewood, W. (2007). Communicative and task-based language teaching in East Asian classrooms. *Language Teaching, 40*(3), 243–9.

Long, M. H. (2015). *Second language acquisition and task-based language teaching*. John Wiley & Sons.

Mochizuki, N., & Ortega, L. (2008). Balancing communication and grammar in beginning-level foreign language classrooms: A study of guided planning and relativization. *Language Teaching Research, 12*(1), 11–37.

Moorhouse, B. L. (2020). Adaptations to a face-to-face initial teacher education course 'forced' online due to the COVID-19 pandemic. *Journal of Education for Teaching, 46*(4), 609–11.

Ortega, L. (1999). Planning and focus-on-form in L2 oral performance. *Studies in Second Language Acquisition, 21*(1), 109–48.

Sato, R. (2010). Perspectives reconsidering the effectiveness and suitability of PPP and TBLT in the Japanese EFL classroom. *JALT Journal, 32*(2), 189.

Skehan, P. (2003). Focus on form, tasks, and technology. *Computer Assisted Language Learning, 16*(5), 391–411.

Solares, M. E. (2014). Textbooks, tasks and technology: An action research study in a textbook-bound EFL context. In Ortega, L., & González-Lloret, M. (Eds.), *Exploring technology-mediated task-based language teaching across foreign language contexts* (pp. 79–114). John Benjamins Publishing.

Thomas, M., & Reinders, H. (2012). *Task-based language learning and teaching with technology*. Bloomsbury.

Van de Guchte, M., Braaksma, M., Rijlaarsdam, G., & Bimmel, P. (2016). Focus on form through task repetition in TBLT. *Language Teaching Research, 20*(3), 300–20.

Van de Guchte, M., Rijlaarsdam, G., Braaksma, M., & Bimmel, P. (2019). Focus on language versus content in the pre-task: Effects of guided peer-video model observations on task performance. *Language Teaching Research, 23*(3), 310–29.

Willis, J. (1996). *A framework for task-based learning*. Harlow.

Ziegler, N. (2018). Pre-task planning in L2 text-chat: Examining learners' process and performance. *Language Learning and Technology, 22*(3), 193–213.

Part 4

E-Assessment during the Covid-19 Pandemic

12

Formative Assessment in Synchronous Language Teaching in Higher Education during the Covid-19 Pandemic

María Luisa Carrió-Pastor

Introduction

This chapter concerns an analysis of the formative assessment carried out for synchronous activities on a course forming part of the master's degree in Languages and Technology at the Universitat Politècnica de València, Spain, during the Covid-19 pandemic. The decision was taken to employ formative assessment for this course because of the occurrence of lockdown periods due to the pandemic. Additionally, after an extensive review of the assessment literature, I found that several researchers, such as Black and Wiliam (2006, 2009), Tillema (2010), Hamodi et al. (2015), Talanquer (2015), Meusen-Beekman et al. (2016), Andersson and Palm (2017) and Van der Kleij (2019), have reported that the use of formative assessment had a positive impact on student achievement. Thus, in order to explore the advantages of formative assessment, some activities on academic writing to be delivered in a Spanish course were designed.

The key idea in this proposal is to see formative assessment in foreign-language teaching as part of the students' learning process, as it facilitates their communicative skills and their engagement in self-assessment and peer assessment. As stated by Black and Wiliam (2006), 'It [formative assessment] may be peculiarly effective, in part because the quality of interactive feedback is a critical feature in determining the quality of learning activity, and is therefore a central feature of pedagogy' (p. 100). Here, I consider whether formative assessment is equally effective while pandemic-related restrictions are in place, when students cannot communicate in as straightforward a fashion with their teachers and peers. Feedback and collaborative work are two of the most important aspects of formative assessment, and, in response to pandemic-related restrictions, immediate feedback and classroom collaboration has to be designed with the use of technology in mind.

Taking all these aspects into account, in this study, formative assessment activities were designed to overcome pandemic-related difficulties for students in language learning, with the design also taking into account the results of previous studies.

Thus, the main objectives were as follows: first, to identify the strengths, weaknesses, opportunities and threats – a SWOT analysis – of the use of formative assessment in academic writing activities on a course on Spanish as a foreign language during the Covid-19 pandemic; and, second, to suggest ways to extend and/or improve the use of formative assessment, if possible. The research questions considered in this chapter are as follows:

1. Is formative assessment able to improve communication in learning Spanish as a foreign language? If so, in what ways?
2. What consequences does the Covid-19 pandemic have for formative assessment?

To answer these questions, this chapter is divided into different sections. First, in this introduction, the general aims and research questions of this study are identified. In the next two sections, previous studies on foreign-language teaching in higher education and formative assessment are described. This is followed by a description, in the 'Methods' section, of the material designed for the formative assessment employed with a group of students and the design of the survey itself. Then, the results of the study are provided and discussed, and finally, the objectives and the research questions as well as post-Covid lessons are addressed in the 'Conclusion'.

Foreign-Language Teaching in Higher Education

Foreign-language teaching has long been a major focus of interest for many researchers (Carrió-Pastor & Alonso Almeida, 2014; Oxford & Oxford, 2009). Teaching strategies (Carrió-Pastor, 2019; Oxford, 2011), how to improve language acquisition and motivation (Carrió-Pastor & Mestre Kleijn, 2014; Carrió-Pastor, 2016a; Foster-Cohen, 2009) and the role of technology (Burston, 2014; Butler-Pascoe, 2011; Carrió-Pastor & Romero Forteza, 2014; Romero-Forteza & Carrió-Pastor, 2015) are some of the most widely studied issues in such research. However, none of these studies considered the possibility of teaching a foreign language during a pandemic, and the Covid-19 pandemic has shown that teachers need to be ready to adapt their curricula in response to such difficult situations. During the pandemic, materials have had to be modified and online teaching became a must. When that happened, technology and how to make best use of it in teaching constituted two key issues for teachers. Learners' self-directed use of technology was crucial while teachers had an essential role to play in encouraging and guiding students 'concerning the use of possible technology-enhanced materials for learning' (Lai, 2015, p. 74). Also, providing students with the tools to perform collaborative work (Aydin & Yildiz, 2014; Carrió-Pastor, 2015) and to maintain contact with classmates was crucial during lockdown periods.

In 2022, it seems that the situation is edging towards normality and teachers do not need to rely so much on technology, but the importance of adapting materials for online teaching remains. It is certainly true that the design and use of a number of technologies for teaching has proliferated in a very short time. Their impact has been wide-ranging, with millions of users taking advantage of technologies such as podcasting, collaborative apps, social media and so on. Yet, even before the Covid-19 pandemic, the use of technology was already a necessary part of effective foreign-language teaching, as many researchers such as Warschauer and Meskill (2000), Chapelle (2003, 2010), Kukulska-Hulme and Traxler (2005), Iskander (2007), Carrió-Pastor and Skorczynska (2015) and Carrió-Pastor (2016b) have shown.

Researchers have paid particular attention to the methodology and the activities employed in virtual environments (Barjis et al., 2012; Carrió-Pastor, 2019; Godwin-Jones, 2011; Oxford & Oxford, 2009; Romero-Forteza & Carrió-Pastor, 2014). Other studies have focused on the innovative character of e-learning (Aydin & Yildiz, 2014; Iskander, 2007), and yet others on how to integrate virtual environments more effectively into language teaching (Barjis et al., 2012; Burston, 2014).

Learners must be central to every process within foreign-language teaching, as 'researchers should carry out their research by taking into account students' needs and the language requirements of their educational level' (Carrió-Pastor, 2016b, p. 256). Most foreign-language learners in higher education are digital natives of virtual environments, and they expect university teachers to use technology in daily teaching. This expectation has increased due to the circumstances of the pandemic. All materials, including activities, assessment tools and so on, have now been adapted to online teaching even when used in non-lockdown periods (i.e. in face-to-face classes). At the beginning of the Covid-19 pandemic, adapting teaching materials to online teaching was challenging, but it is important to remember that assessing students at home was equally difficult. In lockdown periods, the fact that learning and assessment had to continue 'as normal' despite the extreme external situation was a very tough task for teachers. In those circumstances, the use of formative assessment and of technology became issues of great interest for foreign-language teaching.

Formative Assessment

There are several aspects to consider when planning assessment: principally, what, who and how we assess. In the case of academic writing, Aull (2015) indicates that what we must assess are different parts of discourse, such as

1. use of noun phrases and cohesive ties as they contribute to claim development and 'formal style',
2. qualification and certainty markers as they contribute to a 'formal' and 'objective' tone, and
3. rhetorical moves as they contribute to topic, claim and counter-claim development (p. 63).

Once it is decided what we are to assess, which will depend on the curriculum and the desired degree of difficulty, we must consider the characteristics of the students to be assessed: their ability in a foreign language, their previous knowledge, their expectations, their age, whether they are in higher education, the degree they study and so on.

After the 'what' and the 'who', the final key topic in assessment is the 'how' – that is, what kind of assessment practice should be chosen. For example, teachers may decide to use traditional assessment practices, known as summative assessment, or teachers can change 'towards more open, performance-oriented types of assessment that show competence in the professionally relevant outcomes' (Gulikers et al., 2013, p. 116), such as formative assessment, which is also known as assessment for learning (AfL; Marshall, 2010).

Formative assessment has been implemented to varying degrees in higher education study programmes by many researchers, such as Black (2010, 2015), Black and Wiliam (2006, 2009), Talanquer (2015), Meusen-Beekman et al. (2016), Andersson and Palm (2017), Van der Kleij (2019), Yin and Buck (2019), Granberg et al. (2021) and Carrió-Pastor (2021). These studies highlight the benefits of implementing formative assessment: for example, programmes change from a traditional, input-based curriculum to one based on target competencies. In this regard, Andersson and Palm (2017) indicate that 'formative assessment strategies share the common core of modifying teaching and learning based on identified student learning needs, but may include an emphasis on different aspects of formative assessment' (p. 93). The different aspects might be different activities, the feedback given to students, or the role of teachers or students in the process and so on. All the studies cited concerning formative assessment emphasize the extended learning opportunities it offers, potentially improving student achievement.

Formative assessment encourages self-regulation in learners – that is, the capacity to decide what activity will be more fruitful for them. As Xiao and Yang (2019) have said, 'Self-regulated learners are able to define their goals of learning and pursue actions of knowledge on their own initiative [...] formative assessment and feedback have the potential to help students become self-regulated learners' (pp. 39–41). In this sense, students have the agency to decide on the following step in their learning.

Some researchers have also highlighted the importance of technology in formative assessment, as students can gain immediate feedback (Fernando, 2018, 2020; Gikandi et al., 2011; Pellegrino, 2010; Wilson et al., 2017). Technology improves AfL, facilitating collaboration among peers and teachers and students, although these authors also report that some students may feel less motivated if the interaction in the assessment process is unsuccessful.

In higher education, technology in formative assessment has been used with positive results (Gikandi et al., 2011), which is unsurprising given that students frequently use technology to acquire knowledge more generally in their lives. University students have the capacity to self-regulate their learning and are cognitively capable of deciding on the next step to take (Granberg et al., 2021). More specifically to the topic of this study, Lai (2015) refers to the self-directed use of technology for language learning and emphasizes the decisive role of teachers in this process.

Here, I report on my study of the importance and effects of formative assessment on university students, and additionally, I consider the impact of the Covid-19 pandemic on the results of this survey. The procedure followed in this study is based on a prior literature review, mentioned above, including studies which show how to design and implement formative assessment in language teaching classes.

Methods

Participants

This study centres on the analysis of the linguistic performance of thirty-six Chinese students enrolled on the master's degree in Languages and Technology at the Universitat Politècnica de València, Spain. Students need to have a B2 level (upper-intermediate level) in Spanish to enrol on this programme. The students' (male and female) ages ranged between twenty-one and thirty-four years, and they came from a wide variety of backgrounds, with education or work experience in the fields of fine art, business, literature, languages and so on.

During the academic years of 2019–20 and 2020–1, classes were delivered in Spanish via a Sakai-based online platform, known as PoliformaT; Microsoft Teams was used for online meetings during lockdown periods and for some collaborative activities. In this way, students were able to carry out different activities that involved interaction, peer assessment and collaboration, communicating in Spanish with their peers. Technology was crucial to perform all the planned formative assessment activities, due to lockdown periods in Spain and also later, even when students were able to attend in-person classes wearing masks. At that time, they still could not sit close to their other classmates and so technology was required to undertake all the activities designed for peer assessment.

Materials

Thus, the material compiled for this chapter consists of the formative assessment activities used in one course of the above-mentioned master's degree. The activities were inserted into the course units for students to complete as they advanced in their learning process. They consisted of ten assignments and two multiple-choice tests to be carried out by students following the AfL method. Thus, the assignments and tests were discussed with students, explaining the different sections and the main difficulties and giving immediate feedback.

Nineteen students undertook the activities in 2019–20 and seventeen in 2020–1. The course was taught in the second semester, so students continued their instruction at home during the lockdown period in 2019–20, whereas they were able to attend in-person classes, with Covid-19 restrictions, in 2020–1. Due to restrictions on the collation of material from students, the content had to be adapted, and formative assessment was adopted for the course due to health considerations. Previously, summative assessment had been employed for this course, although students were also able to work collaboratively in groups and in pairs.

Thus, overall, the material gathered for this study was composed of 360 assignments and seventy-two multiple-choice tests, together with reports written by each student, reviewing the formative assessment activities they had undertaken. Additionally, the answers to two questionnaires, in which the three teachers of the subject and students gave their opinion on the formative assessment activities, were gathered. In the questionnaires, students and teachers had to identify their attitude to formative assessment in a Likert scale on a continuum from strongly agree to strongly disagree.

Procedure

During this study, there was a strong emphasis on learning, reducing the focus on performance, errors and correction, in accordance with previous research on formative assessment and feedback (Hansen, 2020). The material was designed by the three teachers in charge of the subject. Ten assignments and two multiple-choice tests were prepared, which were to be answered in PoliformaT by students (see a detailed description below). The nature of formative assessment activities was taken into account – that is, they had to be explained before they were done and discussed after students finished them. The first step after designing and producing the material was to identify the collaborative formative assessment procedure to be used. One of the key aspects was feedback, and for this, the work of Nicol and Macfarlane-Dick (2006) regarding formative assessment and their seven principles of good feedback practice was drawn on. For these authors, the most important thing is for students to be proactive rather than passive during class time. The principles considered in this study were that good feedback (Hansen, 2020, p. 3)

1. helps to clarify what good performance is;
2. facilitates the development of self-assessment in learning;
3. delivers high-quality information to students about their learning;
4. encourages teacher and peer dialogue around learning;
5. encourages positive motivational beliefs and self-esteem;
6. provides opportunities to close the gap between current and desired performance; and
7. provides information to teachers that can be used to help shape teaching.

A focus on these seven principles of good feedback entails a change to more traditional approaches, which mainly emphasize on ensuring students attain the desired knowledge or benchmark. In this way, formative assessment fosters collaborative work between teachers and students, as it is based on feedback.

These principles shaped the design of the formative assessment activities in this study. Further aspects considered during the assessment – carried out in class or via Teams during the scheduled sessions – included setting language learning goals, using activities that elicited evidence of language learning, dialogical interaction, peer review and use of technology and linguistic feedback on task-related processes. Importance was placed on whether students were proficient in specific aspects: that is, the number of correct answers was less important than whether the students reached the learning goals. Also, their desire and effort to learn was also taken into account in the formative assessment process: both their competency and their willingness to learn were assessed.

The main aim in all this was to increase students' self-awareness of their linguistic strengths and weaknesses and to teach them to work collaboratively in order to improve their written communication skills, fostering self-regulation of their performance.

Thus, assessment and feedback were carried out by all those involved: by each student, by their classmates and by the three teachers.

The following procedure, based on Hansen (2020), was followed to carry out formative assessment for the assignments and tests. First, the teachers presented the test/assignment, highlighting the aspects to be evaluated and asking students to check that they understood the key points. Then, the assignment/test was introduced (Principle 1) and the academic goals and the main purpose of the assignment or test were described to motivate students; any queries were also addressed (Principle 5). The teachers highlighted the importance for students of self-assessment and reflection when completing the test or assignment (Principle 2).

In this sense, correct answers were not the only important factor to take into account in the assessment, but rather also how students reflected on their performance during a review carried out with teachers and peers (Principle 3). Afterwards, the students started working individually. After finishing the assignment or test, students were given a short break. When they returned to the classroom, a review began. This took the form of an interactive review of all the questions and possible answers in the case of the assignments and the correct answers in the case of the tests.

The answers were discussed in the classroom. It was difficult at the beginning of the course, but when the students learnt that a percentage of their mark depended on their contribution and interaction with the teachers, participation increased (Principle 4). During this time, students self-assessed each assignment or task and were asked to suggest how to self-direct their learning process (Principle 2) by writing it down and sending their report to their teachers. The aim was for the students to consider how they answered the questions and the ways in which they could improve their language proficiency (Principle 6). Meanwhile, teachers considered which areas needed the most attention in language learning, whether there were some areas for improvement after undertaking the assignment or test and other such issues (Principle 7). In the case of the multiple-choice tests, students were aware of how they had performed immediately, but regarding the assignments, the teachers had to first review the assignments and reports after the interactive session.

After the analysis of all the formative assessment activities carried out in the synchronous sessions over the two academic years, the results were gathered and placed in an assessment grid, taking the following aspects taken into account: teachers' assessment, self-assessment, self-regulation and feedback. Students had to reflect on their perception of self-assessment and self-regulation when answering the assignments or doing the tests, submitting their reflections, which were part of the assessment, to teachers.

Of the twelve formative assessment activities (ten assignments and two tests), students needed to complete seven to pass the course. Finally, when all the formative assessment activities were finished, students were asked to answer a questionnaire to express their opinion about formative assessment, self-regulation and the impact of the Covid-19 pandemic on their learning process. Additionally, teachers responded to a questionnaire to indicate aspects to be improved on in the formative assessment procedure and their perception of the impact of the Covid-19 pandemic on the assessment process. This last aspect was important as students were not able to sit close to each other at any time, meaning that discussion with their peers had to take place online even when they were in the classroom. Initially, peer assessment in the classroom was included within the assessment grid, but after considering the circumstances surrounding the pandemic, it was decided to eliminate peer assessment and base the final assessment on self-assessment, teacher assessment and feedback only.

Next, the strengths, weaknesses, opportunities and threats of formative assessment activities during the Covid-19 pandemic are described as well as the way in which this anomalous situation influenced language teaching practices and use of technology.

Results and Discussion

Table 12.1 shows an assessment grid, showing the different dimensions of formative assessment taken into account by teachers during the process: these can be seen across the top row of the grid, with the assessed activities carried out during class time being listed on the left side of the table. After gathering all the activities undertaken by students and the notes taken by teachers during the review of the activities and the student reflections, teachers filled in the grid for each student, inserting comments about the different assignments and tests. The grid content was also discussed later with the students who failed the course, to provide them with further feedback.

As this is a qualitative analysis, the different results associated with this chapter's objectives are discussed below. Table 12.1 shows the grid that was used by the three teachers of the subject to share the evaluation of each student. Each teacher wrote a comment on each section (teacher assessment, self-assessment, feedback needed,

Table 12.1 Assessment Grid Used to Indicate the Results of the Assessed Activities for Each Student

Activities	Teacher Assessment	Self-Assessment	Feedback Needed	Self-Regulation
Assignment 1				
Assignment 2				
Assignment 3				
Assignment 4				
Assignment 5				
Assignment 6				
Assignment 7				
Assignment 8				
Assignment 9				
Assignment 10				
Test 1				
Test 2				

self-regulation) related to every assignment and test done by each student. After that, teachers had a meeting in which all the comments on students were discussed and an assessment of projects by consensus was delivered.

Identification of Strengths, Weaknesses, Opportunities and Threats

After analysing and correlating the results from the assignments and tests, the self-assessment reports and the students' and teachers' questionnaires, the strengths of formative assessment can be said to be the following:

1. a common learning arena was created;
2. students felt they could communicate in the target language and practised by using it;
3. students felt more motivated to answer the tests/assignments correctly because the answers were discussed with their peers; and
4. the teachers involved in the survey were viewed very positively.

In contrast, the weaknesses identified during the study were as follows:

1. the participation of all students in a review of the activities was difficult;
2. formative assessment was more time-consuming than traditional assessment;
3. some students did not participate in real self-assessment; and
4. the ability of some students to communicate was poor, and they could not express themselves properly.

The following opportunities were identified:

1. formative assessment improved the use of technology;
2. teachers had the opportunity to discuss the assignments and tests with students and they were able to change them if students did not consider them valuable;
3. assessment was not seen as a threatening tool by students, as they were part of the process; and
4. the ability to promote self-directed learning during periods of lockdown was crucial.

Finally, the following threats regarding formative assessment were found:

1. some teachers, who were informed about the study, did not believe that the focus on learning rather than achievement benefitted knowledge acquisition;
2. in the case of foreign-language learning, students needed to be proficient enough in the language to participate in the review and discussion that formed part of formative assessment; and
3. standard evaluation was generally suitable to draw up a list of students eligible for access to degrees, to obtain grants, and so on, whereas formative assessment offered a vaguer interpretation of how proficient students were.

Ways to Extend and/or Improve Formative Assessment

In this survey, it was found that Chinese students considered their participation in the review of their tasks to be impolite. At the beginning of the sessions, it was difficult to show them how to review their assignments, as culturally, they were not used to this procedure. Thus, students should be instructed in formative assessment in a collaborative way to participate in the classroom, interacting with peers and teachers.

Additionally, the formative assessment process requires longer periods of time explaining the procedure to students, and technology could be used to optimize the whole process, limiting these interactions and enabling self-assessment of most of the assignments. For the assessment, peers could also play a greater role, assessing their classmates' assignments.

The students' responses to the questionnaires and their self-assessment reports revealed that they enjoyed the discussion of the activities and the insights they were able to gain into why they failed some tests or assignments. One possibility for formative assessment in a foreign language could be to carry out oral exams for the whole process. In this method, the teacher would make notes on the assessment grid (Table 12.1) and the students would participate in the assessment orally. This would mean that teachers would not have to devote much time marking all the assignments and tests.

Improvement of Communication in Spanish as a Foreign Language

All the Chinese students were eager to communicate and practise their Spanish, but at the beginning, it was not an easy task to convince them of the need to discuss their assignments. As the students started taking responsibility for and increased their involvement in the assessment processes, they felt more motivated in the classroom and tried to participate even more to obtain higher marks.

In the questionnaires, they reported that they felt more comfortable with formative assessment as they were able to express their feelings, and they valued how the teachers helped them to understand how to answer the assignments and tests.

Students tried to communicate and report on the formative assessment activities, as can be seen in the example below:

> porque en español, son hay formal e informal para hablar, es decir, para los estudiantes británicos que estudian español, considerarán si el español es similar al inglés se compara la lengua materna con la que se está aprendiendo no estoy seguro pero creo que sí :)

> [because in Spanish, to be formal and informal speaking ways, that is, for British students who study Spanish, they will consider if Spanish is similar to English mother tongue is compared with the one being learnt I am not sure but I think it is true :)].

In the report, the Chinese student explains the answer to the assignment, trying to express herself, but her limited command of Spanish was sometimes an obstacle for the

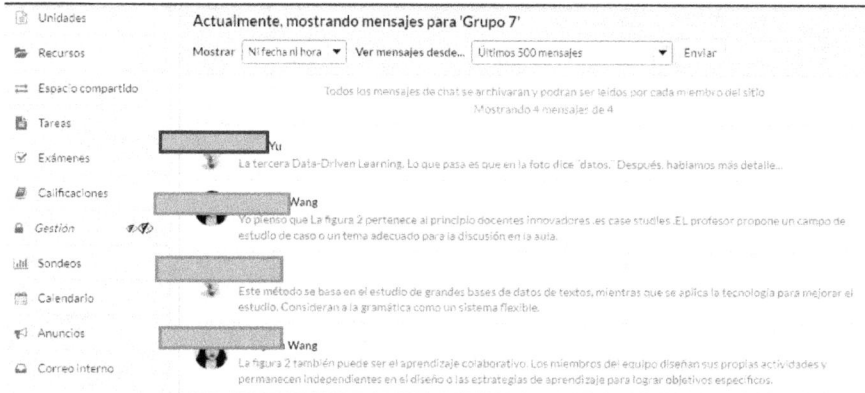

Figure 12.1 Collaborative chat for formative assessment

discussion and review process. Another example of a collaborative task can be seen in Figure 12.1, in which students use the chat facility in PoliformaT to communicate with each other and work in pairs during the Covid-19 pandemic.

This collaborative activity encouraged communication among students and forced them to use Spanish even when their mother tongue was Chinese. Although it was not considered in this study, it was noticed by teachers that students were still able to interact with their classmates despite the Covid-19 pandemic. In the questionnaire, 90% of the students reported that they liked these collaborative activities as it allowed them to communicate in a foreign language. The three teachers had a positive attitude in the questionnaire regarding formative assessment, but one of them reported some stressful situations when some students did not communicate effectively, not participating in the assignments. Two of the three teachers stated that there were demotivating sessions during lockdown.

Oral communication in Spanish occurred during class time when the teacher asked the students questions during the review after a formative assessment activity. Written communication was performed in the course chat and forum, when completing the assignments and when writing the report on the review of formative assessment.

Consequences of the Covid-19 Pandemic for Formative Assessment

Some students preferred to perform formative assessment activities during Teams sessions in 2019–20, a fact that limited the effectiveness of the assignment reviews, as teachers could not be so interactive. In this study, only the students who decided to be in the classroom were selected, to avoid these interferences. In 2020–1, all the students were in the classroom: communication flowed and topics could be discussed more easily, and assignments could be reviewed in a more satisfactory manner. An example of this can be seen in Figure 12.2, from the course forum.

The collaborative activities shown in Example 1 and Figures 12.1 and 12.2 had to be carried out in a way that avoided physical contact, in Teams or via the course chat

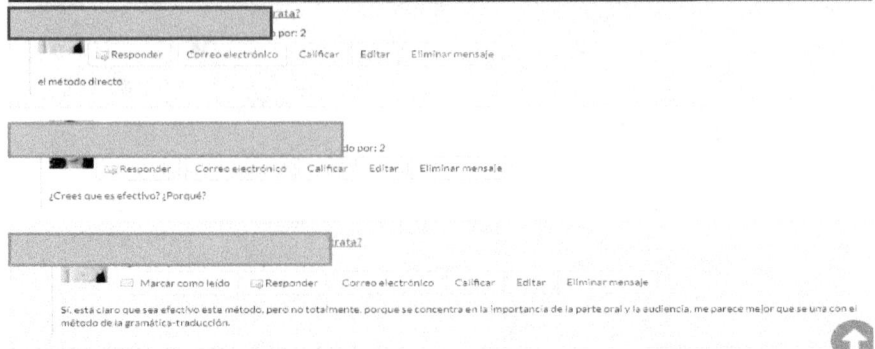

Figure 12.2 Teacher–student communication in the class forum during the Covid-19 pandemic

or forum in PoliformaT, but students were able to communicate with their peers and receive feedback from teachers to self-regulate the activities they needed to complete.

Post-Pandemic Lessons

This survey has identified the benefits of formative assessment, which are similar to those reported in previous studies, but new light has been shed on them due to the circumstances surrounding the Covid-19 pandemic; this can also be taken into account in future studies. The discussion and collaborative work performed in the classroom were carried out using technology, forcing students to communicate in Spanish as the teachers were monitoring the chat facility and forum.

Additionally, implementing the seven principles of feedback proposed by Nicol & Macfarlane-Dick (2006) was challenging, but they helped to organize the formative assessment process during lockdown. Moreover, the grid used by teachers to assess students, focusing on aspects such as self-assessment, teachers' assessment, self-regulation and feedback, could be of interest for other researchers or practitioners of formative assessment.

Conclusions

This study aimed to identify ways in which self-regulation, technology and feedback might be organized to support formative assessment. The SWOT analysis revealed that there are many opportunities and strengths, indicating the benefits of formative assessment. These benefits were also referred to by teachers and students in their responses to the questionnaires completed at the end of the course. Yet the weaknesses and threats identified must be addressed in order to improve the design of future formative assessment activities, and the opportunities identified during the study must be taken advantage of. Thus, the results extracted here are consistent with those of Gikandi et al. (2011), Hamodi et al. (2015) and Andersson and Palm (2017), who highlighted the benefits of implementing formative assessment activities.

The students were able to practise Spanish in formative assessment activities despite the difficulties in communicating that some of them had. At the end of the semester, in both academic years, the students' command of the language had improved. In fact, a future study could involve a comparison of their level of Spanish when they start and finish the course. Students were forced to practise Spanish in the classroom and gradually felt more relaxed in doing so. They were more fluent in the final assignments, and the students highlighted the fact that they had been able to communicate in Spanish as a positive.

Finally, I think that formative assessment has been particularly beneficial during the pandemic, as the students have been able to collaborate and communicate with their peers and teachers even during lockdown. Even when students were not able to attend classes in person, they felt part of the class, and when the classroom was not the place where they could learn and improve their performance, they were still able to have contact and interact with each other, practising their foreign-language skills. It was also an opportunity to self-regulate the rhythm of their learning.

This study was performed in a very special situation, during the Covid-19 pandemic, and there are limitations that could be addressed in future studies. For example, the number of students studied here could be increased or the materials used described in more detail. But the main aim of this study was to describe how formative assessment in synchronous language teaching in higher education during the Covid-19 pandemic was used, and further analyses could address the limitations of this study.

References

Andersson, C., & Palm, T. (2017). The impact of formative assessment on student achievement: A study of the effects of changes to classroom practice after a comprehensive professional development programme. *Learning and Instruction, 49*, 92–102. https://doi.org/10.1016/j.learninstruc.2016.12.006.

Aull, A. (2015). Connecting writing and language in assessment: Examining style, tone, and argument in the U.S. Common Core standards and in exemplary student writing. *Assessing Writing, 24*, 59–73.

Aydin, Z., & Yildiz, S. (2014). Using wikis to promote collaborative EFL writing. *Language Learning & Technology, 18*(1), 160–80.

Barjis, J., Gupta, A., Sharda, S., Bouzdine-Chameeva, T., Lee, P. D., & Verbraeck, A. (2012). Innovative teaching using simulation and virtual environments. *Interdisciplinary Journal of Information, Knowledge, and Management, 7*, 237–54.

Black, P. (2010). Formative assessment. In P. Peterson, E. Baker, & B. McGaw (Eds.), *International encyclopedia of education* (pp. 359–64). Elsevier.

Black, P. (2015). Formative assessment – an optimistic but incomplete vision. *Assessment in Education: Principles, Policy & Practice, 22*(1), 161–77. https://doi.org/10.1080/0969594X.2014.999643.

Black, P., & Wiliam, D. (2006). Developing a theory of formative assessment. In J. Gardner (Ed.), *Assessment and learning* (pp. 81–100). Sage.

Black, P., & Wiliam, D. (2009). Developing the theory of formative assessment. *Educational Assessment, Evaluation and Accountability, 21*, 5–31. https://doi.org/10.1007/s11092-008-9068-5.

Burston, J. (2014). The reality of MALL: Mobile assisted language learning. *Language Learning & Technology, 10*(1), 9–16.

Butler-Pascoe, M. E. (2011). The history of CALL: The intertwining paths of technology and second/foreign language teaching. *International Journal of Computer-Assisted Language Learning and Teaching (IJCALLT), 1*(1), 16–32.

Carrió-Pastor, M. L. (2015). Do online collaborative activities foster autonomy on second language reading and writing? *Language Teaching Tomorrow, 1*, 1–6.

Carrió-Pastor, M. L. (2016a). Should peer assessment be included in foreign language testing? The role of motivation in testing. In M. L. Carrió-Pastor (Ed.), *New challenges for language testing: Towards mutual recognition of qualifications* (pp. 61–76). Cambridge Scholars Publishing.

Carrió-Pastor, M. L. (Ed.). (2016b). *Technology implementation in second language teaching and translation studies*. Springer.

Carrio-Pastor, M. L. (Ed.). (2019). *Teaching language and teaching literature in virtual environments*. Springer.

Carrió-Pastor, M. L. (2021). Análisis comparativo del uso de marcadores metadiscursivos en la evaluación formativa y sumativa online. *Tejuelo, 34*, 261–92.

Carrió-Pastor, M. L., & Alonso Almeida, F. (2014). English as a second language: Variations and pedagogical implications. *Procedia – Social and Behavioral Sciences, 116*, 377–81.

Carrió-Pastor, M. L., & Mestre Behavioural, E. (2014). Motivation in second language acquisition. *Procedia – Social and Behavioral Sciences, 116*, 240–4.

Carrió-Pastor, M. L., & Romero Forteza, F. (2014). Second language writing: Use of the World Wide Web to improve specific writing. *Procedia – Social and Behavioral Sciences, 116*, 235–9.

Carrió-Pastor, M. L., & Skorczynska, H. (2015). Collaborative learning and communication technologies in teaching business English. *Procedia – Social and Behavioral Sciences, 178*, 32–7.

Chapelle, C. A. (2003). *English language learning and technology. Lectures on applied linguistics in the age of information and communication technology*. John Benjamins Publishing.

Chapelle, C. A. (2010). Research for practice: A look at issues in technology for second language learning. *Language Learning and Technology, 14*(3), 27–30.

Fernando, W. (2018). Show me your true colours: Scaffolding formative academic literacy assessment through an online learning platform. *Assessing Writing, 36*, 63–76. https://doi.org/10.1016/j.asw.2018.03.005.

Fernando, W. (2020). Moodle quizzes and their usability for formative assessment of academic writing. *Assessing Writing, 46*, 1–6. https://doi.org/10.1016/j.asw.2020.100485.

Foster-Cohen, S. (2009). *Language acquisition*. Palgrave Macmillan.

Gikandi, J. W., Morrow, D., & Davis, N. E. (2011). Online formative assessment in higher education: A review of the literature. *Computers & Education, 57*, 2333–51. https://doi.org/10.1016/j.compedu.2011.06.004.

Godwin-Jones, R. (2011). Emerging technologies: Mobile Apps for language learning. *Language Learning and Technology, 15*(2), 2–11.

Granberg, C., Palm, T., & Palmberg, B. (2021). A case study of a formative assessment practice and the effects on students' self-regulated learning. *Studies in Educational Evaluation, 68*, 1–10. https://doi.org/10.1016/j.stueduc.2020.100955.

Gulikers, J. T. M., Biemans, H. J. A., Wesselink, R., & van der Wel, M. (2013). Aligning formative and summative assessments: A collaborative action research challenging teacher conceptions. *Studies in Educational Evaluation, 39*, 116–24. https://doi.org/10.1016/j.stueduc.2013.03.001.

Hamodi, C., López Pastor, V. M., & López Pastor, A. T. (2015). Medios, técnicas e instrumentos de evaluación formativa y compartida del aprendizaje en educación superior. *Perfiles educativos, 147*, 146–61.

Hansen, G. (2020). Formative assessment as a collaborative act. Teachers' intention and students' experience: Two sides of the same coin, or? *Studies in Educational Evaluation, 66*, 1–10.

Iskander, M. (Ed.). (2007). *Innovations in E-learning, instruction technology, assessment and engineering education*. Springer.

Kukulska-Hulme, A., & Traxler, J. (Eds.). (2005). *Mobile learning: A handbook for educators and trainers*. Routledge.

Lai, Ch. (2015). Modeling teachers' influence on learners' self-directed use of technology for language learning outside the classroom. *Computers & Education, 82*, 74–83.

Marshall, B. (2010). Formative assessment and instructional planning. In P. Peterson, E. Baker, & B. McGaw (Eds.), *International encyclopedia of education* (pp. 365–8). Elsevier.

Meusen-Beekman, K. D., Brinke, D. J., & Boshuizen, H. P. A. (2016). Effects of formative assessments to develop self-regulation among sixth grade students: Results from a randomized controlled intervention. *Studies in Educational Evaluation, 51*, 126–36. https://doi.org/10.1016/j.stueduc.2016.10.008.

Nicol, D. J., & Macfarlane-Dick, D. (2006). Formative assessment and self-regulated learning: A model and seven principles of good feedback practice. *Studies in Higher Education, 31*, 199–218.

Oxford, R. (2011). *Teaching and Researching Language Learning Strategies*. Pearson Education.

Oxford, R., & Oxford, J. (2009). *Second language teaching and learning in the net generation*. University of Hawai'i at Manoa.

Pellegrino, J. W. (2010). Technology and formative assessment. In P. Peterson, E. Baker, & B. McGaw (Eds.), *International encyclopedia of education* (pp. 43–7). Elsevier.

Romero Forteza, F., & Carrió-Pastor, M. L. (2014). Virtual language learning environments: The standardization of evaluation. *Multidisciplinary Journal for Education, Social and Technological Sciences, 1*, 135–52.

Romero Forteza, F., & Carrió-Pastor, M. L. (2015). Estudio de la efectividad de la formación online en lenguas. *E-Aesla, 1*, 1–8.

Talanquer, V. (2015). La importancia de la evaluación formativa. *Educación Química, 26*, 177–9. https://doi.org/10.1016/j.eq.2015.05.001.

Tillema, H. (2010). Formative assessment in teacher education and teacher professional development. In P. Peterson, E. Baker, & B. McGaw (Eds.), *International encyclopedia of education* (pp. 563–71). Elsevier.

Van der Kleij, F. M. (2019). Comparison of teacher and student perceptions of formative assessment feedback practices and association with individual student characteristics. *Teaching and Teacher Education, 85*, 175–89. https://doi.org/10.1016/j.tate.2019.06.010.

Warschauer, M., & Meskill, C. (2000). Technology and second language teaching. In J. Rosenthal (Ed.), *Handbook of undergraduate second language education* (pp. 303–18). Lawrence Erlbaum.

Wilson, J., Roscoe, R., & Ahmed, Y. (2017). Automated formative writing assessment using a levels of language framework. *Assessing Writing, 34*, 16–36. https://doi.org/10.1016/j.asw.2017.08.002.

Xiao, Y., & Yang, M. (2019). Formative assessment and self-regulated learning: How formative assessment supports students' self-regulation in English language learning. *System, 81*, 39–49. https://doi.org/10.1016/j.system.2019.01.004.

Yin, X., & Buck, G. A. (2019). Using a collaborative action research approach to negotiate an understanding of formative assessment in an era of accountability testing. *Teaching and Teacher Education, 80*, 27–38. https://doi.org/10.1016/j.tate.2018.12.018.

13

E-Portfolios as a Technology-Enabled Assessment: Surviving or Accommodating Covid-19

Ricky Lam, Marcus Lau and Joanna Wong

Introduction

Since March 2020, people from different walks of life have experienced unprecedented challenges owing to the Covid-19 pandemic. Nearly every part of the globe has suffered from the impacts of Covid-19 in one way or another, including the economic downturn (large-scale lay-offs in aviation and tourism), political disputes among nations (differing measures to control the coronavirus), collapse of public health systems (severe lack of infrastructure in hospitals) and even change in individual lifestyles (surging consumption of sanitizers and face coverings; phenomena of social isolation and working from home). In education, teachers and students have encountered similar hardships, including a sudden shift to remote teaching without much preparation (i.e. literacy to teach online), a prolonged period of class suspension (i.e. home-based learning), postponement of large-scale standardized testing due to lockdown and cancellation of most overseas exchange programmes because of stringent travel restrictions.

Throughout the first six months of the pandemic, students' school attendance, dropout rates, academic performance and self-efficacy beliefs had reportedly plummeted drastically, especially when compared to the pre-Covid-19 era (Santibañez & Guarino, 2021). Likewise, some teachers have stated that they only marginally managed to teach with educational technologies – namely, videoconferencing software and gamified mobile apps – because they lacked school support and sufficient training to fine-tune their pedagogies to conduct remote teaching (Cheung, 2021; Reich, 2021). In L2 education, there has been emerging scholarship reporting on how individual teachers have strategically coped with online teaching and learning by manipulating various common learning management systems (e.g. Moodle, Google Classroom or Mahara) and videoconferencing software (e.g. Microsoft Teams, Zoom or Google Meet; Moorhouse & Beaumont, 2020). These tools can serve as e-Portfolio hosts, which assist students in managing and reflecting upon their language learning on and off campus efficiently. Since the turn of the century, e-Portfolios have been mainly used in the tertiary sector, yet their applications in K-12 contexts have been gaining traction recently (Lam, 2021a). Regardless of this research, little has been done to investigate how L2 teachers utilize learning management systems or equivalent e-Portfolio software to evaluate students' learning. To fill this gap, this chapter first showcases how two secondary-level teachers attempted e-Portfolio assessment and then evaluates the extent to which their e-Portfolio applications aligned with L2 teaching and assessment productively. The following section presents a tripartite framework to theorize the e-Portfolios approach.

Rationale behind the E-Portfolio Approach

This section unpacks the idea of social constructivism in relation to assessment *for* learning and assessment *as* learning when e-Portfolios serve as a classroom-based formative assessment tool.

Social Constructivism

Vygotsky (1986) proposed the theory of social constructivism, which emphasizes one's cognitive development as socially constructed. His theory is related to three major aspects of education, including the view of knowledge, the view of learning and the view of assessment, which dovetail with the qualities of e-Portfolios when applied formatively. Regarding the view of knowledge, social constructivism refers to how students make sense of learning through active participation in a community of practice. These participatory actions are likened to students' dynamic engagement in creating, compiling and showcasing multimodal artefacts in their e-Portfolios. Vygotsky further stated that teachers and students are advised to co-construct knowledge collaboratively, because linguistic knowledge and skills are externally mediated semiotic resources which go against the transmission model of instruction. Hence, knowledge co-construction becomes a key goal in e-Portfolio programmes, which promote the benefits of a community of practice in L2 learning – namely, task-based and/or cooperative learning approaches.

As to the view of learning, Vygotsky believed that students learn best if they work with a more capable other, for example, high-calibre peers, teachers, parents or caregivers. The acts of observing, interacting and learning from advanced peers are referred to as the Zone of Proximal Development, which is, by far, the most prominent tenet of social constructivism (Jones & Saville, 2016). To ensure effective L2 learning, scholars proposed that students need constant scaffolding if they were to identify their learning gaps with multiple sources of feedback. These socio-constructivist views of learning can be captured in e-Portfolio compilation processes, wherein teachers play the role of facilitators to support students' learning and students play the role of apprentices to master L2 skills. The social dynamics among students and other stakeholders enhance the students' uptake of coping strategies to close the learning gaps in the portfolio compilation process, including problem-solving and critical thinking skills (Dann, 2018).

About the view of assessment, social-constructivists emphasize the importance of evaluating learning processes more than learning products. They consider that language assessment is low stakes, collaborative, continuous and feedback-rich to facilitate regular review and adjustment of one's own L2 learning development. These beliefs are shared by most e-Portfolio advocates in their scholarship (see Lam, 2021a; Yancey, 2019). From social-constructivist perspectives, assessment tasks are supposed to be authentic and contextualized, which are relatable to students' life experiences and their frames of reference. Assessment should also be an integral part of L2 learning, so that self-assessment, peer assessment and self-reflection could become a rich repertoire of students' learning strategies that nurture their metacognitive capacity. Since e-Portfolios usually include the above three assessment events as key components, they may transform the assessment-as-measurement paradigm into the *assessment-as-inquiry* paradigm, which empowers students to be life-long learners, critical thinkers and independent team players (Serafini, 2000). The ensuing subsection reveals how assessment *for* learning characterizes the formative potential of e-Portfolios as a classroom-based assessment.

Assessment for Learning

Socio-constructivism and assessment *for* learning share a lot of commonalities. Assessment *for* learning refers to effective classroom teaching that supports students' learning, happening in real time and facilitating contingent classroom interactions (Allal, 2020). Similar to what most social-constructivists suggested, assessment *for* learning is interactive, dialogic, student centred and enquiry oriented, which is likely to enhance learner autonomy, classroom interactions with peers and the teacher and ongoing L2 learning development (Klenowski, 2009). Within the context of e-Portfolios, students are given multiple opportunities to revise and upgrade their works in progress owing to delayed scoring, whereas summative evaluation only takes place when the learning artefacts are deemed satisfactory for submission. Moreover, students are encouraged to create their artefacts to fulfil the learning outcomes as stipulated in the course/programme assessment rubrics. These digital artefacts can be validated by multimodal feedback and continuous self-reflection as reliable learning evidence. Because of that, students can celebrate the merits of assessment *for* learning epitomized in e-Portfolio assessment, including active learner engagement, learning as dialogic and development of skills to monitor learning (Jones, 2012). Although assessment *for* learning practices encapsulated in e-Portfolio programmes are chiefly formative, their pedagogical properties could help improve students' summative assessment results eventually. The following subsection links up assessment *for* learning and assessment *as* learning, in which the latter is a core component of e-Portfolios that fosters reflective thinking.

Assessment as Learning

Assessment *as* learning is a subset of assessment *for* learning. It is one form of formative assessment which enables students to take charge of their learning eagerly, critically and independently. As compared to assessment *for* learning, assessment *as* learning is considered personal, idiosyncratic and reflective, although at times it occurs in close collaboration with peers and teachers – namely, through peer assessments and guided instruction (Lam, 2018). Other assessment scholars state that assessment *as* learning could be an individual as well as a collaborative process, in which the teacher and students set goals, share assessment criteria and evaluate learning through dialogues and self- and peer-assessment tasks before students reflect upon their evidence of learning independently (Clark, 2012). Because assessment *as* learning emphasizes learner agency and metacognition, e-Portfolios provide students and teachers with a sustainable platform to carry out self-reflection and self-regulated learning. To reap the benefits of assessment *as* learning, it is suggested to teachers that they incorporate the elements of creation, curation and reflection into the e-Portfolio assessment process, so that students are likely to enhance their creativity, self-regulated capacity, agentic engagement and evaluative thinking ability throughout the decision-making processes in L2 learning. After all, students' metacognitive skills undergird the formative potential of e-Portfolio assessment. The next section describes the attributes, systems, types, advantages and limitations of e-Portfolio assessment.

Qualities of E-Portfolio Assessment

The attributes of e-Portfolio assessment align with its theoretical underpinnings as discussed in the above sections. Unlike its printed counterparts, e-Portfolio or e-Portfolio assessment is a new genre (a brand new discourse), requiring students and teachers alike to acquire another set of viewing/browsing, composing, inferring and grading experiences (Yancey, 1996). This is because e-Portfolio compilation expects learners to have a moderate level of digital literacy (e.g. ability to operate fundamental Web 2.0 application tools). Besides the mastery of technological skills, students need to create and organize relevant learning artefacts to fulfil the course/programme requirements.

Other significant attributes of e-Portfolios are interactivity, collaboration and reflection. Interactivity refers to a synchronous or asynchronous feedback environment, in which students interacting with students and teachers interacting with students provide each other with instant/delayed, multimodal feedback through forums, chat rooms, discussion groups, social networking sites, messaging apps (e.g. WhatsApp) and videoconferencing software (e.g. Microsoft Teams; Cummins & Davesne, 2009). Such interactive modes expedite peer communications, enhance instructional effectiveness and alleviate misunderstandings on certain challenging teaching points. Collaboration is about teachers' scaffolded instruction when students need initial input and guidance from a more capable other. Collaboration involves self-, peer- and teacher assessments throughout an e-Portfolio journey, in which students frequently interact with others via rubric sharing, goal setting, progress reviewing, and adjustment making. This collaborative mode is usually exhibited in the communicative language teaching methodology (Cheung, 2021). Reflection is one of the key elements of iterative e-Portfolio processes besides creation, curation and revision. E-Portfolios can connect teaching and assessment formatively through reflection, because the act of metacognition promotes deep learning, self-evaluative skills and learner independence in order that teaching and performing self-reflection become a central part of the designated English curriculum.

Since e-Portfolio assessment includes the elements of assessment *for/as* learning, it may direct teachers' and students' attentions from the outcomes of learning to the process of learning. Such a shift to the formative purpose of assessment, alongside delayed scoring, serves to provide a learning *space* for students to infer, select and enact multimodal feedback to improve their L2 development (Yancey, 2015). In a word, e-Portfolios are likely to balance the formative and summative purposes of assessment, especially when the latter tends to predominate in an exam-driven culture (i.e. e-Portfolios as a tool of large-scale standardized testing). E-Portfolios are also evidence based, transforming students' artefacts into systematic learning evidence by way of self-reflection and digital feedback. The process of validating learning evidence is crucial because it warrants a moderate to high level of validity and reliability of e-Portfolio assessment (Belgrad, 2013).

In assessment scholarship, there are three prevailing e-Portfolio systems and three common types of e-Portfolios. According to Yancey (2004), these three portfolio systems comprise the following: (a) online assessment systems, such as institutional portals, subscribed learning management systems or weblogs; (b) print versions uploaded – for instance, students type their works on Microsoft Word and then upload those files as digital archives; and (c) web-based portfolios, including social media (e.g. Facebook), customized e-Portfolio software (e.g. Seesaw) and open-source systems. Likewise, there are three types of e-Portfolios – namely, working, assessment and showcase e-Portfolios (Stefani et al., 2007). Working e-Portfolios enable students to monitor and review learning for improvement. They are inherently formative, usually not involving summative grades. They also provide students with continuous feedback, so it is longitudinal by design. Assessment e-Portfolios are mainly used for course/programme evaluations. They are graded and high stakes, generating feedback to students in the form of marks/grades/commentaries relating to rubrics and assessment outcomes. Yet, assessment e-Portfolios are usually short-term or one-off. Showcase e-Portfolios represent students' best abilities or performances. They are used for college admissions and job applications. This type of e-Portfolio is professional, personalized and highly technological (i.e. those in architecture and journalism).

The advantages of e-Portfolios are numerous. First, e-Portfolios are compact, as they occupy almost no physical storage space. Second, they are conveniently editable and revisable, and easy for sharing both online and offline. Third, they are extremely accessible and sustainable as long as learners/users pay the Wi-Fi and software subscription fees. After all, e-Portfolios are well known for their longevity. Fourth, e-Portfolio compilation assists students in developing a sense of achievement and improves their self-efficacy beliefs in learning. Fifth, the multimodal feature of e-Portfolios caters for learner diversity and promotes creativity. Because students may be restrained by the conventional format of portfolios, which emphasize literacy skills, e-Portfolios permit them to express themselves through graphics, sounds, motions and images in lieu of writing. Speaking of limitations, teachers may find it taxing to verify student authorship owing to the collaborative nature of e-Portfolios. Second, grading e-Portfolios and constructing rubrics are cognitively demanding when compared to grading students' single essays. Third, the protection of student privacy remains a thorny issue, since students' reflective pieces and their biographies will become public once published online. Fourth, certain template-driven e-Portfolio tools are likely to restrict autonomy in L2 learning by requiring students to comply with a set of key performance indices (Torrance, 2012). Fifth, the timeliness of feedback provision (i.e. frequency, focus and medium) remains a cause for concern, especially when teachers are already overloaded with heavy pedagogical and administrative commitments. Sixth, in certain less-privileged education contexts, the infrastructure could be absent and students and teachers may lack basic training in developing e-Portfolios; thus, the use of technology would interfere with test validity. Regardless of these caveats, e-Portfolios are still considered a promising tool to support language teaching and assessment during the pandemic. To better understand the formative properties of e-Portfolios, we now look into two classroom vignettes and identify how two teachers experimented with their e-Portfolio approaches.

Two Classroom Vignettes

To contextualize this section, we introduce the role of English instruction in Hong Kong school settings. Chinese and English are official languages in the territory. Both languages are compulsory subjects in K-12 education. Although Hong Kong is considered a bilingual city, English enjoys a higher status and is used as a medium of instruction in nearly one-third of all primary-level and secondary-level schools, including top-tier, government-funded, private and international ones. In normal English lessons, literacy and oracy skills are taught, but teachers tend to emphasize literacy skills and grammar teaching owing to an exam-oriented culture. E-learning has been promoted by the Education Bureau for two decades, but it is largely limited to the use of e-books, PowerPoint slides and game-based learning apps. Teachers and students had rarely experienced online teaching and learning before the pandemic, because like elsewhere in the world, face-to-face teaching was the norm. Besides, e-assessment is neither frequently practised nor considered practical due to a lack of expertise, resources, training and communal consensus, not to mention the issues of fairness and proctoring in such a complex undertaking.

To complicate the scenario further, class suspension in Hong Kong schools occurred four times because of the large-scale student protests and four waves of the Covid-19 pandemic between November 2019 and April 2021. The first class suspension happened in mid-November 2019 for a week; the second between the first week of February and late May 2020; the third between early July and the third week of September 2020; and the fourth from the second week of December 2020 till the second week of March 2021. Then, school reopening was in stages. After the fourth wave, only one-third of students in each school were allowed to have half-day face-to-face classes. Following the Easter holiday break (the second week of April 2021), also at the time of writing, two-thirds of students in each school were permitted to resume normal classes. If schools want to reopen completely, teachers have to get mandatory Covid-19 tests once every two weeks to guarantee they are coronavirus free. If one confirmed case is reported, school premises have to close down for fourteen days and close-contact persons need to undergo mandatory testing and quarantine. As of mid-September 2021, the Education Bureau allows schools to resume whole-day face-to-face classes, provided that over 70% of the total number of teaching/non-teaching staff members (two jabs) and students (one jab aged twelve to seventeen years and two jabs aged over eighteen years) in a school get vaccinated. Against this backdrop, we look into how two novice teachers, Manson and Jackie (pseudonyms) initiated the e-Portfolio approach in their classrooms.

Manson

Manson is a locally born Cantonese and received education in Hong Kong. He has taught English in a secondary school with Chinese as the medium of instruction for two years. His students' academic abilities range from average to slightly below average, and their English proficiency is approximately between B1 and B2 levels with reference to the Common European Framework of Reference (CEFR). Regardless of their limited proficiency, the students are willing to learn English from Manson, especially when they are preparing for the standardized school-leaving exam one year later. Prior to this research project, Manson has learnt about the basic principles of e-Portfolios from his university study. He also kept a paper-based portfolio for his English compositions, notes and exercises when he was a senior secondary school student. Although his own portfolio experience was not pleasant (using portfolio as a folder rather than a learning companion), he was passionate about trying out e-Portfolios, especially when class suspension got in the way of daily teaching and learning.

At first, the rationale for Manson's e-Portfolio programme was to facilitate assignment collection during class suspension. From February to May 2020, Manson attempted to adopt the process writing approach when he taught the most frequently tested genre – argumentative essays – on Zoom. Since his Grade 11 students were not capable, Manson required them to draft one paragraph of the essay per day and upload it on Google Classroom before the class ended. By so doing, he could check on students' mastery of the target genre almost instantly, since he could give students written feedback within the same day. After students received his feedback, they would revise the text before they proceeded to the next paragraph on the following day. Manson emphasized that students felt less embarrassed when receiving individual electronic feedback as compared to the collective feedback that he used to present in front of the whole class. E-Portfolios expedited teacher–student communications during distance teaching and enabled Manson to monitor students' writing progress in a timely manner.

Although e-Portfolios captured the essence of formative assessment – namely, multi-drafting, synchronous feedback and text revision – Manson thought that they were not able to replace summative assessment. It was because in his school, Google Classroom was only regarded as a digital storage platform for daily homework and other formative tasks. Conventional in-person exams eventually took place in late June 2020 after the school reopened. Manson added that the principal did not encourage teachers to conduct any formal, graded e-assessments on Zoom or on Google Classroom for fear of cheating, plagiarizing and ghostwriting. Thus far, no online exams were held in Manson's school and nearby secondary schools. Despite the advantages of utilizing Google Classroom as e-Portfolios, Manson admitted that during online teaching, students were reticent and there were fewer interactions to promote formative assessment, for example, peer feedback. According to our observations, Manson designed lots of engaging tasks with diverse online tools, such as Mentimeter, Kahoot and Breakout Room on Zoom. Nonetheless, the student–student and student–teacher interactions remained inadequate.

When piloting e-Portfolios, Manson encountered two challenges. One was a lack of computer training. Manson told us that the information technology team in his school did not offer in-house training to teachers. His knowledge and skills about the application of e-Portfolios for teaching and assessment were mostly self-taught. At times, he consulted his former university friends when he came across some technical problems. Despite this, the school offered each student an iPad to facilitate distance learning. Another challenge was incessant interruptions caused by four class suspensions over one and a half years. Manson recounted that after each suspension, it took students almost ten days to get used to daily classroom routines, for example, submission of classwork, homework and other written tasks in hard copies. In fact, these challenges motivated Manson to continue with e-Portfolio assessment even when face-to-face teaching resumed in March 2021, because he required students to compile all quizzes, worksheets and composition drafts on Google Classroom for the purposes of ongoing learning review and book inspection. Generally, Manson's students were positive about e-Portfolios, especially for the storage and progress check purposes. They also became more computer literate as they learnt how to edit their writings online.

Jackie

Like Manson, Jackie was raised and brought up locally. She obtained a bachelor's degree in teacher education. Jackie has taught English in a school with English as the medium of instruction (categorized as a high-ranking school) for two years. Jackie's students, mostly in Grades 8 and 9, were unmotivated to learn English, although their English proficiency was equivalent to the B2 level of CEFR. Jackie said that her students had low assignment submission rates and performed poorly in online quizzes during the pandemic. Jackie had not heard about e-Portfolios until she joined this research project. She felt that e-Portfolios were user-friendly and pedagogically viable, facilitating students' organization of learning materials and teachers' supervision of students' learning developments. Jackie analogized e-Portfolios to 'a record of learning progress', which helped students review, reflect and adjust their learning. Albeit impressed by the benefits of e-Portfolios, Jackie thought that students might suffer from information overload because they had to upload or organize too many files, folders, topics, learning tasks and assessment types.

In Jackie's school, Google Classroom was adopted as the default learning management system. Jackie's e-Portfolio programme was built upon Google Classroom by alternating between the sorting of learning materials by 'types' (contents) and then by 'cycles' (timeline). In her first attempt (February to May 2020), she set up the e-Portfolio system on Google Classroom by organizing the teaching and learning materials (those for flipped learning) by types – namely, reading, writing, integrated skills, grammar, language arts and so on. However, at the start of September 2020, one senior colleague told Jackie to re-organize the instructional materials by cycles in order that students might find it convenient to upload and access their learning tasks. Although Jackie firmly believed that sorting by task types was more organized than sorting by teaching cycles, she eventually followed her colleague's idea. Interestingly, students preferred materials being sorted by cycles because they were forgetful and it was so much faster for them to retrieve their assignments by dates.

Contrary to face-to-face instruction, Jackie claimed that she could include e-learning elements into e-Portfolio assessment, for example, Quizlet (a web-based learning app), Google Forms (a survey administration tool) and Kahoot. These digital tools were likely to arouse students' interests in learning. Jackie told us that during in-person teaching, she had no time to apply these interactive learning apps in the lesson since she was fully occupied with administrative duties and there were limited face-to-face contact hours (around thirty minutes for actual instruction after handling classroom management matters). While Jackie was in favour of e-Portfolios, she had concerns about the mode of written feedback. When providing online feedback, Jackie felt that she could only compose a statement or two next to students' paragraphs on the Google Forms. Such online marking experience was nothing compared to handwritten feedback, in which Jackie could circle, underline or highlight students' errors in an elaborated manner. She stated that on-screen marking could not replace conventional paper-and-pen marking.

Notwithstanding the modality of feedback, Jackie remained affirmative about the use of e-Portfolios. She was confident in managing the e-Portfolio software through learning by doing. Since she considered herself a tech-savvy teacher, she took the lead in discussing how to manage the e-Portfolio system with her fellow colleagues. After a one-year trial, Jackie was rather proficient in using Google Classroom. However, she realized that e-Portfolios had drawbacks too – namely, with respect to insufficient synchronous teacher–student interactions and a long wait time for students to collect her feedback. This was the reason why she continued to explore e-Portfolios even after the school reopened. In order to implement e-Portfolio assessment smoothly, Jackie reckoned that teachers needed to understand the overall design of e-Portfolio tools – that is, the interface or function which could enhance student levels of engagement and motivation. She further added that giving clear instructions to students concerning how to operate the e-Portfolio tool was indispensable. It was because at the outset, Jackie's students had difficulties when managing their e-Portfolio accounts like uploading files on the right folders.

After describing Manson's and Jackie's vignettes, we evaluate their e-Portfolio approaches with reference to our tripartite framework created for this chapter.

Critical Evaluation of Classroom Vignettes

With minimal technological support, Manson and Jackie innovated process writing and interactive e-learning apps, respectively, through Google Classroom. They involved students in online classes and assisted them to make sense of their language learning (Manson's class – genres of argumentative essays and Jackie's class – vocabulary items of the pandemic). Manson and Jackie encouraged students to learn from a more capable other (either their classmates or the teacher) via various peer assessment tasks, albeit not very effective, because some students remained taciturn. Although both teachers believed in the benefits of process approaches to language learning and assessment, they still attached great importance to the territory-wide school-leaving exam (in Manson's case) and the syllabus of the internal final exam (in Jackie's case). Despite being resource deprived and exam driven, Manson and Jackie confidently followed the socio-constructivist principles in their application of e-Portfolio assessment – namely, knowledge co-construction and the Zone of Proximal Development.

Teaching-wise, Manson and Jackie exhibited sound assessment *for* learning practices, such as delayed summative scoring, enhancement of e-Portfolio accessibility (sorting materials by time) and provision of timely/continuous feedback. Speaking of feedback, both gave students feedback promptly. For instance, Manson provided students with online feedback within the same day, whereas Jackie wrote detailed commentary on Google Forms. Irrespective of these good practices, both teachers chiefly resorted to the online written feedback. In fact, they could have considered other feedback modalities – namely, auditory (podcasts) or visual (augmented reality clips). Although Manson's and Jackie's online teaching was interactive and student centred, the format of their e-Portfolio programmes remained top-down and managerial, leaving students little room to be creative, independent and reflective. The role of teacher was reduced to an affectionate commander, whereas the role of student, to a content contributor. To look closely at the e-Portfolio designs, the two teachers underscored the technical aspect of e-Portfolios (i.e. portfolio management) more than their learning aspect (i.e. how to facilitate students to compile, curate and reflect on evidence of learning). Such a *technician* view of language assessment should gradually shift to a *specialist* view if teachers aspire to develop a sustainable e-Portfolio culture (Lam, 2021b).

Regarding assessment *as* learning, Manson and Jackie paid less attention to this significant area, because their e-Portfolio programmes emphasized record keeping and database learning management as opposed to ownership and metacognition. Manson's and Jackie's Google Classrooms were developed against an audit culture, where both teachers and their students were accountable to the principals rather than to themselves. In other words, students constructed the e-Portfolios in fulfilment of external coursework requirements. They had no ownership of their creations even though they spent so much time and energy in organizing their artefacts. Involving students in early decision-making processes and negotiating with them about the programme content could, no doubt, enhance ownership in e-Portfolio assessment. Likewise, it is beneficial to persuade students to self-evaluate and then self-reflect upon their language learning, since reflective practices undergird the entire e-Portfolio approach. The act of metacognition (self-assessment or self-reflection) plays a crucial role in enhancing learner agency in the e-Portfolio journey, provided that students (not their teachers) are at the centre of the teaching, learning and assessment process (Lee, 2016). In the penultimate section, we discuss the post-pandemic lessons learnt from the two vignettes.

Post-Pandemic Lessons Learnt

On evaluation of the two vignettes, we found that three post-pandemic lessons were learnt: (a) refocusing on the potentials of e-Portfolios, (b) upgrading of teachers' e-assessment literacy, and (c) sustaining the applications of e-Portfolios. For (a), teachers may redesign their e-Portfolio pedagogy in such a way that more collaborative tasks are included to facilitate teacher–student and student–student co-construction of knowledge. Peer learning and cooperative learning are prioritized in order to promote a community of practice and the Zone of Proximal Development among students. By so doing, learning tasks could be transformed into assessment tasks, which target creative, analytical problem-solving and evaluative skills. These higher-order thinking skills are likely to advance students' learning. To achieve assessment *for/as* learning by e-Portfolios, dynamic use of multimodal feedback, be it self-, peer or teacher feedback, should be adopted to bridge the learning gaps as identified by students during the process of e-Portfolio compilation. After all, the giving, receiving and enacting feedback for learning within an interactive online environment is a complicated undertaking, which takes time and effort to acquire. Integrating a self-reflection component into e-Portfolio assessment is essential, given that self-reflection fosters student metacognition and learning-how-to-learn capacity.

For (b), Manson and Jackie were confident and proficient in delivering their English lessons. In remote teaching, other than sound instructional approach, teachers may need up-to-date and regular information technology training in e-assessment in general and e-Portfolio assessment in particular. Currently, most teachers have no trouble in conducting online lessons with popular web-based videoconferencing tools, such as Zoom, Microsoft Teams, Google Meet and so on. Nonetheless, teachers may not know how to use those common tools and other learning management systems to assess students' learning both formatively and summatively, especially the latter. Giving synchronous feedback via various e-Portfolio software tools (e.g. Seesaw, Schoology or Padlet) requires the uptake of hands-on experiences as well as technological principles. On this note, teachers are expected to develop their e-assessment literacy by drawing reference to the technological, pedagogical and content knowledge framework with a minor alteration to the last dimension – content knowledge to *language assessment* knowledge.

For (c), during the pandemic, e-Portfolios seem to be a viable option for conducting remote teaching, learning and assessment. Although we have no idea when things will return to the normal, sustained use of e-Portfolios in the post-pandemic world is feasible, considering the fact that most e-Portfolio hosts, like Google Classroom, are handy and user-friendly tools that teachers and students can use to continue language teaching and learning without any interruptions. In fact, e-Portfolios could be flexibly adopted alongside face-to-face instruction and assessment, because in-person contact hours remain inadequate. E-Portfolios are likely to serve multiple functions after school: for example, online tutorials for exam preparation, additional consultation meetings, post-assessment feedback sessions or make-up classes due to bad weather or natural disasters. To empower students' life-long learning development, e-Portfolios could serve as an ideal site to help them monitor their language learning holistically and longitudinally even after they graduate, as long as they compile, curate and reflect on their e-Portfolios sustainably.

Conclusion

In closing, e-Portfolios can be used as pedagogical and evaluative tools during the pandemic and post-pandemic periods. They are considered a technology-enabled assessment tool to support classroom-based formative assessment. If used appropriately and proficiently, e-Portfolios are likely to enhance students' motivation, creativity, academic performance and metacognition. In times of the Covid-19 pandemic, classroom suspensions have seriously interrupted teaching, learning and assessment in one way or another. E-Portfolios served as a timely and viable alternative to continue students' learning, although most authentic classroom communications came to a halt. Based on our two vignettes, not only were Manson and Jackie surviving Covid-19 by utilizing e-Portfolio assessment, but they were also adapting it by fine-tuning their e-Portfolio programmes to cater for students' learning needs, to fulfil school expectations and to match their beliefs and personalized pedagogical styles. Undeniably, e-Portfolios have the potential to upgrade first- and second-language instruction, but their full application in Hong Kong and beyond has not been achieved still. Despite uncertainties, there is no doubt that the pandemic does act as a catalyst to promote wider experimentations of e-Portfolio pedagogy and assessment.

Acknowledgements

This work was funded by the Language Fund under Research and Development Projects 2021–22 of the Standing Committee on Language Education and Research (SCOLAR), Hong Kong SAR. The project reference number is (EDB(LE)/P&R/EL/203/12).

References

Allal, L. (2020). Assessment and the co-regulation of learning in the classroom. *Assessment in Education: Principles, Policy & Practice, 27*(4), 332–49. https://doi.org/10.1080/0969594X.2019.1609411.

Belgrad, S. F. (2013). Portfolios and e-portfolios: Student reflection, self-assessment, and goal-setting in the learning process. In J. H. McMillan (Ed.), *Sage handbook of research on classroom assessment* (pp. 331–46). Sage. http://dx.doi.org/10.4135/9781452218 649.n19.

Cheung, A. (2021). Language teaching during a pandemic: A case study of Zoom use by a secondary ESL teacher in Hong Kong. *RELC Journal*. doi:10.1177/0033688220981784.

Clark, I. (2012). Formative assessment: Assessment is for self-regulated learning. *Educational Psychology Review, 24*(2), 205–49. https://doi.org/10.1007/s10 648-011-9191-6.

Cummins, P. W., & Davesne, C. (2009). Using electronic portfolios for second language assessment. *The Modern Language Journal, 93*, 848–67. https://doi.org/10.1111/j.154 0-4781.2009.00977.x.

Dann, R. (2018). *Developing feedback for pupil learning*. Routledge. https://doi.org/10.4324/9781315564210.

Jones, J. (2012). Portfolios as 'learning companions' for children and a means to support and assess language learning in the primary school. *Education 3-13, 40*(4), 401–16. https://doi.org/10.1080/03004279.2012.691374.

Jones, N., & Saville, N. (2016). *Learning oriented assessment: A systemic approach*. Cambridge University Press.

Klenowski, V. (2009). Assessment for learning revisited: An Asia-Pacific perspective. *Assessment in Education: Principles, Policy and Practice, 16*(3), 263–268. https://doi.org/10.1080/09695940903319646.

Lam, R. (2018). Understanding assessment as learning in writing classrooms: The case of portfolio assessment. *Iranian Journal of Language Teaching Research, 6*(3), 19–36. https://dx.doi.org/10.30466/ijltr.2018.120599.

Lam, R. (2021a). E-Portfolios: What we know, what we don't, and what we need to know. *RELC Journal*. https://doi.org/10.1177/0033688220974102.

Lam, R. (2021b). Using ePortfolios to promote assessment of, for, as learning in EFL writing. *The European Journal of Applied Linguistics and TEFL, 10*(1), 101–20.

Lee, I. (2016). Putting students at the centre of classroom L2 writing assessment. *The Canadian Modern Language Review, 72*(2), 258–80. https://doi.org/10.3138/cmlr.2802.

Moorhouse, B. L., & Beaumont, A. M. (2020). Utilizing video conferencing software to teach young language learners in Hong Kong during the COVID-19 class suspensions. *TESOL Journal, 11*(3). https://doi.org/10.1002/tesj.545.

Reich, J. (2021). Ed tech's failure during the pandemic, and what comes after. *Phi Delta Kappan, 102*(6), 20–4. https://doi.org/10.1177/0031721721998149.

Santibañez, L., & Guarino, C. M. (2021). The effects of absenteeism on academic and social-emotional outcomes: Lessons for COVID-19. *Educational Researcher, 50*(6), 392–400. https://doi.org/10.3102/0013189X21994488.

Serafini, F. (2000). Three paradigms of assessment: Measurement, procedure, and inquiry. *The Reading Teacher, 54*(4), 384–93.

Stefani, L., Mason, R., & Pegler, C. (2007). *The educational potential of e-Portfolios: Supporting personal development and reflective learning*. Routledge. https://doi.org/10.4324/9780203961292.

Torrance, H. (2012). Formative assessment at the crossroads: Conformative, deformative and transformative assessment. *Oxford Review of Education, 38*(3), 323–42. https://doi.org/10.1080/03054985.2012.689693.

Vygotsky, L. S. (1986). *Thought and language*. MIT Press.

Yancey, K. B. (1996). The electronic portfolio: Shifting paradigms. *Computers and Composition, 13*, 259–62. https://doi.org/10.1016/S8755-4615(96)90014-6.

Yancey, K. B. (2004). Postmodernism, palimpsest, and portfolios: Theoretical issues in the representation of student work. *College Composition and Communication*, *55*(4), 738–61. https://doi.org/10.37514/PER-B.2013.0490.2.01.

Yancey, K. B. (2015). Grading ePortfolios: Tracing two approaches, their advantages, and their disadvantages. *Theory Into Practice*, *54*, 301–8. https://doi.org/10.1080/00405841.2015.1076693.

Yancey, K. B. (Ed.). (2019). *ePortfolio as curriculum: Models and practices for developing students' ePortfolio literacy*. Stylus. https://lccn.loc.gov/2018033993s.

14

Keeping Them Honest: Assessing Learning in Online and Digital Contexts

Peter Davidson and Christine Coombe

Introduction

The Covid-19 pandemic at the beginning of 2020 brought about a dramatic shift in education as teaching was unexpectedly moved online for many teachers and students with little or no advanced planning. The abrupt move to online teaching saw a concomitant move to online assessment, which brought about an array of additional challenges for teachers. One of the major challenges of online assessment is how to mitigate against academic misconduct in order to ensure that the assessments we implement are valid and reliable. Opportunities for students to engage in academic dishonesty such as cheating, copying, plagiarizing or getting additional outside help from others are exacerbated in an online testing environment, potentially compromising the validity and reliability of an assessment. The purpose of this chapter is to discuss how we can design and implement assessment tasks in order to limit the ability of students to cheat and get outside help and thus maintain an acceptable level of validity and reliability. Specifically, we will look at how different test task types, and the choice of exam topic, can limit the extent to which a student can cheat in an exam and get external assistance on assignments. In the final part of this chapter, we will look at how academic dishonesty can be minimized, and perhaps even eliminated, when taking an online test.

Academic Misconduct

Academic dishonesty and academic misconduct are obviously not new phenomena. As long as there have been tests, there have been students who have sought to boost their test scores through mendacious means. As noted by Coombe (2021) and K12 Academics (n.d.), thousands of years ago, cheating was widespread on the Chinese civil service exam, and if caught, it carried the death penalty for both the examiner and the examinee!! According to K12 Academics (n.d.), academic misconduct can include the following types of fraudulent behaviour:

- Plagiarism: The adoption of original creations of another author without due acknowledgment.
- Fabrication: The falsification of data, information or citations.
- Deception: Providing false information to an instructor concerning a formal academic exercise, for example, giving a false excuse for missing a deadline.
- Cheating: Any attempt to obtain assistance in a formal academic exercise.
- Bribery or paid services: Giving assignment answers or test answers for money.
- Sabotage: Acting to prevent others from completing their work.
- Professorial misconduct: Professorial acts that are academically fraudulent.
- Impersonation: Getting another person to take the exam for you.

Even when we proctored exams face-to-face, students engaged in academically dishonest behaviour, such as hacking into the computer system where the exam was stored and downloading the exam, communicating and colluding with one another during the exam to share answers, accessing the internet during the exam to get answers and/or additional information, using external devices such as mobile phones and smart watches to get answers and additional information, accessing documents and Apps stored on their computer; getting someone else to take their exam for them remotely, and hiring professional agencies to do their assignments and/or assessment tasks for them.

Bushweller (1999) cites some disturbing research on the prevalence of cheating among American high school students. Seventy per cent of the students in this study admitted to cheating on a test at least once, and 95% of those same students were never caught. Dick et al. (2003) cite twelve studies on cheating with mostly college students, which revealed that 75% of college and university students admitted to cheating at least once during their studies. In many of these studies, cheating and academically dishonest behaviours were found to increase with the age of the student at least through to the age of twenty-five years old. As far back as thirty years ago, student cheating was viewed as a significant factor in the university classroom (Cizek, 1999; Michaels & Miethe, 1989; Whitley, 1998) and has been considered a serious problem on university campuses for over a hundred years (Anderson, 1998, as cited in Watson & Sottile, 2010).

If students cheated when they were taking an exam right under our eyes in front of us, imagine what they are doing at home without teacher supervision. Several studies have been conducted on the use of electronic devices and the internet and their relationship to cheating in the college and university environment (Sheard et al., 2003; Dick et al., 2003; Roberts et al., 1997). With the advent of Covid-19 and so many students being required to study and take exams at home, the potential for students to engage in academic dishonesty during assessments has increased exponentially (Kanchan, 2019b; Newton, 2020) as cheating has entered the digital age. According to Watson and Sottile (2010), 'Students today are now part of the "copy paste" generation in which dishonest behavior is only a mouse click away' (p. 2). Opportunities for students to cheat, copy, plagiarize or get additional outside help are clearly exacerbated in an online teaching environment.

Wiley (n.d.) reports that 93% of teachers feel that students are more likely to cheat online than in person. King et al. (2009) found that 73.6% of students felt that it was easier to cheat in an online rather than on a traditional course. Similarly, Watson and Sottile (2010) found that 74% of students found that it was easier to cheat on an online test than on a face-to-face test. It was also found in distance learning research that students who 'feel more distant' are more likely to cheat (Burgoon et al., 2003). In fact, in the *Chronicle of Higher Education*, Jeffrey Young, a professor from the University of Michigan who teaches a course for Coursera, a popular online education platform, states that even students taking free online courses offered by Coursera have reported dozens of incidents of plagiarism, even though the courses bear no academic credit (Bosch, 2012).

The question is, what, if anything, can we do to thwart students' attempts to engage in academic misconduct during their online tests and assessments?

Do We Need to Have Online Exams at All?

Before we consider some approaches to mitigating against academic misconduct in online assessment, we first need to ask ourselves, is it absolutely essential to have an online exam in the first place? Well before Covid-19 struck, Weir (2005) observed that 'the last decade of the twentieth century saw a general decline in the prestige of psychometric, statistically-driven approaches to testing' (p. 56). In a recent polemic article, Staton (2021) reports on a number of examination boards, schools and universities that are doing away with exams altogether, replacing them with more effective means of measuring student performance. Rather than having an online exam where students may engage in academic dishonesty, it may be more constructive to do away with midterm and final exams altogether. They can be replaced with assignments and projects that make it far more difficult for students to cheat than when they are at home with nobody watching them take their online assessments.

For a number of years now, many teachers, academics and test writers have questioned the value of exams as an effective means of assessing students' learning. There has been a move towards authentic assessment which endeavours to replicate in an assessment the type of tasks that students will likely be required to accomplish in real-world settings (Davidson, 2009). As espoused by Lund (1997), 'Authentic assessments require the presentation of worthwhile and/or meaningful tasks that are designed to be representative of performance in the field … and approximate something the person would actually be required to do in a given setting' (p. 25). Davidson and Coombe (2010) maintain that authentic assessment has greater construct validity, content validity and consequential validity than traditional type testing. They further contend that authentic assessment can assess higher-order thinking skills, is contextualized and meaningful, has a positive washback effect and is a better predictor of future performance than traditional assessment.

The usefulness of midterm and final exams has also been called into question with the recognition that assessment can be used to facilitate learning (Davidson & Mandalios, 2009) and with the development of learning-oriented assessment (LOA). An LOA framework recognizes that, in addition to measuring students' performance, another crucial function of assessment is to facilitate learning. As noted by Carless

(2009), 'For all assessments whether predominantly summative or formative in function a key aim is to promote productive student learning' (p. 80). Cambridge Assessment English (n.d.) note that LOA emphasizes that all assessment should contribute in some way to both the effectiveness of learning and the evaluation of learning outcomes, a theme echoed by Saville (2013), who proposes that LOA is a concept that prioritizes and situates learning at the heart of every assessment context. For Purpura (2014), 'An LOA approach to assessment recognizes the symbiotic relationships among external standards, curriculum, instruction, learning, and assessment, and is concerned with the role that these synergies play in understanding learner performance, engagement, learning processes, and the attainment of learning success.' Similarly, Carroll (2017) proposes that LOA should be viewed as a framework which recognizes the dynamic connection between teaching, learning and assessment in order to promote learning.

Even before Covid-19 and the massive migration to online teaching and assessment, the move towards authentic assessment and LOA, both began to make teachers and test writers query the role of exams and the emphasis that should be placed on them. In online assessment where issues of academic dishonesty are exacerbated and test reliability can easily be compromised, we really do need to ask ourselves whether we need to have exams and consider other viable assessment task types.

From a practical perspective, it is often easier to cheat or engage in academically dishonest behaviours in online assessments since the students are not technically 'seen' by the teacher or assessor. This scenario often increases a student's temptation to cheat. Another reason for this temptation is that quite frankly, students are often much more savvy about technology than their teachers, and many are fully aware of the potential for using computers or other technologies for cheating (Rowe, 2004). It is for these reasons and others that we devote the next section to discussing how to mitigate against and even eliminate cheating and academically dishonest behaviours in our students.

Mitigating against Cheating through Assessment Task Types

There are a number of strategies that teachers and administrators can employ to make cheating more difficult for students. One of the most effective ways to mitigate against academic dishonesty on assessments is through the choice of the assessment task types we use. In the classroom, one technique is to require students to complete longer assessment task types that require the teacher to check multiple drafts and provide feedback. This makes cheating and getting outside help more difficult (Harrison, 2020). Such assessment task types may include the following:

- Long answer questions (LAQs)
- Paragraph answers
- Essays
- Projects
- Reports

- Research assignments
- Case studies
- Scenario-based assessment with multiple tasks
- Personalized portfolios
- Pair assessment
- Group assessment
- Presentations

In an exam, avoid or limit those short objective assessment task types that are typically found on tests and exams such as multiple-choice questions (MCQs), true/false questions, matching questions, and gap-fill questions, as these types of questions make cheating easier. Rather, ask students to answer LAQs, paragraph questions and essay questions that cannot be easily copied by other students. Another recommendation we have is to make the online exam an open book exam. Because students in an open book test are able to access their notes and use the internet, you can make the exam more challenging by increasing the amount or types of information you would like students to include on their assessment. You might even consider converting this open book exam into a take home exam and allow students to use their notes as well as information from secondary sources depending on the level of students you have and the types of courses you teach. If you do have to use some objectively scored test items like the ones cited above on your tests, make sure you use functions of computer-based testing to prevent or minimize cheating, like the randomization feature where you can mix up or randomize the order of questions as they appear on the test as well as the randomization of the response options that appear in MCQs. The creation of item banks to make it possible for students taking the same exam to have parallel versions of that exam is also a recommended strategy.

Mitigating against Cheating through Testing Topics

Another method that can be used by teachers to reduce the likelihood of students getting outside help on assessments is to personalize and localize the topics of the assignments. For example, you could personalize a nutrition assignment by asking students to track and evaluate their own weekly dietary intake. They could be required to take photos of the different meals they eat throughout the day. This would make it difficult to find such an assignment on the internet which they could copy and paste. It would also make it difficult for someone else to do this assignment for them.

An example of localizing a topic for a business report would be a focus on the problems of congestion in the parking lots of the school or university where the students study. Students could be required to identify the extent of traffic congestion at different parking lots and come up with solutions to overcome the problem. Again, finding such a ready-made assignment on the internet would be virtually impossible, and it would be difficult for an outsider who was not familiar with your educational context to write such an assignment for a student.

Yet another assignment that both personalizes and localizes the assessment task was used in a basic research methods course which focused on the conceptualization, development, administration and analysis of a survey on a topic that interested students. Five localized topics were shared with students, and their first task was to select a topic that appealed to them and their group members. The topics they were provided with were relatively general, and it was their responsibility to narrow them down before their project began.

Mitigating against Cheating in Online Exams

We would strongly recommend using an online proctoring company to mitigate against cheating in an online exam. We have heard of many cases of teachers admirably trying to manage an online exam themselves, getting students to record themselves taking an exam using their cell phones and unsuccessfully attempting to monitor them all. It is just not possible or feasible for teachers to oversee all of their students taking an exam effectively using this low-tech approach. Fortunately, there are a multitude of companies that provide online proctoring services, including Eklavvya, Examity, Honorlock, Mercer | Mettl, Proctor360, ProctorCam (Pearson), ProctorFree, Proctorio, ProctorU, ProV, PSI, Questionmark and Respondus. The best online proctoring companies will adhere to the guidelines discussed in what follows (Kanchan, 2019a; Cluskey et al., n.d.).

Use Stringent Online ID Authentication

When students take an exam at home, it is easy for them to get an impersonator to take the exam on their behalf. To mitigate against this, it is essential to employ multiple, rigorous online ID authentications before the exam begins. This can be accomplished using a live proctor to verify photo ID against the person taking the exam, or can be more effectively achieved by the computer using facial recognition tools, biometric tests, keystroke authentication and asking questions to confirm the identity of the test taker.

Use a Secure Browser

When implementing an online exam, the use of a Secure Browser is an essential step in mitigating against cheating. A secure browser makes it more difficult for test takers to cheat because it has the potential to do the following:

- It can disable ports for external devices so that test takers cannot access information contained on flash drives or other external devices.
- It can block internet browsing so that test takers cannot access the internet to obtain information or search for answers, or contact each other to ask for answers. If the exam does require test takers to access certain apps or websites, these can be pre-defined and whitelisted to allow test takers to access them.

- It can block the use of unauthorized software so test takers cannot open programs to obtain information that can help them answer questions.
- It can restrict navigation control so that test takers can only answer the questions and not do anything else.
- It can deny test takers access to keyboard shortcuts, copy and paste and so on so that they cannot share questions and answers with one another.
- It can disable screen capture, screen recording, screen sharing and screen mirroring so that test takers cannot share questions and answers with one another or get outside help to answer questions.
- It can disable the printer so that test takers cannot print out the exam, which helps to keep the exam more secure and not in the public domain.

As we can see above, using a secure browser can significantly inhibit a test taker's ability to cheat in an online exam. However, as a stand-alone measure, using a secure browser is not sufficient to stop test takers from engaging in academic misconduct. Test takers can still access resources on other devices or use printed material to copy from. Consequently, additional measures are required to thwart test takers' ability to cheat in an online exam.

Use Mobile Phone Prevention Technology

Mobile phone usage during an online exam is a huge problem. According to a study conducted by McAfee (2017), 'Almost half of students (47%) claim to have seen or heard of another student using a connected device in the classroom to cheat on an exam, quiz, project or other assignment – with 21% admitting to doing it themselves.' Mobile phone prevention technology blocks test takers from using their mobile phones and other devices during an online exam. It can detect any device which a test taker is logged into during an online exam and shows signs of activity, such as opening a web browser, adding another layer of security to stop students from cheating during an online exam.

Use Test Leak Prevention Technology

Back in the Spring 2018 semester, a dean of one of the faculties in a local university sent an email thirty minutes before the final exam was to commence notifying faculty members about a serious exam leak. He informed faculty that a live exam had been compromised and the final exam and all of its answers had been leaked. He said that he had just downloaded these supposedly secure exam materials from the students' WhatsApp page, where he was moonlighting as a student. Suffice it to say that that particular final exam was not run that day. When students were asked about this, they said it was incredibly easy for them to hack into the system to access their exams. One student boasted that her eight-year-old brother had done it for her. Unfortunately, this was not an isolated incident, as there are many instances of people hacking into systems where exams are stored and making these available. In 2015, hackers downloaded the TOEFL test in China and sold it online (Siqi, 2015; Wei, 2015). Pednekar (2017) reports that in India, five major exams were leaked on WhatsApp in five days. So clearly there is a need to employ test leak prevention technology. Test leak prevention technology (see, e.g. Honorlock) scans the internet to report, block or remove websites that contain test questions and answers, providing yet another level of online exam security.

Use an Online Proctor

Another crucial method to significantly reduce cheating during an online exam is to use an online proctor that allows teachers to monitor their students while they are taking the exam, or it records them while they are taking the exam, allowing the teacher to go back and watch the recording if required. Some online proctoring services not only record students taking the exam, but also record what is on the students' screen while they are taking the exam and use a 360-degree camera to record what is happening in the exam room; they also record the audio in the exam room while the student is taking the exam.

There are three different types of online proctors that can be used:

- Live online proctoring, where the proctor can observe all of the test takers on their computer monitor in real time: This is obviously only suitable for small groups of students as the proctor is required to monitor all of the test takers.
- Recorded proctoring, where each student is recorded taking the test, and the proctor can observe each test taker at a later time: The major disadvantage of this method is that it is incredibly time-consuming for the proctor, and as such it is also very expensive.
- Automated advanced proctoring, where students are recorded and an artificial intelligence (AI) algorithm continuously monitors the test takers: Any suspicious behaviour such as excessive moving of the head, the test taker disappearing from the screen or an additional person being present is flagged. The AI algorithm generates a credibility index to identify those test takers who may have compromised the integrity of the test due to their anomalous or at times suspicious behaviour. The proctor is then alerted to this in a report and can check the recording of the test taker at a later date. This method has proved to be the most effective of the three online proctoring methods, especially for large groups of test takers.

Mitigating against Cheating before, during and after an Exam

Before the Exam

If you are required to have online exams because it has been mandated from upper administration, we would recommend keeping the weighting of these online exams as low as possible, so that if students do cheat, the impact on their overall test scores will be minimal. There are a number of things that you can do before the assessment to try and discourage students from engaging in academic dishonesty and to make it more difficult for them to cheat later on during the assessment.

Firstly, you can raise students' awareness of academic integrity and get students to sign an academic integrity contract or an honour code. While some have questioned the value of getting students to sign an honour code (Greenberg, 2015), research indicates that it does have a significant impact on reducing student academic misconduct (Callahan, 2011; McCabe et al., 2002). Students who were reminded of their moral and ethical obligations by signing an honour code before they took a test cheated less than students who did not sign an honour code. Research has demonstrated that schools that have honour codes have lower rates of cheating than other institutions by around 25%, provided that the honour code is made a pivotal part of campus culture (Barthel, 2016). As such, flying the flag that 'students who cheat, only cheat themselves' might be a deterrent to cheating for some students.

There are a number of other, more practical strategies that teachers can employ before an exam in order to maintain academic integrity. For example, they can prepare different versions of the exam, which would make it very difficult for students to share answers. Another strategy is to have a pool of test items which the computer randomly selects from, so each student would get different questions, again making it virtually impossible for students to share their answers with one another. One other thing that teachers could do before the exam to limit the chances of the exam being compromised is to set passwords for entry into the exam and only give it to students before the exam begins.

During the Exam

There are also a number of things that can be done while students are actually taking the exam to mitigate against academic misconduct (Budai, 2020):

- Offer the online exam only once at a set time so that students cannot tell other students the content and the answers to the exam.
- Set a strict time limit for the exam in order to not allow students time to collude with each other to share answers or to search the internet or use other devices to search for answers.
- Set a strict time limit for each question so that students do not have time to look at their notes, other questions on the test or the internet to help them answer questions. If you are using MCQs, it has been shown that forty-five to sixty seconds is sufficient time for students who know the material to be able to answer the question.
- Randomize the order of the questions to make it difficult for students to copy from each other if they are taking the exam together on nearby computers or to contact each other remotely and share answers. If students do try to collaborate, all of their questions will be in a different sequence which would make cheating more difficult.

- Randomize the order of the answer choices or response options on objective test items such as MCQs to make the sharing of correct answers even more challenging.
- Present your exam questions one at a time. Having only one question on the computer screen at one time makes taking a screen shot of the whole exam more difficult.
- Do not allow students to backtrack. This will reduce the ability of students who finish the exam early to go back to questions and do a search on Google or check their notes to search for answers.
- Set the exam to auto-submit so that the exam is submitted when the time is up to prevent students from taking longer than the time allocated or to use that time to contact students also taking the exam with answers.

After the Exam

There are also a number of things that we can do after an online exam to mitigate against cheating and to maintain academic integrity of an exam. Firstly, delay score availability to all test takers until all students have taken the online exam, including the make-up assessment. Secondly, delay any feedback that you give to students until all students have completed the online exam. Obviously, if you give feedback before all students have completed the online exam, there is a chance that students who received the feedback could collude with those students still taking the exam. Thirdly, a teacher can check predicted online exam scores if available with achieved online exam scores. If there are major discrepancies, it would be pertinent for the teacher to investigate further. Finally, do not use the same exam the next time you teach the same class. Students may have copied questions or even memorized them, and they can easily tell the next cohort of students the questions and answers. You need to completely rewrite the exam questions the next time you implement an exam for the same course or expand the item bank for that course.

Post-Pandemic Lessons

At the time of writing this chapter, the Covid-19 outbreak has brought about significant disruptions to our personal and professional lives. In that time, we have learnt a number of valuable post-pandemic lessons about online assessment:

- Increasing numbers of students will likely take online assessments in the future.
- Opportunities for students to cheat, copy, plagiarize or get additional outside help are exacerbated in an online teaching environment.
- The vast majority of teachers feel that students are more likely to cheat online than in person.
- Students say that it is far easier to cheat in an online test than it is on a test that is proctored face-to-face.
- Large-scale online assessments can be implemented efficiently and effectively.
- Online assessments can maintain an acceptable level of reliability and validity.

- Online assessments have a number of advantages over traditional face-to-face exams, and these advantages should be used to their full potential.
- Technological advancements have resulted in AI proctoring, which has proven to be highly effective at preventing academic misconduct.
- Other measures apart from AI proctoring, such as test task type and the choice of test topic, can also be utilized to effectively mitigate against academic dishonesty.
- Students will likely find new ways to thwart our best efforts to mitigate against cheating during online exams.
- Technological advancements will need to be continually developed to make it more difficult for students to cheat in an online exam.
- Although the focus of this chapter was on mitigating against cheating on online assessments, other forms of academic dishonesty need to be highlighted and taken into consideration. For example, teachers and students need to be trained in the use of anti-plagiarism software so that they are aware of what constitutes plagiarism. Proper attention should also be paid to appropriate and accurate ways of citation and referencing.

Conclusion

Covid-19 has brought about many significant changes in all our lives, and the move to online teaching and testing has thrown up an array of challenges for teachers. One of the major challenges we face is to mitigate against academic dishonesty as much as we can and ensure the validity and reliability of our assessments. Given the propensity of students to engage in academic dishonesty during an online exam, we must begin by asking ourselves if we actually need to implement an online exam in the first place. If we must implement online exams, we cannot just administer the same exam with the same questions to all students. We can significantly mitigate students' ability to engage in academic misconduct and get outside help in online assessment through careful consideration of the assessment task types we use and through the choice of topics of the assessment. This chapter has also outlined a number of strategies that teachers can utilize before, during and after an online exam to mitigate against academic dishonesty, which we hope will provide a way to ensure the academic integrity of our online assessments. However, we also need to bear in mind the fact that, despite our best efforts, some students will still be able to find ways around all of the measures that we have put in place to mitigate against academic misconduct, and the validity and reliability of some online exams will be compromised. It is our sincere hope that we will have made it more difficult for those students who skirt our efforts to protect the integrity of our online assessments.

References

K12 Academics. (n.d.). Academic dishonesty. Retrieved 22 November 2021, from https://www.k12academics.com/academic-dishonesty.

Barthel, M. (2016, 20 April). How to stop cheating in college. *The Atlantic*. Retrieved 22 November 2021, from https://www.theatlantic.com/education/archive/2016/04/how-to-stop-cheating-in-college/479037/.

Bosch, T. (2012) Why would someone cheat on a free online class that doesn't count toward anything? *SLATE Future*Tense*. Retrieved 22 November 2021, from https://slate.com/technology/2012/08/coursera-plagiarism-why-would-students-cheat-in-a-free-online-class-that-doesn-t-over-academic-credit.html.

Budai, S. S. (2020). Fourteen simple strategies to reduce cheating on online examinations. Retrieved 22 November 2021, from https://www.facultyfocus.com/articles/educational-assessment/fourteen-simple-strategies-to-reduce-cheating-on-online-examinations/.

Burgoon, J., Stoner, M., Bonito, J., & Dunbar, J. (2003, January). Trust and deception in mediated communication. *36th Hawaii International Conference on System Sciences*.

Bushweller, K. (1999, April). Generation of cheaters, *The American School Board Journal*, 186(4), 24–32.

Callahan, D. (2011, 25 May). Why honor codes reduce student cheating. *Huffpost*. Retrieved 22 November 2021, from https://www.huffpost.com/entry/why-honor-codes-reduce-st_b_795898.

Cambridge Assessment English. (n.d.). Retrieved 22 November 2021, from https://www.cambridgeenglish.org/research-and-validation/fitness-for-purpose/loa/.

Carless, D. (2009). Learning-oriented assessment: Principles, practice and a project. In L. H. Meyer, et al. (Eds.), *Tertiary assessment and higher education student outcomes: Policy, practice and research* (pp. 79–90). Ako Aotearoa.

Carroll, B. A. (2017). A learning-oriented assessment perspective on scenario-based assessment. *Teachers College, Columbia University Working Papers in Applied Linguistics & TESOL*, 17(2), 28–35.

Cizek, G. J. (1999). *Cheating on tests: how to do it, detect it and prevent it*. Lawrence Erlbaum.

Cluskey, G. R., Ehlen, C. R., & Raiborn, M. H. (n.d.). Thwarting online exam cheating without proctor supervision. *Journal of Academic and Business Ethics*, 1–7.

Coombe, C. (2021, 5 February). *Looking to the future of English language assessment* [Plenary presentation]. Nile TESOL Conference.

Davidson, P. (2009). Authentic assessment in EFL classrooms. In C. Coombe, P. Davidson, & D. Lloyd (Eds.), *The fundamentals of language assessment: A practical guide for teachers* (2nd ed., pp. 213–24). TESOL Arabia.

Davidson, P., & Coombe, C. (2010). Setting real standards using authentic assessment in an EAP context. In J. Mader & Z. Urkun (Eds.), *Proceedings of the IATEFL Testing, Evaluation and Assessment SIG conference: Establishing and maintaining standards* (pp. 16–21). IATEFL.

Davidson, P., & Mandalios, J. (2009). Assessment for learning. In C. Coombe, P. Davidson, & D. Lloyd (Eds.), *Fundamentals of language assessment* (pp. 47–52). TESOL Arabia.

Dick, M., Sheard, J., Bareiss, C., Carter, J., Joyce, D., Harding, T., & Laxter, C. (2003, June) Addressing student cheating: Definitions and solutions. *ACM SIGCSI Bulletin*, 35(2), 172–84.

Greenberg, S. H. (2015, 28 May). Why colleges should ditch honor codes. *The Washington Post*. Retrieved 22 November 2021, from https://www.washingtonpost.com/posteverything/wp/2015/05/28/why-colleges-should-ditch-honor-codes/.

Harrison, D. (2020). *Online education and authentic assessment*. Retrieved 22 November 2021, from https://www.insidehighered.com/advice/2020/04/29/how-discourage-student-cheating-online-exams-opinion.

Kanchan, R. (2019a). *How to prevent cheating in online exams with 7 proctoring technologies*. Retrieved 22 November 2021, from https://mettl.com/en/online-remote-proctoring.

Kanchan, R. (2019b). *Ten clever ways students cheat in online proctored exams*. Retrieved 22 November 2021, from https://blog.mettl.com/cheating-in-online-exams/.

King, C., Guyette, R., & Piotrowski, C. (2009). Online exams and cheating: An empirical analysis of business students' views. *Journal of Educators Online, 6*(1), 1–11.

Lund, J. (1997). Authentic assessment: Its development and applications. *Journal of Physical Education, Recreation and Dance, 68*(7), 25–8, 40.

McAfee. (2017). Cybersecurity 101: Top takeaways from our back to school study. Retrieved 22 November 2021, from https://www.mcafee.com/blogs/mobile-security/back-to-school-study/?utm_campaign=Consumer&utm_source=twitter&utm_medium=spredfast&utm_content=blog#sf102832612.

McCabe, D. L., Treviño, L. K., & Butterfield, K. D. (2002). Honor codes and other contextual influences on academic integrity: A replication and extension to modified honor code settings. *Research in Higher Education, 43*, 357–78.

Michaels, J., & Miethe, T. (1989). Applying theories of deviance to academic cheating. *Social Science Quarterly, 70*(4), 870–85.

Newton, D. (2020). *Another problem with shifting education online: cheating*. Retrieved 22 November 2021, from https://hechingerreport.org/another-problem-with-shifting-education-online-cheating/.

Pednekar, P. (2017). *5 Papers leaked in 5 days: Now, HSC maths and statistics papers out on WhatsApp*. Retrieved 22 November 2021, from https://www.hindustantimes.com/mumbai-news/5-papers-leaked-in-5-days-now-hsc-maths-and-statistics-papers-out-on-whatsapp/story-LWHmttr08lVvJLMBH8Vo0H.html.

Purpura, J. E. (2014). *What is LOA?* Retrieved 22 November 2021, from http://www.tc.columbia.edu/tccrisls/what-is-loa/.

Roberts, P., Anderson, J., & Yannish, P. (1997, October). *Academic misconduct: Where do we start?* [Paper presentation]. Annual Conference of the Northern Rocky Mountain Educational Research Association, Jackson, WY, USA. Retrieved 22 November 2021, from https://files.eric.ed.gov/fulltext/ED415781.pdf.

Rowe, N. C. (2004, Summer). Cheating in online student assessment: Beyond plagiarism. *Online Journal of Distance Learning Administration, 2*, 2. Retrieved 22 November 2021, from https://ojdla.com/archive/summer72/rowe72.pdf.

Saville, N. (2013, December). *The CFR and Learning Oriented Assessment (LOA)* [Paper presentation]. CFR Conference, Higher Colleges of Technology, Dubai, United Arab Emirates.

Sheard, J., Markham, S., & Dick, M. (2003). Investigating differences in cheating behaviours of IT graduate and undergraduate students: The maturity and motivation factors. *Higher Education Research and Development, 22*(1), 91–108.

Siqi. C. (2015). *TOEFL questions, answers leaked in China: Reviewer*. Retrieved 22 November 2021, from https://www.globaltimes.cn/content/905501.shtml.

Staton, B. (2021). Educators around world seek to take axe to exam-based learning. *Financial Times*. Retrieved 22 November 2021, from https://www.ft.com/content/9d64e479-182c-4dbd-96fe-0c26272a5875.

Watson, G., & Sottile, J. (2010). Cheating in the digital age: Do Students cheat more in online courses? *Online Journal of Distance Learning Administration, 13*(1), Spring.

Wei, S. (2015). *TOEFL exam scores in doubt after leak.* Retrieved 22 November 2021, from https://www.chinadaily.com.cn/china/2015-02/02/content_19468099.htm.

Weir, C. J. (2005). *Language testing and validation.* Palgrave Macmillan.

Whitley, B. (1998). Factors associated with cheating among college students: A review. *Research in Higher Education, 39*(3), 235–73.

Wiley. (n.d.). *Academic integrity in the age of online learning.* Retrieved 22 November 2021, from http://read.uberflip.com/i/1272071-academic-integrity-in-the-age-of-online-learning/1?.

Part 5

Beyond Emergency CALL, Post–Covid-19 Lessons

15

Moving Back into the Classroom while Moving beyond Current Paradigms: Lessons for Post-Covid Language Education

Melinda Dooly

Introduction

Throughout the history of education, there have always been small pockets of advocates (some might say visionaries) who have called for the integration of technology into everyday teaching practices. The tools in question have changed with the times, of course. In Babylonia, clay tablets were used for students to copy lessons (Spar, 1988). When wet, they could be erased and used more than once. This practice evolved into the use of slate tablets coupled with chalk. Then, in 1801, it is believed that a geography teacher in Edinburgh, Scotland, James Pillans, came up with the idea of hanging a large slate in the front of his class, a practice which soon became ubiquitous with most schools across the world well into the 1970s (when whiteboards gained popularity; see Muttappallymyalil et al., 2016).

Interestingly, these tools were not initially used for educational purposes. The Babylonian clay tablets were first employed for commercial and governmental purposes (e.g. keeping accounts of taxes); similarly, the chalkboard was used in London's financial district to list the names of debtors in hopes of shaming them into payment (as chronicled by John Francis in 1850). Moreover, the introduction of 'new' technology into education has always been met with detractors. In 1830, students at Yale were expelled after refusing to be examined on mathematical theorems on a chalkboard instead of through the older traditional examination method of oral recitation (Williams, 2019). And while it is far more complicated to find examples of students rebelling against the use of clay tablets, it is not a far stretch to imagine Babylonian scholars and their families begrudging the added economic burden of procuring the tablets and stylus necessary for lessons (Flaxton, 2015).

This abbreviated jaunt through the history of technology in education is, of course, anecdotal, and even a bit whimsical. However, it serves to highlight how the integration of the most current technology of the time is never frictionless and that adjustment to change is neither automatic nor without glitches and may even involve pushback from the main stakeholders: teachers, students, parents and even the community at large. This is true when transformation takes a rather leisurely pace of adoption and adaptation, as was the case of chalkboards in schools. We have seen the challenges for change multiplied and magnified by the need for rapid adaptation brought about by Covid-19. The pandemic led to the shutting down of schools for extended periods, and teachers had to pivot almost immediately from in-person teaching to online around the world, especially during the first year of the pandemic (2020–1). Still, as Hodges et al. (2020) point out, a distinction is best made between online education and *emergency* remote teaching.

Recommendations and general takeaways for teachers having to make this unprecedented rapid transition to online teaching, which includes for many teachers a significant learning curve regarding use of technology, have already been well documented (Chan et al., 2021). Whittle et al. (2020) propose a framework identifying eight key issues regarding emergency remote teaching: hidden curriculum, student engagement, loss of teacher social presence, loss of student social presence, learner agency, synchronicity, instability of expectations and parental connections. Emerging studies are already demonstrating how the rapid move from teaching 'face-to-face' to online has been fraught with many challenges, not least of which is the intent by many teachers to transfer more 'traditional' teaching methods to digital contexts. This is not to belittle the gains in technology familiarity that have inevitably occurred during this world crisis. Indubitably, innumerable teachers have increased their techno-pedagogical know-how, have gained confidence in their technological abilities and will bring this knowledge and positive attitude back into the face-to-face classroom in the (hopefully) near future.

Still, there is a need to push beyond these parameters of merely thinking about technical teacher know-how; this does not guarantee true innovation in pedagogy. The world is now obliged to take a close look at necessary changes to society for the upcoming post-pandemic century regarding the issues highlighted by Whittle et al. (2020). It seems that this is an opportunity for teachers (and teacher educators) to propose an alternative paradigm for twenty-first century learning as well. The time will come – or as some reports claim, this moment has already arrived – when students begin demanding classes with flexible timetables (lessons that do not require 100% face-to-face contact hours), flexible assignments and learning options tailored to the individual, and all using technology that is now familiar to most.

This chapter will first briefly discuss pedagogical themes that have long been present in educational research but that have been spotlighted during the Covid crisis. It will then discuss potential areas for innovation that are still under-explored by language teachers as high-impact technology quickly moves into many people's daily lives, before synthesizing the key lessons learnt for language education during the pandemic.

Looking Back to Go Forward

Much has been said about the twenty-first century teacher. Interestingly, one of the most common features mentioned is that the leading-edge teacher should use student-centred, inquiry-based teaching approaches – the same characteristics asserted by Dewey (1916) more than a hundred years ago in his proposal for a transformative educational framework. In this model, he argued that the role of education is to provide developmental opportunities for the individual. Significantly, from 2020 to 2021, numerous support documents for educators adjusting to online teaching also tend to highlight student-centred practice. And yet this shift from a 'transmission mode of pedagogy' to more 'participative experience' (Thomas et al., 2013, p. 7) has been the backbone of learning design for computer-assisted language learning (CALL) for several decades.

Other support documents, workshops and (almost ironically) online courses for teachers published in 2020 deal with how to use communication technology effectively. Again, these are not new technologies; they have been around for years, and pockets of practitioners have been integrating them into their teaching for decades (Dooly & Vinagre, 2021). In particular, it is important to consider the experience of educators working in distance education – a few universities began offering courses in the 1980s and 1990s (e.g. University of Toronto in 1984, Trident University International in 1993). Easier, quicker and more economical access to the internet around the world ushered in a much wider swathe of universities offering partial or full online degrees in the early to mid-2000s. Another area of studies which has contributed significantly to a growing body of knowledge regarding blended learning (online and in-class) is telecollaboration (also known as Tele-tandem and virtual exchange). Warschauer's (1996) conference proceedings are widely viewed as setting the foundations for research in this area. Now, in 2020–1, as a result of the emergency remote teaching, many of the results of these studies are being corroborated by teachers around the world.

There is consensus that much of the success of online teaching and learning is related to the relatively lower costs of educational delivery when compared with more traditional teaching methods, resulting in more widespread educational options for a more comprehensive socio-economic group. These changes have also resulted in a greater variety of subject options and, inevitably, a wider range of quality, as control of these options is decentralized. (It has been argued that this online 'democratization' of content has resulted in higher standards as the content is now open to a greater number of potential reviewers, although many educational governing bodies might argue the opposite). Global access to online education has also meant a greater variety in learner profiles and possibilities of interaction between students from around the world. Nonetheless, these positive attributes of greater access to and subsequent democratization of learning have also been contrasted with the higher rate of student attrition, learner isolation and increase in non-expertise in educational delivery (Miller, 2014).

Much of what is being published as findings resulting from the emergency remote teaching often feel predictable for the smaller pocket of researchers working in distance and telecollaborative education. This underscores how slowly our current education workforce struggles to catch up with technological innovation and social problems, as well as learning from what other practitioners are doing. A brief, cross-national comparison of studies and reviews of changes in teacher education demonstrate that, in general, educational approaches have almost always lagged decades behind socio-technological change (Blin & Munro, 2008; Hargreaves, 2005; Ketelaar et al., 2012; Mutch, 2012; Tiwari, 2016).

Too often, transformation in learning science has been incidental – nudged by external factors rather than through systematic research initiated from within and by researchers in education working ahead of the curve (Glenn, 2009). Teachers need to be willing to learn from those who have gone before them. One might even put forth that the world of education took part in a worldwide collective experience of incidental learning as a result of the pandemic. So, what has this collective experience corroborated regarding previous research on technology-enhanced language teaching and learning? Our next section aims to provide a digest (inevitably partial) of some of the main points regarding online language learning environments and general pedagogical aspects gleaned through the recent decades of online teaching research and practice.

Online Language Teaching and Learning: The Importance of Learning Design

Many experienced teachers who had always worked within in-person classroom environments suddenly found themselves having to take decisions on how best to make this transition. Arguably this shift is not unlike the uncertainty felt by newly graduated teachers during the first months or years after joining the workforce of educators (Redding, 1995). Luckily there were and are a large number of easily accessible handbooks and guidelines, many of which were written for online teaching or blended learning environments long before the pandemic (e.g. numerous American universities published Open Access online handbooks for their teachers between 2015 and 2018). Books and guides on teaching languages through online technology have also been available from the mid-2000s onwards (see Anderson, 2008; Dooly, 2008; Meskill & Anthony, 2010). These books cover many of the aforementioned areas of concern for teachers who have had to shift to online teaching during the pandemic. These volumes cover themes such as understanding the main theoretical foundations for teaching and learning in online environments, developing an effective infrastructure, establishing positive interaction patterns, dealing with economic and accessibility factors, delivery, assessment, quality control and supporting collaborative learning, timing, task design and content sequencing, affordances and limitations of online learning environments and promoting team work.

Admittedly, there have been significant technological advances since the publication of many of the aforementioned books, but the underlying pedagogical principles withstand the march of time. Many of the points outlined in these books are echoed in the guidelines for emergency remote teaching during the Covid crisis. To wit, Meskill and Anthony's (2010) words still ring true a decade later:

> Excellent language teaching is often likened to arranging and conducting a complex musical score ... However ... the critical player in the language learning

alchemy remains talented educators ... Regardless of the medium, the tools and the algorithms, language development depends on the humanware, that is, you, the teacher. (pp. 188–9)

This brings up another key takeaway from the body of research on technology-enhanced teaching. It is not so much the tool or even the technological know-how that is essential for learning gains in digital environments. What is more crucial is the teacher know-how.

A growing body of studies also point to task design in technology-enhanced language teaching as one of the most relevant areas for successful language learning. This corroborates expert interviews, carried out during the Covid-19 pandemic, regarding online distance education in general (Rapanta et al., 2020). In the summary of their answers, the experts all pointed to the prominence of 'careful design of activities' (p. 937). Similarly, in online language education, the task design is often put forth as one of the most crucial aspects to take into consideration for successful language learning (Kurek & Müller-Hartmann, 2017; Meskill & Anthony, 2010).

Online language learning environments must be carefully scaffolded, and this can be daunting when planning natural language use in a digital environment, especially when working with lower-level learners. This means that the teacher should try to identify key language aims (lexicon, language chunks) for each task, lesson or project (if planning a longer-term telecollaborative project, for instance). These may be part of the overall learning objectives or these may be part of the sub-tasks that help the learner achieve other aims in a longer project. For instance, the teacher may present the students with the necessary formulaic target language (e.g. 'I didn't understand that, can you repeat please?') in order to collaborate with an online partner in a jigsaw language task. These language chunks are needed in order to complete an online collaborative language lesson but may not be the main learning objectives (incidental learning). Ideally, the teaching strategies will integrate the needed lexical items or language chunks in various modes of communication (Council of Europe, 2018). For instance, the activity may include reception (understanding instructions, understanding other online participants) as well as production (sustaining a work-oriented dialogue) in order to complete the task. They may also include socio-pragmatic aspects (e.g. politeness), which are necessary communication skills for learning with others online.

Another important feature of planning for language learning online is the identification of the different objectives of the task itself. Some activities may combine several goals, but there should be at least one principal aim for each planned activity (in other words, online language learning is not merely a question of 'chatting together online'). This resonates with more recent guidelines that have emerged during the Covid-19 lockdown (OECD, 2020) regarding the need for clear, attainable learning outcomes. To provide a simple example, a task cycle design may principally aim to draw the learners' attention to specific forms of the target language (focus on form) through the use of enhanced images (e.g. with embedded hotspots); this task in turn provides support or reinforcement for expected language reception or production in a subsequent task.

Other task designs may aim to provide opportunities for incidental focus on form (Loewen, 2005), in which case the learners have fewer limitations for language use and more possibilities of unplanned language exposure. This plays into the very nature of online communication, which is often referred to as 'authentic', contextualized language learning (and is often touted as one of the main benefits of technology-enhanced language learning; Dooly & Vinagre, 2021). However, these potential moments of unanticipated language use can be a bit intimidating for new teachers, especially if the target language is not their L1. If viewed as teachable moments (Glasswell & Parr, 2009), these can potentially be scaffolded by training the learner beforehand to take notice of unknown words, gaps in communication or other problems (incidental attention to form) that occur during technology-enhanced interactions. These can then be integrated into other lessons or as self-paced post-activity work, wherein the learner explores and resolves as many linguistic gaps as possible before the next online encounter. Students can even be given the responsibility of helping the teacher pinpoint key *teachables* for themselves and their peers by taking note of their doubts, gaps in communication or difficulties in comprehension. Planning a whole-class post-session analysis of recordings or transcripts of exchanges that have been anonymized is an excellent way to promote this type of incidental attention to language.

Moreover, a careful diagnosis of keywords or chunks that can be introduced to learners *before* they begin the main learning sequences of the project or gradually as the project unfolds can help students with anxiety or fear of failure in online environments (related to the concept of affective filter; see Krashen, 1986). Preparing students for potential miscommunication also helps in expectation management regarding what the exchanges might be like and demonstrates that they do not need to be afraid of failure, another key issue that has been documented in Covid-19 teaching guidelines (Whittle et al., 2020).

Ample (but scaffolded) contact and exposure with the target language teaching has been highlighted as essential for effective technology-enhanced language teaching. Studies show that significant repetition is needed (reception and production) of the language before learners can use the word or phrase appropriately in a different, less-controlled environment. However, exposure does not mean merely hearing or repeating words over and over. Repetition must take place in a variety of meaningful contexts. For instance, for beginner-level learners, the activity of greetings at the beginning and end of short telecollaborative sessions ('hello', 'how are you?', 'bye', 'see you next time', etc.) can eventually be transferred to other contexts (online or face-to-face situations). As experience with technology-enhanced language teaching has shown over the decades, the repetition of hearing and using the target language in digital contexts that allow interaction with other speakers outside the school is far more beneficial than the repetition – often decontextualized and rote – that frequently takes place in a wall-bounded classroom.

In summary, prior publications on studies and praxis of language education in digital environments corroborate many of the conclusions currently being drawn regarding successful emergency remote teaching (Hodges et al., 2020). The design of the learning environment is as crucial for online learning as it is for in-class learning. Paradoxically, technology-enhanced language learning design does not begin with the technological resources (Dooly, 2008; Kurek & Müller-Hartmann, 2017). Good language learning design must first take into account the learning (and learner) context (where, who and when), learning goals (what are the main aims of both the activity and the overall course), the teacher (style, techno-pedagogical skills; Mishra & Koehler, 2006), timing (of delivery, performance, deadlines, etc.), the specific tasks or activities to be carried out, scaffolding necessary for the tasks to be completed (both for communication and other cognitive demands such as world knowledge, transdisciplinary content, etc.), the interaction (teacher–learner, learner–learner, learner–other external speaker) and, finally, corollary to this last item, the most adequate communication channel(s).

Teacher, Learner and Collaborative Interaction

Given the number of publications on online education in the past two to three decades, one might ask which conceptual dimensions have emerged as essential for successful technology-enhanced teaching and learning. First and foremost, expert practitioners underscore the notion of 'well-being'. This also resonates with the recent publications regarding how best to deal with emergency remote teaching (Lorenza & Carter, 2021). Well-being applies to both teachers and students and ranges from ensuring time limitations on workload (e.g. planning, implementing and evaluating for teachers; tasks and homework for learners) to an in-depth understanding of how learning styles can have an impact on the online student (although it must be recognized that this factor is not limited to online learning environments). Studies in distance and blended learning pinpoint these major factors for overall student and teacher well-being (Popescu et al., 2021): course design (including institutional and technological infrastructure); the interaction (teacher–learner, learner–learner, etc.); learner aptitudes, attitudes and performance (e.g. preferred styles, technological know-how, intrinsic and extrinsic motivation, tolerance of ambiguity, autonomy); individual traits (e.g. introvert or extrovert) and external factors (e.g. access to technology, low-stress environments for study, time factors, other personal responsibilities). In short, online teaching requires very similar competences that are required in face-to-face teaching as learning paradigms shift from a sense of transmission of knowledge to the constructivist paradigm of mutually shared and collaborative knowledge building (Blayone et al., 2017; Thomas et al., 2013).

Data indicates that these types of collaborative environments can have a significant impact on learning (Dooly & Sadler, 2020; Jesionkowska, 2020). This concept is related to the notion of 'social presence', which draws from prior work carried out on Communities of Inquiry (see Garrison, 2016). This theoretical shift places emphasis on the notion that being digitally connected is as authentic as face-to-face interaction, thereby acknowledging student agency and affectivity, and underscoring the social presence within a community of online learners, versus a more transactional sense of non-visible other-to-other in cyberspace. The advance in synchronous communication technology (e.g. videoconferencing tools) has helped promote this as online teaching has progressed from slower, text-based interactions to more synchronous, oral exchanges. As Blayone et al. (2017) explain, in order to promote social presence and collaborative learning (rather than transactional distance teaching), online learning environments must help first '(a) build interpersonal relationships; (b) promote distributed responsibility for refining knowledge through challenging feedback that triggers cognitive dissonance; and (c) encourage divergent thinking' (p. 8).

Similarly, research in online education highlights the importance of autonomy. It is increasingly acknowledged that technology in language education can help advance learner autonomy (Fuchs et al., 2021). According to Lamy and Hampel (2007), learner autonomy is directly related to learner presence, identity and the motivation to participate in the learning process, which must be assiduously *supported* (not forced) by the online teacher. This also implies mitigation of learner anxiety. 'At one level anxiety can be linked to learners' sense of aloneness, contextual deprivation and anonymity in online environments' (Lamy & Hampel, 2007, p. 85). The online teacher's role in lowering levels of anxiety and promotion of social presence and feeling of community can have a deep impact on eventual positive outcomes of the entire online learning process. This implies that the teacher is sensitive to the flow of communication from the beginning till the end of the course, from initial welcoming and ice-breaking activities to discussing, negotiating and modelling 'good practices' in online communication. Teachers must also provide timely feedback and follow-up to interventions, prodding reluctant participants to take part in the interactions while reminding others who may monopolize online discussions that they should follow norms of turn taking that have been agreed upon by the participants. These lessons learnt through years of technology-enhanced language teaching are now validated by the multiple reports on good remote teaching during the pandemic (OECD, 2020).

Where Do We Go from Here?

High-impact, quickly evolving technology holds the potential to revolutionize teaching and learning. One rapidly growing area is extended reality (XR): real and virtual combined environments and human–machine interactions generated by computer technology and haptic devices. XR is expected to become reality (pun intended) for many sectors in the near future. Estimates put the XR industry market size at more than $209 billion by 2022 (Scribani, 2019), principally in entertainment, marketing, real estate and remote work (Trinon, 2019). Noticeably, there is little mention of XR in education apart from specific training for highly technical (and quite lucrative) areas such as military training (Koźlak et al., 2013; Lele, 2013) or piloting (Trinon, 2019).

This corroborates the argument that our current education workforce often finds itself struggling to catch up with technological innovation. Faced with limited knowledge of how to harness today's latest advances in high-impact technology, there is a noticeable gap in educators' ability and willingness to efficiently engage with novel learning scenarios such as platforms for XR-enhanced teaching. While it is acknowledged that the costs of the hardware and software that comprise XR devices are, for the moment at least, inaccessible for the majority of teachers and educational communities, it is well documented that as technology costs come down and products become available for mainstream consumption, these tools are more readily accepted by educators.

Experts in XR discuss the rapid advances that have already been made in education. XR use can lead to deeply realistic avatars that will revolutionize collaborative learning spaces, including online learning environments. Arguably, the lessons we have already learnt during decades of blended language teaching (e.g. virtual exchange) and more recently, the techno-pedagogical gains brought about by the emergency remote teaching will be important cornerstones for adopting new XR teaching and learning environments.

Still, there has not been much work on the integration of XR into language education, despite arguments regarding the motivation of embodied engagement with target lingua-cultural simulated environments. In 2012, Ibañez et al. published their work on a game-like 3D multi-user virtual world that simulated a 'typical' street in Madrid. The motivation of the learner-avatars was to explore their surroundings and eventually find and enter a virtual rendition of *El Prado* Museum. However, no language learning results were made available. A more recent study found that learners who had been presented with input from the target language (English) through 360° video viewing outperformed another group who had not had immersive videos as part of the language input (Repetto et al., 2021). Other studies suggest that the sense of presence that occurs in immersive environments may support situated learning by providing greater opportunities for language students to associate lexicon and formulaic chunks to specific context, thereby increasing both memory association and contextualized use (Ou Yang et al., 2020). Gruber and Kaplan-Rakowski (2020) found that XR can help reduce foreign language anxiety. In short, it seems that soon the time-honoured use of role play in language classrooms can get a heightened veneer as students take on embodiment through avatars in culturally significant environments!

Lessons Learnt

A key lesson learnt is that we mustn't throw the baby out with the bath water. Students and teachers have expressed their desire to return to in-class environments (Lorenza & Carter, 2021); however, at the same time, there is a growing call for selecting 'best practices' that have emerged from not only this 'collective experiment' of online teaching, but also experiences from practitioners who have worked in this field since the mid-1990s (Rapanta et al., 2020). In particular, there is a call for blended environments that bring in features from flipped instruction, collaborative learning (e.g. telecollaboration) and in-class instruction (Dooly & Sadler, 2020) for effective technology-enhanced language teaching that adapts to today's learners' needs. It has already been underscored that the emergency remote teaching guidelines which have been proposed differ considerably in focus from pre-Covid frameworks for online teaching. Pre-Covid recommendations emphasize careful elaboration of 'processes, planning, implementation and evaluation' (Carr-Chellman, 2016, p. xiv), whereas emergency remote teaching is generally understood as a temporary organization of teaching in response to a crisis (Hodges et al., 2020). Yet there are inevitably lessons to be learnt which can draw from diverse bodies of research as the world slowly returns to the classroom.

Firstly, this implies critical reflection of how technologies are being used both inside and outside of the classroom. Do the activities (both in-person and online; with and without technology) fully support learner-centred activity? Does the technology-enhanced learning design clearly delineate the learning aims and accommodate the teacher and learner styles for technology-supported (and non–technology-supported) teaching and learning? Does the design fully support all the necessary interactions online and offline? As teachers advance from the emergency remote online context, we must apply our fortified confidence and techno-pedagogical skills to leverage the constructive potential that technology holds in a combined nexus of 'traditional' in-class settings and digital learning environments.

Sadly, perhaps one of the most painful lessons learnt during the Covid-19 lockdown is that the 'digital divide', which has been observed and remarked for decades, has been exacerbated by the educational crisis brought on by schools being shuttered across the globe. The 'digital divide' – made even more evident with the Covid-19 epidemic – has been documented for decades. The socio-economic and political inequality, in large part due to lack of access to 'key knowledge', has been referred to as 'the ingenuity gap' (Homer-Dixon, 2000) or the gap between 'information haves and have-nots' (Norris, 2001) as society began to truly see the impact of the first 'digital age' (associated with the beginning of access to personal computers).

Recent studies on the impact of the pandemic are already reporting larger disparities in education provoked by lack of digital access in homes and communities across the globe. Teachers need to proactively inform themselves regarding their students' technology access. Individualized learning plans (ILPs) need to take into account not only a learner's cognitive, emotional or physical strengths and weaknesses, but should also comprise sociocultural and socio-economic factors, including time management and access to the technologies expected to be used in the lessons. And while this may seem contradictory, XR may eventually be pivotal in helping level the playing field in language education. Providing publicly accessible XR environments for language learning can open the door for uncountable learners who would not otherwise have the means to immerse themselves in the lingua-cultural environments that ensure opportunities of exposure to and practice of other languages. This manner of pioneer thinking is essential. As we slowly return to the classroom, it will be important to continue employing the creative problem-solving that was so abundant during the lockdown and to remain inquisitive about innovative opportunities that will bring the world into the language classroom in the most enriching ways possible.

References

Anderson, T. (2008). *The theory and practice of online learning*. Athabasca University Press.
Blayone, T. J. B., van Oostveen, R., Barber, W., DiGiuseppe, M., & Childs, E. (2017). Democratizing digital learning: Theorizing the fully online learning community model.

International Journal of Educational Technology in Higher Education, 14(13), 1–16. Last accessed date 7 October 2022, from https://doi.org/10.1186/s41239-017-0051-4.

Blin, F., & Munro, M. (2008). Why hasn't technology disrupted academics' teaching practices? Understanding resistance to change through the lens of activity theory. *Computers & Education, 50*(2), 475–90. Last accessed date 7 October 2022, from https://doi.org/10.1016/j.compedu.2007.09.017.

Carr-Chellman, A. (2016). *Instructional design for teachers: Improving classroom practice* (2nd ed.). Routledge.

Chan, R. Y., Bista, K., & Allen, R. M. (2021). *Online teaching and learning in higher education during COVID-19. International perspectives and experiences.* Routledge.

Council of Europe. (2018). *Common European framework of reference for languages: Learning, teaching, assessment. Companion volume with new descriptors.* Council of Europe.

Dewey, J. (1916). *Democracy and education: An introduction to the philosophy of education.* MacMillan.

Dooly, M. (2008). *Telecollaborative language learning. A guidebook to moderating intercultural collaboration online* [2008/online 2013]. Peter Lang.

Dooly, M., & Sadler, R. (2020). 'If you don't improve, what's the point?' Investigating the impact of a 'flipped' online exchange in teacher education. *ReCALL, 32*(1), 4–24. Last accessed date 7 October 2022, from https://doi.org/10.1017/S0958344019000107.

Dooly, M., & Vinagre, M. (2021). Research into practice: Virtual exchange in language teaching and learning. *Language Teaching*, 1–15. Last accessed date 7 October 2022, from https://doi.org/10.1017/S0261444821000069.

Flaxton, N. (2015). *Greetings noble sir.* Andrews UK Limited.

Fuchs, C., Dooly, M. & Hauck, M. (2021). Autonomy and technology: Potential game-changers in language education. An introduction. In C. Fuchs, M. Hauck & M. Dooly (Eds.). *Language education in digital spaces: Perspectives on autonomy and interaction* (pp. 1–15). Springer.

Francis, J. (1850). *Chronicles and characters of the stock exchange.* W. M. Crosby & H. B. Nichols Publishers.

Garrison, D. R. (2016). *Thinking collaboratively: Learning in a community of inquiry.* Routledge.

Glasswell, K., & Parr, J. M. (2009). Teachable moments: Linking assessment and teaching in talk around writing. *Language Arts, 86*(5), 352–61.

Glenn, J. C. (2009). Introduction to the futures research methods series. In J. C. Glenn & T. J. Gordon (Eds.), *Futures research methodology – V3.0* (pp. 1–106). The Millennium Project.

Gruber, A., & Kaplan-Rakowski, R. (2020). User experience of public speaking practice in virtual reality. In R. Z. Zheng (Ed.), *Cognitive and affective perspectives on immersive technology in education* (pp. 235–49). IGI Global.

Hargreaves, A. (2005). Educational change takes ages: Life, career, and generational factors in teachers' emotional responses to educational change. *Teaching and Teacher Education, 21*, 967–83. Last accessed date 7 October 2022, from https://doi.org/10.1016/j.tate.2005.06.007.

Hodges, C., Moore, S., Lockee, B., Trust, T., & Bond, A. (2020, 27 March). The difference between emergency remote teaching and online learning. *Educause Review.* Last accessed date 7 October 2022, from https://er.educause.edu/articles/2020/3/the-difference-between-emergency-remote-teaching-and-online-learning.

Homer-Dixon, T. F. (2000). *The ingenuity gap.* Knopf.

Ibañez, M. B., Delgado-Kloos, C., Leony, D., García Rueda, J. J., & Maroto, D. (2012). Learning a foreign language in a mixed-reality environment. *IEEE Internet Computing, 15*(6), 44–47.

Jesionkowska, J. (2020). Designing online environment for collaborative learning in a scientific community of practice. In M. E. Auer & T. Tsiatsos (Eds.), *The challenges of the digital transformation in education. Proceedings of the 21st International Conference on Interactive Collaborative Learning (ICL2018) – Volume 2* (pp. 176–85). Springer.

Ketelaar, E., Beijaard, D., Boshuizen, H. P. A., & Den Brok, P. J. (2012). Teachers' positioning towards an educational innovation in the light of ownership, sense-making and agency. *Teaching and Teacher Education, 28*(2), 273–82. Last accessed date 7 October 2022, from https://doi.org/10.1016/j.tate.2011.10.004.

Koźlak, M., Kurzeja, A., & Nawrat, A. (2013). Virtual reality technology for military and industry training programs. In A. Nawrat & Z. Kuś (Eds.), *Vision based systems for UAV applications* (pp. 327–34). Springer.

Krashen, S. D. (1986). *Principles and practice in second language acquisition.* Pergamon Press.

Kurek, M., & Müller-Hartmann, A. (2017). Task design for telecollaborative exchanges: In search of new criteria, *System, 64*, 7–20. Last accessed date 7 October 2022, from https://doi.org/10.1016/j.system.2016.12.004.

Lamy, M.-N., & Hampel, R. (2007). *Online communication in language learning and teaching.* Palgrave Macmillan.

Lele, A. (2013). Virtual reality and its military utility. *Journal of Ambient Intelligence and Humanized Computing, 4*(1), 17–26. doi:10.1007/s12652-011-0052-4.

Loewen, S. (2005). Incidental focus on form and second language acquisition. *Studies in Second Language Acquisition, 27*(3), 361–86. Last accessed date 7 October 2022, from https://doi.org/10.1017/S0272263105050163.

Lorenza, L., & Carter, D. (2021). Emergency online teaching during COVID-19: A case study of Australian tertiary students in teacher education and creative arts. *International Journal of Educational Research Open, 2*(2), 1–8. Last accessed date 7 October 2022, from https://doi.org/10.1016/j.ijedro.2021.100057.

Meskill, C., & Anthony, N. (2010). *Teaching languages online.* Multilingual Matters Textbooks.

Miller, M. D. (2014). *Minds online: Teaching effectively with technology.* Harvard University Press.

Mishra, P., & Koehler, M. J. (2006). Technological pedagogical content knowledge: A framework for teacher knowledge. *Teachers College Record, 108*(6), 1017–54. Last accessed date 7 October 2022, from https://doi.org/10.1111/j.1467-9620.2006.00684.x.

Mutch, C. (2012). Curriculum change and teacher resistance. *Curriculum Matters, 8*, 1–8. Last accessed date 7 October 2022, from https://doi.org/10.18296/cm.0145.

Muttappallymyalil, J., Mendis, S., John, L. J., Shanthakumari, N., Sreedharan, J., & Shaikh, R. B. (2016). Evolution of technology in teaching: Blackboard and beyond in medical education. *Nepal Journal of Epidemiology, 6*(3), 588–92. Last accessed date 7 October 2022, from https://doi.org/10.3126/nje.v6i3.15870.

Norris, P. (2001). *Digital divide: Civic engagement, information poverty, and the internet worldwide.* Cambridge University Press. Last accessed date 7 October 2022, from https://doi.org/10.1017/CBO9781139164887.006.

OECD. (2020). *Strengthening online learning when schools are closed: The role of families and teachers in supporting students during the COVID-19 crisis.* OECD. Retrieved 2

October 2021, from https://read.oecd-ilibrary.org/view/?ref=136_136615-o13x4bk owa&title=Strengthening-online-learning-when-schools-are-closed&_ga=2.58028 586.1278673125.1634750216-1156029269.1634750215.

Ou Yang, F.-C., Lo, F.-Y. R., Chen Hsieh, J., & Wu, W.-C. V. (2020). Facilitating communicative ability of EFL learners via high-immersion virtual reality. *Educational Technology & Society, 23*(1), 30–49. Last accessed date 7 October 2022, from https://www.jstor.org/stable/26915405.

Popescu, E. F., Tătucu, M., & Dobromirescu, V. (2021). Students' well-being in online education in Covid-19 context. *International Journal of Education and Research, 9*(2), 1–10. Last accessed date 7 October 2022, from http://ijern.com/journal/2021/February-2021/01.pdf.

Rapanta, C., Botturi, L., Goodyear, P., Guardía, L., & Koole, M. (2020). Online university teaching during and after the Covid-19 crisis: Refocusing teacher presence and learning activity. *Postdigital Science Education, 2*, 923–45. Last accessed date 7 October 2022, from https://doi.org/10.1007/s42438-020-00155-y.

Redding, R. E. (1995). Cognitive task analysis for instructional design: Applications in distance education, *Distance Education, 16*(1), 88–106. Last accessed date 7 October 2022, from https://doi.org/10.1080/0158791950160107.

Repetto, C., Flavia Di Natale, A., Villani, D., Triberti, S., Germagnoli, S., & Riva. G. (2021). The use of immersive 360° videos for foreign language learning: a study on usage and efficacy among high-school students. *Interactive Learning Environments*. Last accessed date 7 October 2022, from https://doi.org/10.1080/10494820.2020.1863234.

Scribani, L. (2019, 16 January). What is extended reality (XR)? *Visual Capitalist*. Retrieved 14 October 2021, from https://www.visualcapitalist.com/extended-reality-xr.

Spar, I. (Ed.). (1988). *Cuneiform texts in the Metropolitan Museum of Art. Volume I: Tablets, cones, and bricks of the third and second Millennia B.C.* Metropolitan Museum of Art.

Thomas, M., Reinders, H., & Warschauer, M. (2013). Contemporary computer-assisted language learning: The role of digital media and incremental change. In M. Thomas, H. Reinders, & M. Warschauer (Eds.), *Contemporary computer-assisted language learning* (pp. 1–12). Bloomsbury.

Tiwari, D. (2016). *Paradigm shifts in the pedagogical approaches: Andragogy-heutagogy-synergogy*. IGI.

Trinon, H. (2019). *Immersive technologies for virtual reality – case study: Flight simulator for pilot training* [Unpublished master's dissertation]. University of Liège. Last accessed date 7 October 2022, from http://hdl.handle.net/2268.2/6443.

Warschauer, M. (1996). *Telecollaboration in foreign language learning: Proceedings of the Hawaii symposium (technical report, 12)*. University of Hawai'i Press.

Whittle, C., Tiwari, S., Yan, S., & Williams, J. (2020). Emergency remote teaching environment: A conceptual framework for responsive online teaching in crises. *Information and Learning Sciences, 121* (5/6), 311–19. Last accessed date 7 October 2022, from https://doi.org/10.1108/ILS-04-2020-0099.

Williams, D. B. (2019). *Stories in stone: Travels through urban geology*. University of Washington Press.

16

Deconstructing the 'Normalization' of CALL: Digital Inequalities, Decolonization and Post-Pandemic Futures

Michael Thomas

Introduction

Technologies have been promising to 'transform' education for rather a long time (Laurillard, 2013). CALL has grown exponentially over the past three decades and is now a well-established sub-field of second-language acquisition supported by national and international researchers and practitioners. Growing out of the more widespread availability of personal home computers in the early 1980s, nearly two decades ago Stephen Bax (2003) looked forward to what he called the 'normalisation' of digital technologies in language education, arguing that there would come a time in which language learners would find them 'in every classroom, on every desk, in every bag' (p. 21). The technologies would become normal parts of teaching in much the same way that pens and paper had achieved their modern-day invisible status.

'Normalization' was partly a critique of what Bax called 'the wow factor', by which he meant the all too familiar short-term hype that often surrounds the emergence of new technologies in education that tends to take precedence over syllabus and learner needs. This is a history that spans several hype cycles in education, from educational radio through interactive whiteboards to virtual reality over the past one hundred years. Moreover, Bax's understanding of 'normalization' was recognition at the turn of the new millennium that CALL technologies typically involved a 'once-a-week' session in a separated computer lab as part of a formal language course, if facilities allowed, or a CD-ROM to support out-of-class autonomous learning. Few language classes at that time were taught entirely online, and where technology was used, it was more likely to be used for delivering language teacher training courses through distance learning. These courses often used asynchronous discussion boards more than videoconferencing as neither the applications nor the internet were reliable enough to sustain prolonged, high-quality video streaming. Where CALL applications were used, it was likely to be carried out by a small group of technology enthusiasts and innovators in any one educational institution rather than by the majority of language teachers.

Jump forward nearly two decades, and language educators find themselves in the midst of an unprecedented global health emergency, which no one could have envisaged, impacting on teaching and learning in quite the ways it has done to date. While digital technologies have seen equally unprecedented rates of adoption as a result of the pandemic, leading some to indicate that they have now been 'normalized', it is important to recognize the existing digital inequalities both within nations as well as between them that Covid-19 has highlighted. While there are increasingly high rates of technology adoption for devices such as smartphones (and this presents opportunities for mobile learning), it would not be accurate to describe them as being 'in every classroom, on every desk, in every bag', and the notion of 'normalizing' technology adoption requires closer examination in relation to disabilities, social class, race, ethnicity and gender, not merely in low-and-middle-income countries (LMICs), but also in the so-called developed world, where significant digital inequalities also exist. If CALL is to progress further as a field, it needs to recognize the social and material realities of teaching and learning, not merely focus on the technologies, and to deconstruct rather than merely accept 'normalized' assumptions and ways of using them.

In this context, this chapter considers several key questions for language educators that have emerged as a result of the pandemic: What will the legacy of the 'exodus to online education' be for the future of language learning within an increasingly neoliberal international marketplace in which digital technologies play a key supporting role? Does the pandemic present language educators with the opportunity to reflect on alternative futures based not only on the discourse of endless digital innovation and enhancement, but also on sustainable, socially just and inclusive technological practices? In order to address these questions, this chapter explores the implications of the wider 'critical turn' or 'techlash' taking place in the field of digital education for CALL and aims to examine the prospects of CALL in a post-pandemic future (Selwyn, 2017).

Normalization Revisited

Writing shortly after the first wave of Covid-19 lockdowns had begun in March 2020, Jody Greene acknowledged the scale and rapidity of the transformation that had taken place in such a short period of time in her college in the United States:

> Anyone even minimally involved in teaching or supporting teaching ... has over the past week witnessed a quiet revolution ... in which instructors have turned to teaching centers and instructional design units, as well as to colleagues, professional organizations, social media and Internet search engines, to learn *together* about a range of digital tools they will need to use to teach remotely and about the design consequences of those choices. Teaching center staff who have been shouting into the wind about the benefits of learning communities can't help but smile as the entire collegiate instructional workforce scrambles to find the nearest Hangout or Zoom teaching happy hour. (Lederman, 2020)

While Greene identifies several positive implications arising from the pandemic, especially those related to 'learning together' in 'communities of practice' and the newfound enthusiasm with which the potential of digital technologies has been greeted, there is also an underlying acknowledgement of the need to overcome previous generations of resistance or indifference.

Also writing in March 2020, Jones (2020) argued from his perspective on UK higher education that 'Covid-19 offers a chance' for education 'to redefine its relationship with the public, and for ... managers to reset their relationship with staff'. Both Greene's and Jones's perspectives are interesting in that they draw attention to the significant resistance that technology integration in education had often faced in the decades prior to the pandemic, as well as the realization that education requires a 'reset', a period of reflection to 'redefine' its vision and key relationships. Both of these perspectives are at odds with the unproblematic and often celebratory hype that surrounds the use of language learning technologies, much of which is borrowed from the fetishization of consumer-oriented 'techno-culture' found within wider Western society.

While Greene was writing about the wider field of educational technology, the scene she describes also captures the changes which took place among language educators around the world. Although practitioners and researchers in CALL had been exploring the potential of digital technologies with increasing regularity, prior to the pandemic, it had made few inroads into formal education. Indeed, the history of CALL tells a story of it as a rather 'specialist interest' driven by a constantly changing array of new technologies. At its worst or most challenging, CALL research has been trying to explore technologies which in some cases have changed (or even disappeared) by the time the research study has been concluded or a new academic year has begun (Freddi, 2021).

Anyone suggesting at any point two years ago that language classes in universities around the world would, within a matter of weeks, as Greene notes above, take their entire course portfolio online would not have been believed. Even taking one face-to-face course online would have been met in some contexts in higher education with massive resistance from teachers, learners, administrators and parents who naturally privilege the benefits of presence-based learning given the increasingly high tuition fees paid for a campus experience.

The Covid-19 public health crisis has indeed brought about a rapid change in the way digital technologies are used in language teaching. In many cases, it has resulted in a form of 'emergency remote teaching' using videoconferencing platforms; however, rather than sustainable forms of online pedagogy, and rather like previous iterations of the web, from the read/write Web 1.0 to the symbiotic Web 4.0, it has focussed on a small range of what are now called 'platform' technologies. Hegemonic examples from the period of Covid-19 include Zoom and MS Teams, whereas in Web 2.0, for example, this was primarily Google, Wikipedia and YouTube from among many other applications that served a similar purpose (Greenhow et al., 2009). In this sense, while this period has been hyped as 'normalization' to use Bax's (2003) term, it clearly masks the digital inequalities which the pandemic has shone a light on and requires a constantly vigilant approach that 'problematises' technology, rather than one that merely envisages them one day becoming 'invisible'.

The swift transition to emergency online teaching demonstrated the effectiveness of contemporary videoconferencing and fast internet connections, which came to the rescue of hundreds of millions of students and teachers around the world. Although the pandemic has promoted the use of digital technology platforms, it has not dealt effectively with how to translate 'being online' into sustainable practices capable of achieving greater integration in skills work and syllabi envisaged by Bax. Indeed, Bax (2003) defined 'normalization' in terms of a 'stage when a technology is invisible, hardly even recognised as a technology, taken for granted in everyday life' (p. 23). By 'invisible', Bax meant that technology will, therefore, no longer have a primary role and that pedagogy will thus have gained the upper hand:

> CALL will reach this state when computers (probably very different in shape and size from their current manifestations) are used every day by language students and teachers as an integral part of every lesson, like a pen or a book. Teachers and students will use them without fear or inhibition, and equally without an exaggerated respect for what they can do. They will not be the centre of any lesson, but they will play a part in almost all. They will be completely integrated into all other aspects of classroom life, alongside coursebooks, teachers and notepads. They will go almost unnoticed. Most importantly, CALL will be normalised when computers are treated as always secondary to learning itself, when the needs of learners will be carefully analysed first of all, and then the computer used to serve those needs ... Technology will then be in its proper place. (pp. 23–4)

Arising from his critique of Warschauer and Healey's (1998) three-phase history of CALL incorporating behaviouristic/structural, communicative and integrative approaches, Bax advocated for a new series of phases: restricted, open and integrated. Restricted CALL mirrored the focus on accuracy in which the role of the computer was largely to replace the teacher as a tool. Open CALL likewise developed the emphasis on communication particularly through the use of up-to-date computer-mediated communication in which computers are still typically accessed via a dedicated computer lab once a week. Bax's notion of integrated CALL represents a significant step change in this respect, as it aims to demonstrate the interconnectedness of language skills and technologies, in which the technologies are used so seamlessly that they have naturally become a part of the fabric of the learning experience. At the time of writing, most teachers and learners continued to work in 'open CALL', and the familiar experience with digital technologies in language learning was still in a dedicated computer lab. Unlike Warschauer and Healey's history of CALL, Bax's approach does not merely accept a linear approach to the three different stages, as he argued that the phases overlap and that the behaviourist learning principles of the restricted phase may also be valuable in other phases (Hubbard, 2021).

Normalization tends to focus too much on the notion of providing hardware but little on the pedagogical strategies required to make integration successful (Bax, 2011). What is often neglected too is the importance of providing sustainable CALL software. Another point of criticism is that CALL tends to support out-of-class and informal learning rather than in-class communicative activities. Nevertheless, normalization is an interesting concept, particularly when viewed in the context of the pandemic and the rhetoric that surrounds the apparent integration of digital technologies. In a TESL-EJ (March 2006 Forum) discussion, Bax elaborated further on it, identifying a more nuanced approach to technology integration that acknowledged many of the digital inequalities and political aspects associated with technology integration in the educational marketplace:

> An example: a Middle East country (which I will call X) where I worked some six years ago received millions of dollars (Canadian, as a matter of interest) to buy computers for its schools. The Minister of Education spoke to me excitedly about this and assured me that all teachers and students would soon be using the Internet daily and with huge benefit. I felt that there was something missing … Last year went back to do a study of aspects of the country's schooling and found not one computer being used regularly in language classes. In fact most were under lock and key, occasionally used to teach computing. What went wrong? There had been training. But one thing at least which seemed to me to be missing was the decision to integrate the use of computers into the syllabus.

The pandemic has done a great deal to refocus teachers' minds on the contradictions of digital education, including the overemphasis on the potential at the expense of lessons learnt from technology integration research over the past two decades. Lessons learnt from the pandemic to this extent are not new and call for more effective teacher training with respect to digital pedagogies and how to achieve an effective blend between face-to-face and online learning, as the balance between synchronous and asynchronous learning is already well-established in CALL research (Son, 2018).

If the global pandemic had occurred a decade ago, it is unlikely that learning technologies would have been sufficient in an era of lower bandwidth and no smartphones. Students now positioning themselves as customers may demand their money back if the experience of online education is poor, and this is not out of the question, given the haste with which face-to-face course materials have been turned quickly into online materials. Moreover, while once it was thought that teaching online would save valuable teacher time and resources, research suggests that in order to go beyond mere transmission modes of pedagogy through lecture capture, it actually requires a significant investment of time and resources and administrative capability to turn face-to-face lessons into sustainable digital pedagogies (Laurillard, 2013). Is this a CTRL-ALT-DELETE moment that makes teachers question everything about the globalized educational marketplace for language learning? Is this an opportunity for online education to improve its reputation given there is less competition from face-to-face courses on campus? Or will the wholesale use of online education prove that it is after all a second-class citizen to presence-based instruction? For universities, is this an opportunity for further privatization and casualization, as they see the initial resistance vanishing before their eyes and perceive this moment of change as a vehicle for extending the flexibility of an already increasingly contract-based and part-time gig economy, particularly evident in the case of language instructors?

Neoliberalism

The pandemic appears to offer a complete reset in the way we think about many of the issues that affect us in CALL teaching and research. It is also a time of opportunities in which language educators need to think carefully about what brought them to this position and what comes next. Does the current situation allow us to think again about the seemingly inevitable and normal way of life that we have all been accepting – travelling to present at an international conference, commuting to work rather than offering the course via videoconference or meeting a student in a virtual world rather than in our offices. As educators we need to reflect on the lessons learnt from the pandemic by considering issues of sustainability, social justice, globalization and the importance of seeing and measuring value, not only through an economic lens, but also through other lenses concerned with individual and collective well-being, inclusivity and how we support students and teachers at the periphery of education and educational institutions and to 'reset' what we mean by education in a time of neoliberal globalization.

There are of course darker sides of the increasing turn towards the use of digital education in the form of big data, algorithms, machine learning and artificial intelligence (AI). The 'datafication' of learning and the growth of learner and teacher profiling which we see in language education is increasingly based on performance-driven, quantitative measures of educational effectiveness. In the UK during the 2020 and 2021 examination crisis, algorithms were used to predict students' final grades, but instead amplified the inequalities in education, health and wealth, giving students in schools from less-advantaged socioeconomic areas lower predicted grades, while higher grades for students from private schools increased significantly (Adams, 2021).

Neoliberalism is the term used to describe many of the aspects of this debate captured above, and it is deeply intertwined with the values that have become all-pervasive in thinking about higher education in the UK. The neoliberal period is defined by several key interlocking themes, including the need to identify new national and/or international markets and the positioning of students as customers within them. This has led to a period with high levels of market volatility affecting all institutions of higher education in similar but different ways, with those at the bottom of the rankings and league tables prone to more upheaval and change as income derives largely from student recruitment and tuition fees. At research-intensive and, more tellingly, teaching-intensive institutions, fluctuations in student recruitment produce an unstable landscape marred by staff redundancy, casualization and insecurity. Educational institutions compete for tuition fee income to survive and retain their staff base, and innovations and marketing campaigns emphasize the employability potential of their graduates. Employability has become a key indicator of the prestige of an institution, and universities are ranked according to the percentage of their graduates who obtain employment within six months of completing their courses. Acquiring technology skill sets to enable them to work with the Fourth Industrial Revolution have become key. Interestingly, while this has led to demotion for liberal arts and social science subjects at the expense of STEM (science, technology, engineering, mathematics), students with language and digital literacy skills continue to be in demand given their attractiveness to international companies. Alongside employability, internationalization has therefore been a strong influence on the direction of educational policy that has shaped the vision, mission and curriculum of English universities.

As a structural support, digital technologies have been key aspects of employability, internationalization and the student experience over the past two decades. Digital technologies are associated with influential discourses about entrepreneurship and innovation. In terms of pedagogy, they are also associated with developments in technologies deriving in large part from the world of business which aim to aid managerialism. In particular, this means the use of standardized approaches to pedagogical content knowledge, such as virtual learning environments and data analytics, both of which were imported from other contexts into education. Within this fiercely competitive model of student recruitment, attracting students through increased marketing offers are sometimes disguised under the umbrella of internationalization, equality, diversity and inclusivity and widening participation. The student experience equates with increased consumer choice.

Within this landscape, digital technologies have been positioned to provide more flexible forms of learning, as well as being used strategically to demonstrate a university's innovativeness and connection with a new generation of tech-savvy students. On the flip side, social media, increased surveillance and cyberbullying are all associated with these new digital cultures (Dede, 2016). Moreover, teaching online is also often identified with similar contradictions, offering both increased flexibility and increased precarity. Digital education has been marked by contradictions rather than simple solutions, then, from massive open online courses (MOOCs) that were originally designed with an emphasis on 'openness', while the reality demonstrates that they tend to attract middle-class graduates rather than students from more disadvantaged backgrounds.

Neoliberalism has become dominant in Western societies since the late 1970s and early 1980s, and is identified with increasing marketization and privatization, particularly in areas of the economy and social life formerly occupied or regulated by the state. While neoliberalism began as an economic philosophy to challenge what was positioned as an inefficient collectivist society, its values became prominent in all areas of social and cultural life. In education, in particular, neoliberalism has led to a transformation in funding models, shifting the responsibility from state funding to individuals who are increasingly positioned as consumers within a marketplace exercising unfettered freedom of choice.

In rejecting the notion of a large state as was evident in governments in the United States and the UK throughout the 1980s, neoliberalism advanced ideas associated with self-regulating free markets. In higher education policy, neoliberalism was encapsulated in moves towards more student choice. For staff, that has also meant more managerial approaches based on a culture of measurement, audit and analytics in which individuals are responsible for their activities rather than their context. Now, academics facilitate courses which have been turned into products in a digital marketplace.

While CALL has been focused on the micro concerns of technology, research has largely been unable to explore the wider neoliberal implications of where the technologies come from and the values that support their introduction and use. In the wider context of educational technology, there has been a more recent critical turn or 'techlash' against the overhyped status of digital technologies as advanced by neoliberal education policy (Selwyn, 2017). This has not yet been seen in CALL which continues to be fixated on research studies exploring the use of new technologies from AI to extended and virtual reality at the expense of more critically informed sociological studies of technology in the societies under examination (Helm et al., 2015). This agenda continues to ignore the sociopolitical context in which CALL technologies are implemented to fulfil a marketing opportunity or used to collect measurable data about student performance to aid learner profiling, and fewer studies question the ethical dimensions of new technologies given their narrow pedagogical focus. In a double move, language learning and programs have steadily closed in universities, particularly in less commonly taught subject areas, while at the same time those that survive do so because of their potential to aid employability in an increasingly globalized world.

Digital Technologies and Neoliberalism

Like all technologies, CALL technologies are not neutral. Digital technologies are integral to the ideology of neoliberalism. Within the field of education, neoliberalism is evident in the repositioning of students as customers and courses as products. The relentless drive to integrate digital technologies in education has been evident across all sectors, from schools to universities and the commercial language teaching and learning context. It is underpinned by terms that clearly define a prominent deterministic or causal role for technology in 'improving', 'enhancing' or 'assisting' with the improvement of learning (Anwaruddin, 2018).

The marketization of English and English language teaching, which has been by far the most prominent language in CALL research, by such organizations as the British Council has been a powerful channel for neoliberal values around the globe. The promotion of English has been strongly allied to economic arguments about individual and national empowerment. Increasing performance in English proficiency brings with it employability skills that may enhance learners' careers, improving graduate prospects and salaries. Promoted by the UK and the United States as colonial powers, English is the world's lingua franca, and English language teaching, tutoring and teacher education has become big business around the globe. English is thus allied to economic and social development, particularly in LMICs, as English has become the language of science, business, commerce and education. English language teaching and learning has become an important commodity exported by English-speaking countries, and their cultural agencies peddle soft diplomatic power through its influence and their financial assistance and research. Allied to the hegemony of English has been the notion of native speakerism, such that job advertisements and course materials sought to give it prominence.

Digital technologies have been central to neoliberalism in English language education. In English language teaching, the awareness of digital resources and pedagogical tools has become increasingly prominent. English language teacher training courses as well as undergraduate and postgraduate courses now offer specialized modules on technology-enhanced language learning as standard, seeking to bridge the divide between practitioner and theoretical perspectives.

Learning the Lessons of the Pandemic and Conclusions

While the pandemic has demonstrated that language educators were able to engage in online teaching at scale in a short period of time, perhaps their greatest legacy has been to foreground the digital and wider social and educational inequalities relating to class, gender, disability, race and ethnicity (Eubanks, 2018). While CALL research has traditionally focused mostly on English in developed countries, a good deal of research in LMICs has been overlooked. Such research focuses on citizenship and social justice issues related to the UN Sustainable Development Goals (SDGs), dealing in particular with SDG 4 on improving quality education and SDG 5 on gender inequality (Anwaruddin, 2019).

In addition to normalization, Bax (2010) also introduced the term 'difficultator' as an alternative to the widely used and 'normalized' term 'facilitator' that has become prominent with contemporary constructivist learning approaches in the language classroom. A 'difficultator' sits uneasily with the notion that CALL will eventually lead to the seamless 'normalization' and 'integration' of technologies in language education. Indeed, it has more in common with the tradition of critical pedagogy and deconstructionism that calls for the patient, slow and unfashionable critical interrogation of normalized traditions and approaches (Pennycook, 2001).

The Covid-19 pandemic has been valuable in highlighting the way future crises may need responses from educators that are interdisciplinary, drawing on a wide range of skill sets, including those of languages. An alternative vision of CALL, then, one which learns the lessons of the pandemic, will be to explore critically the role of digital technologies in the 'new normal', recognizing that this is always fluid rather than stable, questioning the assumptions of the neoliberal educational institution. Indeed, there is some evidence of a turn towards recognizing the importance of addressing social justice, equality and diversity, interdisciplinary research, project-based learning, and decolonizing the curriculum in educational technology research (Ayers et al., 2009).

In learning the lessons of the pandemic, future research on CALL should also begin to address these concerns, particularly those related to imposing predominantly Western approaches to pedagogy and Western technologies on LMICs, and this is evident in the work on decolonizing the curriculum. Numerous definitions of decolonization have appeared in relation to education:

> Decolonising universities is not about completely eliminating white men from the curriculum. It's about challenging longstanding biases and omissions that limit how we understand politics and society … to interrogate its assumptions and

broaden our intellectual vision to include a wider range of perspectives. While decolonising the curriculum can mean different things, it includes a fundamental reconsideration of who is teaching, what the subject matter is and how it's being taught. (Muldoon, 2019)

More specifically, decolonization is related to the legacy of Western modes of thinking, as Singh (2018) argues:

Decolonisation of the curriculum is a profound project that is concerned with addressing the devastation and ongoing violence that European empires have perpetuated against people, mostly but not exclusively in/from the global south … It is about highlighting ways in which all aspects of the imaginary western superior modes of thinking, being, doing and living are privileged over indigenous knowledge and histories, which are deemed to be primitive, irrelevant to modern life, and irrational.

And it is also concerned with recognizing how this is a more indirect and subtle process in which apparently neutral, normalized or widely accepted assumptions about curricula and technology are used:

Decolonization is the process of undoing colonizing practices. Within the educational context, this means confronting and challenging the colonizing practices that have influenced education in the past, and which are still present today. In the past, schools have been used for colonial purposes of forced assimilation. Nowadays, colonialism is more subtle, and is often perpetuated through curriculum, power relations, and institutional structures. (Centre for Youth & Society, n.d.)

In this sense, critical approaches which seek to decolonize the CALL curriculum engage in a process of continuous reflection on the role of technologies, curricula and education and the contexts in which they are used and recognize this as a responsibility. At the same time significant research on the use of information and communication technologies has taken place in LMICs driven by Anglo-American corporations offering technology solutions to educational systems who have their own indigenous traditions and approaches to education (Traxler, 2018a, 2018b; Traxler et al., 2019).

In turning to consider the role of decolonization, Traxler (2021) has identified ways in which education technologies function as a 'conduit to access knowledge and information' and impact on and 'change many aspects of language and of learning' and that decolonizing educational technology requires root and branch reflections on:

- hardware;
- operating systems and system software;
- applications, especially browsers, Web 2.0, social media and open source, interfaces and interactions;

- dedicated educational technologies especially MOOCs, virtual learning environments and the surrounding and supporting software systems such as plagiarism detection, learning analytics and automated assessment;
- procurement, deployment, training, support, management and maintenance;
- buildings and architecture;
- curriculum design;
- Edtech policy and guidance; and
- cultural and societal expectations.

At each level, the 'normalized' assumptions, values, pedagogies and managerialist philosophy driving much of English language teaching and CALL need to be addressed in terms of decolonization to be able to see any long-standing cultural bias, misrepresentations and elisions within tacit and hegemonic discourse. CALL has often been dominated by the English language, by Western approaches to research and Western technology vendors. Learning the lessons from the pandemic in CALL means deconstructing any attempt to 'normalize' technology and adopting an inclusive, individual approach in place of 'one size fits all' type of teaching and learning. It means creating accessible and diverse CALL curricula, helping students and teachers from diverse contexts to be represented in CALL materials and empowering language learners with the technical, linguistic and cultural skill sets necessary to function as citizens in a diverse and global world. Opposed to the neoliberal use of digital technologies in education, it is important to ask the question in the context of CALL: can digital technologies be used for good to promote an alternate vision based on sustainable and socially just pedagogies?

References

Adams, R. (2021, 10 August). Private schools in England give pupils top grades in 70% of A-level entries. *The Guardian*. Retrieved 14 September 2022, from https://www.theguardian.com/education/2021/aug/10/private-schools-in-england-give-pupils-top-grades-in-70-of-a-level-entries.

Anwaruddin, S. M. (2018). Beyond determinism and instrumentalism: Re-conceptualizing technology for CALL. In J. Perren, K. Kelch, J. Byun, S. Cervantes, & S. Safavi (Eds.), *Applications of CALL theory in ESL and EFL environments* (pp. 22–35). IGI Global.

Anwaruddin, S. M. (2019). Teaching language, promoting social justice: A dialogic approach to using social media. *CALICO Journal, 36*(1), 1–18.

Ayers, W., Quinn, T. M., & Stovall, D. (Eds.). (2009). *Handbook of social justice in education*. Routledge.

Bax, S. (2003). CALL-past, present and future. *System, 31,* 13–28.

Bax, S. (2010). Beyond the 'wow' factor. *Digital education and learning: Opportunities for social collaboration* (pp. 239–56). Palgrave.

Bax, S. (2011). Normalisation revisited: The effective use of technology in language education. *International Journal of Computer-Assisted Language Learning and Teaching, 1*(2), 1–15.

Centre for Youth & Society. (n.d.). Decolonization in an educational context. Retrieved 14 September 2022, from https://www.uvic.ca/research/centres/youthsociety/assets/docs/briefs/decolonizing-education-research-brief.pdf.

Dede, C. (2016). Social media and challenges to traditional models of education. In C. Greenhow, J. Sonnevend, & C. Agur (Eds.), *Education and social media: Toward a digital future* (pp. 95–112). MIT Press.

Eubanks, V. (2018). *Automating inequality: How high-tech tools profile, police, and punish the poor.* St. Martin's Press.

Freddi, M. (2021). Reflection on digital language teaching, learning, and assessment in times of crisis: A view from Italy. In N. Radić, A. Atabekova, M. Freddi, & J. Schmied (Eds.), *The world universities' response to COVID-19: Remote online APACALL Newsletter.* APACALL.

Greenhow, C., Robelia, B., & Hughes, J. E. (2009). Learning, teaching, and scholarship in a digital age: Web 2.0 and classroom research: What path should we take now? *Educational researcher, 38*(4), 246–59.

Helm, F., Bradley, L., Guarda, M., & Thouësny, S. (2015). *Critical CALL: Proceedings of the 2015 EUROCALL conference.* Research-publishing.net.

Hubbard, P. (2021). *An invitation to CALL: Foundations of computer-assisted language learning.* Retrieved 14 September 2022, from https://www.apacall.org/research/books/6/An_Invitation_to_CALL_2021.pdf.

Jones, S. (2020, 31 May). Covid-19 is our best chance to change universities for good. *The Guardian.* Retrieved 14 September 2022, from https://www.theguardian.com/education/2020/mar/31/covid-19-is-our-best-chance-to-change-universities-for-good.

Laurillard, D. (2013). *Rethinking university teaching: A conversational framework for the effective use of learning technologies.* Routledge.

Lederman, D. (2020, March 18). Will shift to remote teaching be boon or bane for online learning? *Inside Higher Ed.* Retrieved 14 September 2022, from https://www.insidehighered.com/digital-learning/article/2020/03/18/most-teaching-going-remote-will-help-or-hurt-online-learning.

Muldoon, J. (2019, 20 March). Academics: It's time to get behind decolonising the curriculum. *The Guardian.* Retrieved 14 September 2022, from https://www.theguardian.com/education/2019/mar/20/academics-its-time-to-get-behind-decolonising-the-curriculum.

Pennycook, A. (2001). *Critical applied linguistics: A critical introduction.* Lawrence Erlbaum.

Selwyn, N. (2017). *Education and technology: Key issues and debates.* Bloomsbury.

Singh, G. (2018). Decolonising education – decolonising the arts curriculum: Perspectives on higher education. Retrieved 14 September 2022, from https://decolonisingtheartscurriculum.myblog.arts.ac.uk/.

Son, J.-B. (2018). *Teacher development in technology-enhanced language teaching.* Palgrave Macmillan.

TESL-EJ. (2006, March). Normalisation of CALL, *9*(4). Retrieved 14 September 2022, from http://tesl-ej.org/ej36/f1.pdf.

Traxler, J. (2018a). Learning with mobiles: The global south. *Research in Comparative and International Education, 13*(1), 152–75.

Traxler, J. (2018b). Digital literacy: A Palestinian refugee perspective. *Research in Learning Technology, 26,* 1–21.

Traxler, J. (2021). *#LTHEchat 220: Decolonising learning technology. Led by Professor John Traxler*. Retrieved 14 September 2022, from https://lthechat.com/2021/11/28/lthechat-220-decolonising-learning-technology-led-by-professor-john-traxler-johntraxler/.

Traxler, J., Khlaif, Z., Nevill, A., Affouneh, S., Salha, S., Zuhd, A., & Trayek, F. (2019). Living under occupation: Palestinian teachers' experiences and their digital responses. *Research in Learning Technology, 27.* https://doi.org/10.25304/rlt.v27.22.

Warschauer, M., & Healey, D. (1998). Computers and language learning: An overview. *Language Teaching, 31,* 51–71.

17

Conclusion: Learning the Lessons from the Pandemic?

Michael Thomas, Karim Sadeghi and Farah Ghaderi

The chapters assembled in this edited volume have explored the different dimensions of teaching and learning foreign languages with digital technologies during the Covid-19 pandemic. Collectively, the book confirms the conclusions of many research studies published in CALL over the past three decades – namely, that the integration of digital technologies is a complex process that can both enable opportunities for communication and collaboration, while also presenting barriers in the form of new skill sets or the lack of technical infrastructure (Bailey & Lee, 2020; Warschauer, 2004). CALL technologies, like those in the wider field of educational technology, remain a volatile and fast-moving area of practitioner enquiry. Moving our field of vision away from the classroom, which is an important aspect of being an educator, it is also necessary to understand the wider socio-economic forces that are shaping digital education (Thomas, 2017; Thomas & Schneider, 2020).

The market for learning technologies is increasingly driven by technology start-ups and EdTech Unicorns (e.g. companies worth over one billion US dollars) that appear and disappear at regular intervals and that adapt technology solutions from other areas, particularly business, in a global marketplace now worth billions of dollars each year. Indeed, while language teachers have been focussing on the micro-level potential of digital technologies to fix classroom-level challenges during the pandemic with their learners, EdTech Unicorns from India to China have grown at a staggering pace. In particular, online tutoring platforms have seen increased rates of growth and renewed interest across all subject areas, particularly in language learning, buoyed by affordable or even free synchronous platforms (Chan et al., 2021). These services include platforms offering gaming, videoconferencing and streaming at the same time as a new wave of hyperbole surrounds the emergence of the metaverse, blockchain solutions, the Internet of Things and Web 3.0.

On the positive side, since 2020, the pandemic has amplified the affordances of digital technologies to connect teachers and learners through platforms such as Zoom and Microsoft Teams (Adedoyin & Soykan, 2020). No respecter of wealth and status, however, the transition to emergency remote online teaching and learning has also been a powerful lens on existing educational inequalities in schools and universities in low- and medium-income countries (LMIC) as well as in wealthier nations, where technology infrastructure is lacking, and access may be determined by a person's postcode or family income. As Warschauer (2003) presciently noted, the digital divide is not simply a problem of access but one perhaps better understood in terms of the term 'digital inclusivity', and educators and policymakers need to consider the sustainability of pedagogical practices and teacher training (pre-service and in-service) if access to digital technologies is to be meaningful in terms of longer-term learning gains (Moorhouse, 2020).

In recognizing the complex nuances of these challenges, the chapters in this book have brought together original research and fresh perspectives from practitioners and researchers in Australia, Hong Kong, Iran, Japan, Italy, Spain, the United Arab Emirates, the United Kingdom and the United States of America to provide insights into the behaviour and perceptions of teachers and learners across a range of educational sectors, from schools to universities. The studies draw on a range of research approaches, from corpus approaches to action research, to investigate this challenging technology-mediated landscape and to identify valuable lessons to be learnt from an unprecedented health and social crisis.

Understanding the past can aid understanding of the present and help educators and educational institutions to prepare for an uncertain future and reduce digital inequalities. On the other hand, it is essential to recognize, as several studies in the book point out, that education alone cannot solve these complex problems of digital access and sustainability, and researchers, practitioners and policymakers will need to work together across disciplines to address these grand challenges (Chan et al., 2021). From the language learning and intercultural education perspective, which will continue to be important in an increasingly globalized world, several lessons in particular stand out from the research assembled in this book, in the areas of pedagogy, technology infrastructure, continuing professional development, and social justice and the digital divide.

Pedagogical Lessons

Perhaps the most significant issue arising from the transition to emergency remote teaching has been the 'intent by many teachers to transfer more "traditional" teaching methods to digital contexts' (Dooly, Chapter 15, p. 214). Research suggests that this cannot be done so simply, and technology-mediated learning requires pedagogies which are sensitive to the technologies being used and the contexts in which they are adopted (Adedoyin & Soykan, 2020). While the transition has led to gains in terms of teacher confidence, expertise and knowledge, students too have acquired insights into the potential affordances of technologies which promote more flexible types of assessment and attendance (see Meskill, Kusumastuti and Guo, Chapter 4, this volume). This may be in the form of blended, flipped or collaborative learning, and more research is needed to explore the longer-term rather than short-term implications of this switch.

While changes of this nature will take time and technologies such as extended reality and virtual reality remain only potential or partial solutions in some parts of the developed world, perhaps the main pedagogical innovations stemming from the pandemic have been (a) the increased opportunity to reflect on the future of pedagogy within the wider context of the future of educational institutions and (b) the type of original and creative thinking and problem-solving that accompanied the transition to remote teaching and online learning.

In this respect, research suggests that synchronous classes need to be more structured and integrate interactional approaches; and more opportunities for discussion should prevail in place of a transmission-based banking model approach (see LaFond, Chapter 2, this volume). Responses from students in several studies in the book also suggest that they were interested in addressing the deficits that online teaching can sometimes bring through the use of breakout rooms and distraction-free spaces on campus based on new models of class scheduling. Students were also aware of the effects of gazing at themselves on a screen for prolonged periods of time in terms of their mental and physical health, and this was especially relevant in language learning, which typically involves more opportunity for physical interaction and movement.

More reflection on the appropriate form of pedagogy, not just digital, was one key aspect of the transition, as was the associated task of considering who is included and excluded from the educational offer. Specifically, this has led to more reflection on the use of asynchronous learning to encourage greater time for reflection among learners. Arising from the latter, as Alm (Chapter 9, this volume) indicates, the extended period of instruction which took place during periods of lockdown emphasized the need to recognize the value of building bridges between learners' formal and informal language learning practices. There is some evidence that during the pandemic, students had more opportunity to engage in autonomous language learning as online tools facilitated this move and greater freedom outside of class. Many students in the studies were also conscious of trying to manage the distractions brought about by the blurring of work and home environments. This was evident in the contribution of Torsani (Chapter 7, this volume), which aimed to recognize the value of autonomous learning in the broader ecosystem of foreign-language education with digital technologies, as well as in particular situations, such as study-abroad programmes, which may benefit from more blended solutions (see Sasaki and Takeuchi, Chapter 6, this volume).

Given the nature of the emergency, the ability of educational institutions to react quickly via their administration was also identified as an inhibiting factor for pedagogical processes (Whittle et al., 2020). Likewise, other aspects of pastoral support for learning, such as that available from parents and guardians, was also important for the move online. Another important consideration was improving the digital literacy of students. This might be through a range of strategies, including giving students early access to resources, scaffolding learning, adopting user-friendly designs and using more personalized teaching and learning strategies to compensate for isolation.

Finally, one of the key areas of pedagogy requiring more understanding is online assessment, where it is important to reflect on new types of performance measurement and academic misconduct to ensure validity and reliability (Newton, 2020; see also Davidson and Coombe, Chapter 14, this volume). The use of more flexible approaches such as e-portfolios was in evidence, and the pandemic may have provided teachers with the need to reflect on assessment practices and identify gaps in their assessment literacy, whether online or offline. Such tools as e-portfolios may provide a resilient form of technology worth investing in as they can be used in face-to-face and offline contexts (Lam, Lau and Wong, Chapter 13, this volume).

Technology Lessons

Several studies highlighted the potential technical challenges encountered by teachers and learners during the transition to remote teaching. Problems included a lack of familiarity with hardware and software, poor connectivity to the internet and online meeting fatigue arising from all day spent staring at screens.

None of these challenges is new to research in CALL or technology-enhanced learning, having been identified by numerous studies over the past three decades, but they were new on such a large-scale (Todd, 2020). Given the appeal of blended learning and more flexible learning now expected by students, educational institutions will need to have the necessary support and infrastructure in place to facilitate this flexibility and to take into consideration the performance of students who do not have access to the internet and required platforms.

Continuing Professional Development Lessons

Significant studies in the field of CALL have underlined the importance of technology education for pre-service and in-service language teachers, as well as effective continuing professional development (Kubanyiova, 2020). Teachers' digital literacy skills, both in terms of knowledge delivery and e-assessment will need continual updating, as will students' creative and analytical skills (Lam, Lau and Wong, Chapter 13, this volume).

A related issue, highlighted by Liontas (Chapter 10, p. 147) is the impact on the psychosomatic health and well-being of teachers as a result of extensive periods of work and study removed from face-to-face contexts. As Liontas writes, the pandemic has had effects on 'stress, anxiety, uncertainty, frustration' as well as 'the risk factor for rising mental health problems impacting one's emotional, social, and physical life … from anxiety disorders to depression to post-traumatic stress disorder (PTSD)'. Several studies on teacher development in this volume clearly underline the need for structured and meaningful continuing professional development in digital literacies that does not simply train teachers how to use technologies but engages them in a critical dialogue about whether they should be used (Ferrari, Chapter 3, this volume).

The pandemic reinforces the lesson that technical skills alone do not enable teachers to adapt to the challenging contexts and risks inherent in any use of technologies in education (Meskill et al., 2020). Alongside pedagogical and content knowledge, teacher training programmes need to consider the soft skills required to adapt and the impact on teacher identity (Liontas, 2020). Related to this is the understanding that the use of technology is not a neutral process; it involves choices, and this requires reflection and cognitive flexibility and ongoing support for teachers (Lomicka & Ducate, 2021). Above all, the importance of continuing professional development for language educators throughout their careers, to enable them to be responsive to a rapidly changing landscape, is a key implication of the move online. This means providing a supportive space to grow, experiment and develop without oppressive forms of performance review.

Social Justice and the Digital Divide

The pandemic has amplified challenges associated with educational inequalities. Numerous newspaper headlines as well as studies have highlighted the plight of students and teachers who have been disadvantaged by not having access to technology to participate reliably in online classes or complete homework (Thomas, 2021).

It is therefore important to acknowledge the critical turn in technology-enhanced learning research, as was evident in the contribution of Morcom and Liu (this volume), and to aim to make CALL researchers aware of how 'a utopian narrative championing smart technology at the center of a pandemic response ... can cause more harm than good', not only in relation to how it represents particular types of students and groups, but 'also to research legitimacy and pedagogical practices'. This was also evident in the research of Cox and Song (Chapter 5, p. 115), which responded to the anxiety caused to immigrant learners when studying in unfamiliar online environments by advocating for teachers to design online pedagogies which 'foster positive emotional experiences'.

Recognizing these challenges to online learning may also lead to approaches involving co-design with students and providing more flexible forms of instruction which do not assume that students are digital natives who understand how to socialize effectively in the online classroom without instructional guidance. Working in partnership with students, it is also essential to consider moves to decolonize the use of educational technologies, to recognize differences in learning and teaching styles across the world and not to impose Western ideas of pedagogy or Western technologies on different countries which have their own well-established traditions of learning and research (Starkey, 2020).

There are also dangers in seeing the move to remote online teaching as overly positive and utopian as they seek to provide more uncritical capital to support tech integration which can damage the legitimacy of non-tech approaches. An approach to technology integration that is based on uncritical determinism requires an alternative vision. As Morcom and Liu (Chapter 8, p. 115) suggest, it can be based on 'care, connectivity, and interaction', in which teachers and learners are given choices about the types of technology they are expected to use, their frequency of use and their purpose.

The pandemic reinforced the social nature of learning and language learning in particular. As Alm (Chapter 9, this volume) suggested, one of the main lessons from the pandemic is that teachers can empower learners to draw on resources from their own social contexts by creating learning environments that support the basic needs of autonomy, competence, and relatedness – creating the conditions for meaningful engagement with language.

Conclusion

The Covid-19 pandemic has led to an opportunity for more critical reflection on the shape of online and offline pedagogy in language learning as in many other disciplines. It also shone a powerful light on the creative potential of human beings to collaborate to solve complex problems in order to keep learning in the midst of great difficulties and complex challenges. Associated to this, the pandemic has placed significant demands on the health and well-being of teachers, students and support staff as they attempt to balance the 'new normal' of working from home. It is not surprising that increases in anxiety and mental health challenges have gone hand in hand with the emergency remote teaching.

On the other hand, the pandemic has been a kind of 'collective experiment' in resilience and supporting oneself and others, and while it has been perceived as something temporary, it has significant lessons to teach educators and those responsible for education that may be more enduring. It is to be hoped that this volume can contribute to these ongoing discussions about the future shape and vision of education in general and language education in particular in an increasingly digitally mediated world and that we can all learn valuable lessons and put them into practice.

References

Adedoyin, O. B., & Soykan, E. (2020). COVID-19 pandemic and online learning: The challenges and opportunities. *Interactive Learning Environments*, 1–13. https://doi.org/10.1080/10494820.2020.1813180.

Bailey, D. R., & Lee, A. R. (2020). Learning from experience in the midst of COVID-19: Benefits, challenges, and strategies in online teaching. *Computer-Assisted Language Learning Electronic Journal*, 21(2), 178–98.

Chan, R. Y., Bista, K., & Allen, R. M. (2021). *Online teaching and learning in higher education during COVID-19. International perspectives and experiences.* Routledge.

Kubanyiova, M. (2020). Language teacher education in the age of ambiguity: Educating responsive meaning makers in the world. *Language Teaching Research*, 24(1), 49–59.

Liontas, J. I. (2020). Understanding language teacher identity: Digital discursive spaces in English teacher education and development. In B. Yazan & K. Lindahl (Eds.), *Language teacher identity in TESOL: Teacher education and practice as identity work* (pp. 65–82). Routledge.

Lomicka, L., & Ducate, L. (2021). Using technology, reflection, and noticing to promote intercultural learning during short-term study abroad. *CALL*, 34(1–2), 35–65.

Meskill, C., Anthony, N., & Sadykova, G. (2020). Teaching languages online: Professional vision in the making. *Language Learning & Technology*, 24(3), 160–75.

Moorhouse, B. L. (2020). Adaptations to a face-to-face initial teacher education course 'forced' online due to the COVID-19 pandemic. *Journal of Education for Teaching*, 46(4), 609–11.

Newton, D. (2020, August 7). *Another problem with shifting education online: Cheating.* Retrieved 14 September 2022, from https://hechingerreport.org/another-problem-with-shifting-education-online-cheating/.

Starkey, L. (2020). A review of research exploring teacher preparation for the digital age. *Cambridge Journal of Education, 50*(1), 37–56.

Thomas, M. (2017). *Project-based language teaching with technology: Learner collaboration in an EFL classroom in Japan*. Routledge.

Thomas, M. (2021). Epilogue: Critical project-based pedagogy and social justice in the post-pandemic university. In M. Thomas & K. Yamazaki (Eds.), *Project-based language learning and CALL: From virtual exchange to social justice* (pp. 283–94). Equinox.

Thomas, M., & Schneider, C. (2020). *Language teaching with video-based technologies: Creativity and CALL teacher education*. Routledge.

Todd, R. W. (2020). Teachers' perceptions of the shift from the classroom to online teaching. *International Journal of TESOL Studies, 2*(2), 4–17.

Warschauer, M. (2003). *Technology and social inclusion: Rethinking the digital divide*. MIT Press.

Warschauer, M. (2004). Technological change and the future of CALL. In S. Fotos & C. Brown (Eds.), *New perspectives on CALL for second and foreign language classrooms* (pp. 15–25). Lawrence Erlbaum Associates.

Whittle, C., Tiwari, S., Yan, S., & Williams, J. (2020). Emergency remote teaching environment: A conceptual framework for responsive online teaching in crises. *Information and Learning Sciences, 121* (5/6), 311–19.

Index

accuracy 5, 152–5, 159, 162
academic dishonesty 197–200, 205, 207
agency 77, 83
anger 59–60, 64, 68
anxiety 60–1, 68
artificial intelligence 1, 104, 204, 232
assessment as learning 184–6, 192
assessment for learning 184–6, 192
asynchronous xx, xxi, 3–4, 13–18, 23–4, 31, 50, 60–2, 67, 143, 155, 186, 227, 231, 243
attitude 59–63, 68–70
authentic assessment 199–200
authentic language 44
autonomy 75, 77–8, 89–100

belief 96, 99–100
blended learning/teaching 215–16, 219, 221

CALL 1–8, 15, 228–37, 241, 244–5
caption 122–3
cheating 197–8, 200–7
collaborative 167–9, 171–2, 176–8
computer-assisted language learning xix, 1, 2, 215
Covid-19 1–4, 6–8, 13–14, 29, 31, 40, 47–9, 59, 62, 75, 77–8, 84, 89, 90–1, 95, 98, 103–8, 112–15, 121, 126, 135–8, 147, 151, 156, 162, 167–74, 177–9, 183, 188–9, 194, 197–200, 206–7, 214, 217–18, 222, 228–9, 235, 241, 246
communicative 44, 50
community of practice 138, 145
complexity 152–5, 162
corpus 106–9, 111
critical consciousness 137
critical participatory action research 135–7
cultural and linguistic diversity (CALD) 104, 106, 114

dialogic 139, 144–5
digital content 44
digital divide 222, 241–2, 245
digital technology 1–7, 146, 230
distance learning 29, 31–2
distraction 15–21, 24–5

E-assessment literacy 193
ecology 90–1, 95–6, 100
EdTech 237, 241
emergency remote learning 43, 45, 48, 241
emergency remote teaching 214–16, 218–19, 221, 241
emotion 59, 61, 64–5
engagement 121–3, 126, 128–32
English as an additional language/dialect (EAL/D) 103–9, 112–15
E-portfolio 183–94
extended reality (XR) 220–2

fatigue 15, 18, 21–2, 25
feedback 167, 170–4, 178
fluency 5, 152–4, 162
focus on form 217–18
formative assessment 167–79

globalization 232

habit 90, 92–100
higher education 167–70, 179
honour code 205

immigrant 59, 61–2, 68–9
inequality 227–9, 231–2, 235, 242, 245
infodemic 106
integration 229–31, 235, 241
intercultural 76–7
Italian as an additional language 29–31
Italian as a second language 29–30
iterative problem solving process 138–9, 144

knowledge construct 137, 139

L2 blogging 123, 128, 131
L2 viewing 122–3, 126, 128, 131
learning management system 183–4, 187, 191–3

mainstream education 29–31, 33–8
migrant student 35
modality 13, 16, 21
modelling 152–7, 160–1
motivation 77, 80, 82, 84
multitasking 15, 17–19, 22

neoliberalism 232–5
Netflix 121–4, 126–7, 132
Non-native English speaking (NNES) 104–5, 115

on-demand 79–80, 85
online 1, 3–8, 13–19, 21–5, 29, 31–41, 43–54, 59–70, 75, 77–84, 90–100, 104–7, 126, 132, 135–48, 151–2, 154–5, 158, 161–3, 168–9, 171, 183, 187–8, 190–3, 197–207, 214–22, 227–31, 233, 235, 241, 243–6
online assessment 199–200, 206–7
online education 214–15, 219–20
online gaming 93, 95–6
online instruction 43–4, 46–50, 52–3
online learning 135–6, 139–40, 144–7
online medium 43, 49, 52
online SA (Study Abroad) 75, 79–84
online tools 91, 96, 98
online tutoring 37, 241
out-of-class 89–91, 93, 95–6, 98–100

pedagogical 14, 24, 136–7, 242–5
perception 59, 63–4, 69
planning 152–62
podcast 1, 142, 169, 192
pre-task 152–8, 160–3
pride 59–60, 64, 68–9
proctoring 202, 204, 207

psychosomatic health and wellbeing 146–7

refugee 59, 61–2, 68–9
remote learning 105

scaffolding 217–19
secure browser 202–3
self efficacy 77, 80–1, 85
self-reflection 193
self-regulation 165, 170, 172–5, 178
shame 59, 64–5, 68
smartphone 228, 231
social engagement 121, 123, 129, 131
social media 44, 47, 49, 52, 90, 92–6, 98–9, 187
socio-cognitive dimension 47
social constructivism 184–5
Spanish as a foreign language 168, 176
STEM (Science, Technology, Engineering, Mathematics) 232
synchronous xxi, 3–4, 14–19, 22–5, 31, 50–2, 135–6, 138–40, 147, 151, 155, 167, 173, 179, 241, 243

task design 216–17
techlash 228, 234
technopedagogy 214
technology in education 213
teacher knowledge 45–6, 49, 52
teaching strategy 29, 32–4, 36, 38
telecollaboration 215, 221
transition 44, 46, 48, 50–2, 55

videoconferencing 183, 186, 193, 241
virtual exchange 215, 221
virtual learning 1, 233, 237

Web 2.0 1, 145, 186
Web 3.0 241
world Englishes 114

Zoom 13, 15–22, 35, 46–7, 50, 62–3, 65, 75, 79–81, 83, 103, 124, 128, 132, 141, 144, 146, 183, 189–90, 193, 228–9, 241

www.ingramcontent.com/pod-product-compliance
Lightning Source LLC
Chambersburg PA
CBHW062123300426
44115CB00012BA/1794